Mormons An Open Book

WRITTEN
BY A MORMON

What you really want to know

ENSIGN
PEAK

Art direction by Richard Erickson.
Cover design by Hint Creative.
Interior design by Barry Hansen.
Production design by Shauna Gibby and Kayla Hackett.

Library of Congress Cataloging-in-Publication Data
Sweat, Anthony, author.
   Mormons : an open book
     pages cm.
   Includes bibliographical references.
   ISBN 978-1-60908-811-8 (hardbound : alk. paper) 1. The Church of Jesus Christ of Latter-day Saints—Doctrines. 2. The Church of Jesus Christ of Latter-day Saints—History. 3. Mormons. I. Title.
   BX8635.3.S94 2012
   289.3'32—dc23   2011050448

Printed in the United States of America
R. R. Donnelley, Crawfordsville, IN
10 9 8 7 6 5 4 3 2 1

Contents

Author's Note vii

Preface ix

Introduction 1

PART 1: MORMON BELIEFS

1 Ten Facts to Know When Meeting a Mormon. 8

2 The Message of Mormonism 10

3 Are Mormons Christian? Latter-day Saints and the Gospel of Jesus Christ . . . 19

4 What Is the Purpose of Life? 29

5 LDS Priesthood Authority and Ordinances 39

6 Mormons and Marriage. 50

7 Mormons and Family 57

8 What Happens inside LDS Temples? 67

9 LDS Scriptures and Sources of Truth 77

10 The Mormon View of the Afterlife 87

PART 2: MORMON HISTORY

11 The History of the LDS Church in Thirty Seconds 96

12 The Joseph Smith Story 98

13 The Book of Mormon 110

14 Latter-day Prophets 122

15 Temple Square 134

PART 3: THE MORMON WAY OF LIFE

16 Mo-cabulary: Understanding Mormon Vernacular 138

17 What Does It Take to Be a Mormon? LDS Standards 147

18 Mormons and Sex 157

19 Mormon Women 164

20 LDS Teenagers 173

21 The Organization of LDS Church Congregations 182

22 A Peek inside a Mormon Worship Service 190

23 Mormons and Missionary Work 194

24 Mormons and Money 203

25 Mormons, Politics, and America 212

26 The Weird and Wonderful World of Mormon Culture 220

Notes 226

Photo and Image Credits 245

Author's Note

This book is written from the perspective of a faithful member of The Church of Jesus Christ of Latter-day Saints and describes the doctrinal positions, beliefs, and practices of Mormonism to those who are interested in our faith. Thus, phrases such as "*we* believe ..." and "*our* standards are ..." or "those of *us* ..." are repeatedly used to represent this plural perspective. However, the fact of the matter is that this general voice is that of a singular person, myself. Therefore, although I am a Latter-day Saint religious educator, I make no pretensions that I speak for the entire membership of the LDS Church or its leadership. I alone am responsible for the content and positions represented in this book.

Anthony Sweat, PhD

Preface

In 2009, the comedian and host of *The Tonight Show,* Conan O'Brien, along with his side-kick, Andy Richter, and drummer, Max Weinberg, did a little song in honor of Mormons. The chorus went, "Oh Mormons, Mormons, Mormons, we haven't got a clue of what you folks believe in, or think or drink or do."[1]

Conan, you are hilarious—and you're not alone.

According to a 2007 Pew Forum poll, 51% of Americans feel that they know "not very much" or "nothing" at all about the Mormon Church.[2] And the most common one-word impression of Mormonism is still "polygamy,"[3] a practice The Church of Jesus Christ of Latter-day Saints abandoned more than one hundred years ago. A 2008 study found that the most common reason given for any antagonism towards Mormonism was not our unique beliefs (only 9% stated that), but that people don't really know *what* we believe (25% listed "ignorance" as the primary cause).[4]

Take this example from a 1989 episode of the classic TV sitcom *Cheers:*

> Rebecca: *[after Carla received a bouquet of flowers]* "Oh, why can't more men send flowers?"
> Sam: "I didn't know Mormons couldn't send flowers."
> Rebecca: "I said 'more men,' not 'Mormons.'"
> Sam: "I know they can't dance."
> Norm: "No, Sammy, that's the, ah, that's the Amish."
> Sam: "Why can't Mormons send flowers?"
> Rebecca: "They can."
> Sam: "What are you talking about?"
> Rebecca: "I just wish someone would send me some . . . roses."
> Sam: "Why does it have to be a Mormon?"
> Rebecca: *[exasperated]* "Oh!"
> Sam: "Some people you just can't discuss religion [with]."[5]

Why can't Mormons send flowers? Actually, we can!

Although many are still confused about what Mormons believe, The Church of Jesus Christ of Latter-day Saints (the official name) continues to grow and receive national and international attention. In fact, the June 2011 cover of *Newsweek* claimed we are experiencing an unprecedented "'Mormon moment'"[6] in America. It seems that more and more people in the general population are curious about Mormonism, our faith, and our values, desiring to know—in the age of Internet indigestion—what we really believe. This book is an attempt to say, in essence, "Hey, this is what we actually believe. You can take it or leave it, but at least now you know."

Perhaps the most important feature of this book is that it is written from the insiders' perspec-

The June 2011 cover of News-week *claimed we are experiencing a "Mormon moment."*

tive—from those who believe it and live it and love it. There are probably many books and people outside the faith who could explain the mechanics, history, conflicts, and nuances of Mormonism, but those books rarely give you the heart and soul of it. For that, you need to talk to those who are moved by the faith. After all, if you wanted to know about and understand the thrill of snowboarding, you'd talk to the snowboarder who rides the snow, not the weatherman who explains where it came from. If you want to really understand Mormonism, then it's best to meet, talk to, and hear from some faithful Mormons. Because, "Oh, Conan, Conan, Conan, we Mormons have a clue of what us folks believe in, and think and drink and do."

We hope you enjoy the following discussion of a growing body of faith in America and around the world: Mormonism.

If you wanted to understand the thrill of snowboarding, you'd talk to a snowboarder. The same is true for Mormonism. If you want to understand it, talk to and hear from a faithful Mormon.

Introduction

Meet the Mormons

If you were standing in a room with one hundred Americans, odds are that one or two of them would be a Mormon.[1] The 2005 *Yearbook of American and Canadian Churches* listed The Church of Jesus Christ of Latter-day Saints as "the fourth-largest denomination in the United States, with more than 5.5 million" American Mormons.[2]

Mormonism is a world-wide faith with over 14 million members, and growing. More Mormons live outside the USA than in it.

In fact, there are more LDS congregations in the United States than there are congregations of Presbyterians, Episcopalians, or Lutherans.[3] And as of 2009, there are more members of the LDS Church in America than there are Muslims, Hindus, or Buddhists.[4] But before you think that the only Mormons are in America, consider this fact: There are more Mormons who live *outside* the United States than in it.[5] Mormonism is a worldwide faith with more than fourteen million members, and growing.[6] If its growth continues over the *next* one hundred years as it has over the *previous* one hundred years, Mormonism is positioned to become the first new world faith since the rise of Islam some 1,400 years ago.

That's our official name. But some people call us "Mormons" because we believe in a book of scripture called the Book of Mormon. Or sometimes we're called "Latter-day Saints" or the "LDS Church" because, to some, saying the entire full name of the Church can be a mouthful, especially in Spanish (La Iglesia de Jesu Cristo de los Santos de los Ultimos Dias . . . anybody have an oxygen mask?).

Although its rise and growth are remarkable, there are still a lot of questions, curiosity, misunderstandings, and misinformation about the LDS Church. What do Mormons believe? What is their message? Are they Christian? What goes on inside their temples? Why the emphasis on families? Do they still dress like pioneers and have funky, long beards?

THE BOOK OF MORMON
ANOTHER TESTAMENT OF JESUS CHRIST

The nickname "Mormon" comes from our belief in the Book of Mormon, Another Testament of Jesus Christ. The Book of Mormon is a volume of scripture comparable to the Bible.

While there are other books about Mormonism, this book aims to give readers an insider's view of Mormonism—without trying to convert or condemn anyone—and tries to present that information in an engaging, visual format so you don't feel like you're being tortured by professor of religion Dr. Putmetosleep. So sit back, relax, look around the room, and meet the Mormons.

260 Million Mormons?

In 1984, noted sociologist Rodney Stark predicted that by the year 2080 there would be any-where between 64 and 267 million Mormons. That was more than twenty-five years ago. So how has his prediction measured up over the past two decades? Surprisingly, in the words of Stark, "It is the high estimate [267 million] that best approximates what has taken place."[7] Although the membership is relatively small by comparison (98.3% of the US and 99.98% of the world are not LDS, let alone *practicing* Mormons), anyone who understands compound growth rates should realize that if membership rates keep up the present pace, it might not be long before being a Mormon is a pretty common thing.

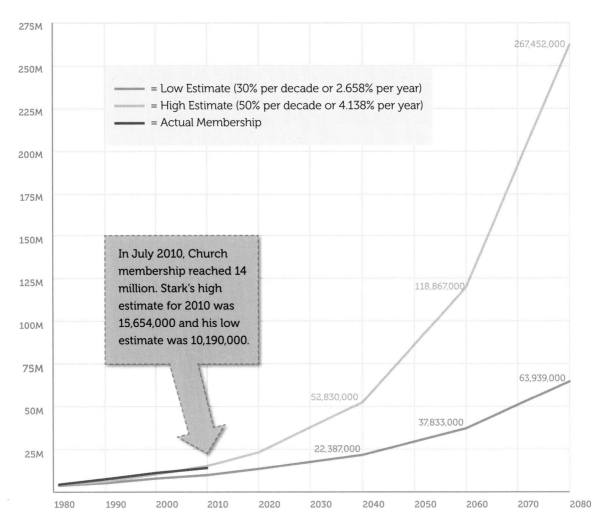

Stark estimated that by the year 2080 there will be between 64 and 267 million Mormons. Current Church growth is in line with the high estimat

Are Mormons Christian?

Asking a Mormon if they believe in Jesus Christ's divinity is like asking Romeo and Juliet if they are in love. To Mormons, it's obvious: The official name of our church is The Church of *Jesus Christ* of Latter-day Saints, and the subtitle to the Book of Mormon is "Another Testament of Jesus Christ." Contrary to what some have claimed, faithful Latter-day Saints love Jesus, believe in His saving divinity, desire to follow His teachings, and rely on His saving grace. (See chapter 3 to learn more about Mormon beliefs related to the Savior Jesus Christ.)

The official name of the Mormon Church is The Church of Jesus Christ of Latter-day Saints.

Is Mormonism a Cult?

If Mormonism is a "cult," then so is any other group that has "a system of religious beliefs and ritual"—which is how the dictionary defines the word.[8] A cult can also be defined as "a religion regarded as unorthodox." Perhaps that's why some people think Mormonism is a cult—because it's a little different in its worship than mainstream Christianity. But using that standard of logic, Mormonism is perfectly orthodox and normal to a Mormon, whereas other ways of religious worship might seem a little different to us. As Mormonism grows and is better understood, the derogatory label of "cult" should fade from civil discourse, just as it faded by those who used to apply it to early Christianity.

MORMYTH:

Mormons live in secluded compounds and don't use electricity.

Which one do Mormons live in?

Answer: False.

Mormons are not throwbacks to a bygone era, hiding out in secluded compounds and wearing pioneer clothing. Some people are shocked when they find out their neighbor is a Mormon because we look so . . . well . . . relatively normal. (How can he be a Mormon? He's an electrical engineer! I thought Mormons couldn't even use electricity!) Mormons are soccer moms and coaches, school teachers, policemen, business executives, doctors, lawyers, artists, writers, politicians, movie and sports stars, and the like. Mormons are simply your common neighbors living a relatively uncommon religion.

Want to see what real Mormons are like? Go to www.mormon.org and read some of their personal profiles.

At www.mormon.org you can read about the lives and beliefs of regular Mormons from around the world and learn why they are Mormons. You can select who you want to read about by age, gender, ethnicity, country, or previous religion. And scattered throughout this book you will find this logo tag:

This will direct you to www.mormon.org, where you can meet a Mormon who is discussing the topics covered in the chapter in which his or her picture is featured.

A White, American Church? Not Anymore

Some people think that Mormonism is a white, American church. Actually, more than half (55%) of Latter-day Saints are *not* Caucasian, and more than half of Church members worship in congregations outside the USA. The LDS Church has more than 28,000 congregations in 177 countries worldwide.[9] Nearly half of the entire country of Tonga are Mormons (46%), and there are two million Mormons in Mexico and nearly a million in Asia.[10] And for those who think that Mormonism's numbers are just due to "generational" growth (i.e., we can trace our genealogy back to Great-great-great-great-grandpa Ezra who knew Joseph Smith), you might also be surprised to know that more than half of current Latter-day Saints are first-generation converts to the Church.[11]

*Think Mormons are mostly white Americans? Guess again.
There are 2 million members in Mexico!*

Is All of Utah Mormon?

Ever been to Utah to ski or hike or work? Well, if you were in a room with a hundred Utahns, sixty of them would be Mormons. Utah has the highest concentration of Mormons anywhere on earth. This is mostly because Utah was the place where the early Mormon pioneers settled and because Salt Lake City is currently the location of the worldwide headquarters of the LDS Church. Although 60 percent of Utah's population is Mormon, that number is actually the lowest on record for the state. The percentage of Mormons in Utah has declined each year for the past two decades, and if the trend continues, less than half of Utah will be Mormon by 2030.[12] Salt Lake City actually has one of the lowest Mormon populations of all Utah cities, with 50 percent of the city being LDS.

60 percent of Utah's population is LDS.

Sixty percent of Utah's population is Mormon. The percentage of Mormons in Utah has declined each year of the past two decades.

Contrary to popular belief, Salt Lake City has one of the lowest Mormon populations of all Utah cities, with 50 percent of the city being LDS.

Part 1:
Mormon Beliefs

1 Ten Facts to Know

Perhaps you've just learned that your new neighbor is LDS, or your sister's brother-in-law is a Mormon, or a guy in your office is a Latter-day Saint. If you don't know much about Mormons and want a quick overview of information, or if you just want to know what to expect when you meet them or talk with them, here are ten things that can help:

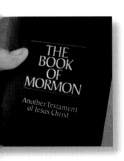

Your Mormon friend won't arrive at your house in a horse and buggy.

1 Mormons are normal people. Your Mormon friend doesn't secretly live in a compound, and he won't arrive at your house in a horse and buggy. He is not part of a cult or an antisocial group. He will be a regular person following his beliefs, just like you follow your beliefs. Feel free to ask him about his family, hobbies, sports, musical tastes, talents, and anything else you would ask a neighbor or friend about their regular life.

2 Mormons believe in salvation through Jesus Christ. Your Mormon friend believes in Jesus Christ and in His saving grace, and she centers her worship on Him. Having faith in the Lord Jesus Christ is the first principle of her religion, and her religious desire is simply to try to follow Jesus' teachings as best as possible. Don't be afraid to talk about Jesus or other Christian principles. As a matter of fact, your Mormon friend would probably love it if you asked her about her feelings on Jesus' divinity. (See chapter 3 for more about Mormons as Christians.)

LDS = Latter-day Saint = Mormon = The Church of Jesus Christ of Latter-day Saints

3 The Mormon Church is The Church of Jesus Christ of Latter-day Saints. Your friend is a Mormon, is LDS, is a Latter-day Saint, and is officially a member of The Church of Jesus Christ of Latter-day Saints—and no, they aren't four different churches: They are all the same thing. It's like how an adherent to Islam is also called Muslim. It's okay to refer to your friend as a Latter-day Saint, or a Mormon, or LDS. And if you use the official name of the Church, you will score bonus points.

4 Mormons don't worship Joseph Smith. Your Mormon friend believes Joseph Smith was a prophet just like other prophets in biblical times. He believes Joseph Smith was the Lord's servant who helped reestablish and restore Jesus' authorized Church, but he doesn't worship Joseph Smith any more than a Catholic worships Peter or a Jew worships Moses. He simply reveres him as a great prophet in modern times. (See chapter 12 for more about the Joseph Smith story.)

5 Mormons are nicknamed after one of their books of scripture, the Book of Mormon. Your Mormon friend believes in a book of scripture called the Book of Mormon, which is another testament of Jesus Christ's divinity. It is a prophetic record translated by Joseph Smith about a people who lived in ancient America. Your friend studies and reads the Book of Mormon, as well as a book of Joseph Smith's revelations called the Doctrine and Covenants. But she also believes in, reads, and studies the Old and New Testaments. So go ahead and talk about the Bible with your friend if you want to—she probably loves the same verses you do. (See chapter 13 for more about the Book of Mormon.)

When Meeting a Mormon

6 Mormons have a *living* prophet. The LDS Church has a living prophet, a man currently on earth that your Mormon friend believes to be God's authorized spokesperson, just like Abraham, Moses, or Isaiah were in their day. This prophet is someone whom your Mormon friend greatly respects and looks to as a servant of Jesus Christ. Ask your friend who the living prophet is today and what subjects the prophet has talked about lately. (See chapter 14 for more about latter-day prophets.)

7 Modern Mormons are *not* polygamists. Your Mormon friend is not a polygamist. He doesn't have three wives, nor does he believe (or wish!) he should. Faithful Mormons haven't entered into polygamous marriages since the 1890s. If you ask him about it, he will probably say something like: "Sure, faithful Mormons followed a revelation to practice polygamy for about fifty years, but ended the practice when a revelation to the prophet told them to stop." Polygamy has about as much modern-day meaning to your Mormon friend's faith as Benjamin Harrison does to your current American patriotism. (Who's Benjamin Harrison? Oh, he was president of the US in 1890.) (See chapter 6 for more about Mormons and marriage.)

Your Mormon friend does not have multiple wives.

8 Mormon women are not subordinate to Mormon men. Contrary to what Shakespeare advocated in *The Taming of the Shrew*, Mormon women are not considered inferior to Mormon men. (Sorry, Petruchio.) Mormon women are independent, highly honored in their role as mothers, have professional careers, think for themselves, serve in leadership positions and in councils in LDS congregations, and, if married, are equal partners with their husbands in governing their families. (See chapter 19 for more about Mormon women.)

9 Mormons don't drink alcohol, coffee, or tea. If your Mormon friend is coming over for dinner, or if you are going out to a restaurant, she will probably graciously refuse tea, coffee, or alcohol. Mormons have a code of health they live by, and they try to abstain from anything that could damage their health, impair their judgment, or be addictive or habit-forming—especially tobacco, alcohol, coffee, and tea. However, Diet Coke is a whole other story ☺. (See chapter 17 for more about LDS standards.)

Your Mormon friend will probably graciously refuse that cup of fresh-brewed coffee.

10 Mormons serve as lay ministers in their local congregations. Odds are your Mormon friend has a "calling" within his or her local LDS congregation—something he or she has been asked to do voluntarily and without compensation. Many Mormons give substantial time each week fulfilling these assignments. Your friend might be called to serve as a Sunday School teacher, or to serve with Mormon youth, or to be a financial clerk for the congregation. Your friend might serve as the president of the women's organization that helps the poor and needy (the Relief Society). Or your friend might serve as the bishop over the whole congregation. Ask your Mormon friend if he or she has a Church calling and how he or she donates time to the local LDS congregation. (See chapter 21 for more about Church organization.)

2 The Message of Mormonism

CHRIST'S ORIGINAL CHURCH HAS BEEN REESTABLISHED ON EARTH.

This is our message to the world in a nutshell. (Or on a billboard for extra emphasis.)

Mormons are known for many things: strong family values, honesty, high moral standards, not drinking or smoking, the Book of Mormon, and even a bizarre affinity for green Jell-O.

However, although it is good that we are known for those things (with the exception, perhaps, of the green Jell-O), our message to the world isn't just family values and moral behavior. Suppose you were asked to summarize what you think the message of The Church of Jesus Christ of Latter-day Saints is to the world—what would you say? If you aren't quite sure, that's all right. You're not alone. A recent study asked a thousand non-Mormons to answer the question, **"To the best of your understanding, what is the main claim of Mormonism?"** Only 14 percent of respondents identified closely what Mormonism's message to the world is.[1] So what is the message of Mormonism? Here it is in three sentences:

During Jesus' life, He organized His Church.
It became corrupted by men.
Jesus has reestablished His Church in our day.

Our message to the world is not only what you find on YouTube under "Mormon Messages" (although those videos are good; watch them). *The* Mormon message is that the Church of Jesus Christ has once again been officially reorganized on the earth. Modern-day prophets have been called. God's divine authority to act in His name has been given again. Ancient truths once lost have been reestablished, and new revelations with additional eternal truths have been given. The promises God made in Old and New Testament times are now extended to all. The world is being prepared for Christ's return to earth. **Simply put, our message to the world is that Christ's original church has been reestablished on earth.**

Jesus Established His Church during His Lifetime

In Jesus' Church He ordained "some, apostles; and some, prophets; and some, evangelists; and some, pastors and teachers" (Ephesians 4:11).

Jesus told His disciples that one of the reasons He was on the earth was to "build my church" (Matthew 16:18). We believe that **Jesus** organized an **actual church** when He was on the earth. He chose and "ordained" (John 15:16) **twelve apostles** to act in His name and laid His hands on their heads and "gave them power" (Matthew 10:1) and **authority.** Jesus' church was "built upon the foundation of the apostles and prophets, Jesus Christ himself being the chief corner stone" (Ephesians 2:20). In Jesus' church, He ordained "some, apostles; and some, prophets; and some, evangelists; and some, pastors and teachers" (Ephesians 4:11). These prophets with their authority oversaw the teaching, doctrine, and ordinances of the Church, and "added to the church daily" (Acts 2:47) those who believed.[2] Therefore, the original Church of Jesus Christ was centered on Christ and was directed by apostles who had authority given to them to act in Jesus' name.

74% 57%

of all Americans believe that men changed the original church of Christ.

of all Christians feel that something went wrong between Christ's establishment of His Church and today.

What Happened to Jesus' Original Church?

Mormons aren't alone in our belief that something eventually went awry with the early church established by Jesus. A 2008 study found that **"74% of all Americans believe that men changed the original church of Christ," and 57% of all Christians feel that something went wrong between Christ's establishment of His Church and today.**[3] There is a lot of scriptural evidence that the original church Jesus organized faced severe threats to its success, both by corruption from within the church and persecution from without.[4] Over time, men altered the original church established by Jesus and made unauthorized changes to its teachings, ordinances, and organization.[5] The Apostle Paul warned of "grievous wolves" entering into the church, "speaking perverse things" (Acts 20:29–30), and predicted that

Christ's return to the earth would not come "except there come a falling away first" (2 Thessalonians 2:3). This "falling away" (or *apostasia* in the original Greek) was brought about as wicked people persecuted the Lord's apostles and killed many of them, resulting in the loss of the power and authority necessary to oversee Jesus' church. With the death of the apostles, men without authority began to change church teachings, organization, and ordinances. **This loss of authority and the resulting unauthorized changes in Jesus' original church is what Mormons call the apostasy.**

One Lord, One Faith—30,000 Churches?

If Jesus' original church was "built upon the foundation of the apostles and prophets" (Ephesians 2:20), then what happened when the foundation was pulled out? The church fell. This is what we believe happened, and we call it the apostasy.

When the church fell, people who had the best of intentions, but who did not claim authority, tried to reform and reorganize the fallen church as they thought it should be. We believe that this is what led to the formation of many different churches, all of which splintered off with various beliefs and perspectives.

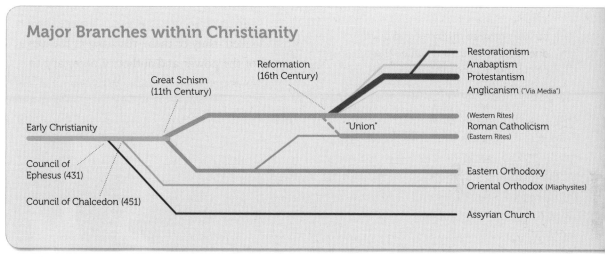

Well-meaning people tried to reform and reorganize, which led to the formation of many different churches.

Today, the *World Christian Encyclopedia* estimates that there are about 34,000 different Christian churches or groups in the world.[10] This is a far cry from the "one Lord, one faith, one baptism" (Ephesians 4:5) of the one original Church of Jesus Christ.

The Enlighteners and the Reformers

After Jesus' original church was corrupted by men, we believe that God set events in motion and inspired many people to prepare the world for the Church of Jesus Christ to be reestablished. Call it the "Reformation." Call it the "Enlightenment." Call it "Freedom." We call it "Alotofreallyamazingthingshappeningtoprepareawayforjesus'churchtocome back." (Put that one in your lexicon.)

Our take on this revolutionizing era of history goes like this: Gutenberg invents the printing press in the mid-1400s. ("Hey, let's print a Bible so more people can read Jesus' teachings!") Coincidentally (we think not), Columbus sails west in the late 1400s. Then, in 1517, Martin Luther nails his theses detailing 95 errors to the church door (Reformation = "You are in error" x 95) and the ball really gets rolling. William Tyndale is inspired by Luther's actions and publishes the Bible in English (an act which costs him his life), giving the "boy who drives the plough"[11] the opportunity to learn the word of God for himself.

Along come other reformers in the 1500s like John Calvin and John Wesley,[12] and, inspired by these reformers, the Puritans take off to America to establish a land with religious freedom. ("Worship the way I want *and* some coastal land? Score!") Soon, by the sacrifices of many and the miracle of heaven, a free and independent nation was born, guaranteeing religious freedom. ("Congress shall make no law respecting an establishment of religion, or prohibiting the free exercise thereof."[13])

We believe all these enlightening, reforming, and liberating events were orchestrated by God to prepare a seedbed for the Church of Jesus Christ to be reestablished on the earth in the latter days. In 1820, the Lord called on a young farm boy in New York named Joseph Smith and revealed truths through him, and eventually The Church of Jesus Christ of Latter-day Saints was restored.

How Does Joseph Smith Fit into This?

In order for Jesus' church to be reestablished on earth, God needed to again call a prophet and give him power and authority. In other words, a restoration of Jesus' divine authority was necessary to reestablish Jesus' church; such a restoration was accomplished through heavenly messengers who had previously held the appropriate authority. (See chapter 5.)

Joseph Smith was prepared and called to be a prophet of the Lord in the latter days and to reestablish God's truth.

Timeline of Enlightenment and Reformation

1525
William Tyndale translates the Bible into English, eventually paying for it with his life.

1492
Columbus sails to the New World.

1440
Gutenberg invents the printing press, making the Bible available to many more people than ever before.

1517
Martin Luther produces his Ninety-Five Theses, initiating the Protestant Reformation.

Here is how we believe that came to be: In 1820, when Joseph Smith was about fourteen years old, he went to a grove of trees behind his home and asked God which of all the existing churches was the Lord's true church and which one he should join. In a heavenly vision, the Lord Jesus Christ and God the Father appeared to him. He was told that, although the existing churches had "a form of godliness" (i.e., all churches taught some truths), none of the existing churches taught the fullness of Christ's truth nor were they recognized as the Lord's original church (Joseph Smith—History 1:18–19). However, because of God's great love for all His children, the time was right to reestablish Jesus Christ's church on the earth.

Similar to the way Noah, Abraham, and Moses were chosen as prophets, Joseph Smith was also prepared and called to be a prophet of the Lord in these latter days and to reestablish God's truth. He was visited by heavenly messengers—including the ancient apostles Peter, James, and John—who laid their hands on Joseph Smith's head and gave him the same power and authority Jesus had given to them. Additional angels visited Joseph Smith, including Moses, Elijah, and Elias,[14] to give him additional authority and to "restore all things" (Matthew 17:11). With this authority, Joseph Smith was directed by Christ to reestablish His church on the earth once more and to call twelve modern-day apostles. **Through repeated revelations to Joseph Smith, Jesus' original ordinances, teachings, and covenants were reestablished.**[15] Once more, the Church of Jesus Christ was established on the earth.

We claim and believe that The Church of Jesus Christ of Latter-day Saints is the very kingdom that Daniel prophesied would "stand for ever" in the last days (Daniel 2:44) and fill the earth. We believe it is the very "restitution of all things" (Acts 3:21) prophesied to take place before Jesus returns to earth. We believe it is "the dispensation of the fulness of times" where God has gathered "together in one all things" (Ephesians 1:10). We believe it is literally and truly the Church of Jesus Christ restored once more.

1776
The Revolutionary War begins as the American colonists seek to free themselves from British oppression.

1820
Fourteen-year-old Joseph Smith goes into a grove of trees to pray and receives what becomes known as the First Vision.

1620
The Mayflower transports the Pilgrims from Plymouth, England, to Plymouth, Massachusetts.

1791
The Bill of Rights, or the first ten amendments to the Constitution of the United States, are ratified. The First Amendment establishes freedom of religion.

Restoration—It Has Nothing to Do with Grandpa's Car

One word that we Mormons use a lot in describing our message to the world is that Jesus' church has been *restored*. This word can be confusing to some people because when we think of restoration, we often think of *Restoration Hardware*, or fixing up an old home, or clicking "restore" on the computer that just crashed, or getting that '69 Mustang painted cherry-red—something that always existed and just needs a bit of fixing up. But when Mormons say that Jesus' church has been *restored*, we don't mean that Jesus' church just got a new coat of theological paint to an already existing organization.

We believe the authorized church of Jesus Christ officially ceased to exist on the earth. Its prophets and apostles were rejected and killed. The authority to act in God's name was not passed on. The tree of Jesus' original church was no longer alive. And it would remain that way until a new seed was planted, prophets were reestablished, authority was reinstated, and the Church's divine organization was rebuilt—or in other words, that Jesus' church was *restored* to the earth.

For Mormons, this ↑ is *not* what we mean when we say *Restoration*. What we mean is this. ↓

We Are Not a New Church— We Are Jesus' Original Church Reestablished

Mormons are not Catholic or Orthodox, Evangelical or Protestant. From our perspective, we are not even a new Church. We believe that we follow the same everlasting gospel that Adam and Eve did. We believe that the plan of salvation we teach (see chapter 4) is the same plan that was taught by Abraham and Moses and Jesus. We believe that we are part of the original covenant, simply reestablished today.

MORMONISM ESTABLISHED YEAR 1 BY ADAM AND EVE

The Cycle of Apostasy and Restoration

God calls a prophet, reveals His truth to him, and gives him authority to work in God's name.

God loves His people—who are now living in generational error—and wants to help them know and come to the truth.

The prophet teaches God's truth ("Thus saith the Lord . . .).

Although the idea of God's people falling away from truth (apostasy) and then God's truth being reestablished (restoration) might seem new to some, we believe this same cycle has happened again and again. (Just read the Old Testament! Come on, children of Israel, can't you stay faithful for just one generation? Please? You just got saved from Pharaoh and now what's this? A golden cow? C'mon!) Here is the pattern, which happened from Adam to Noah to Abraham to Moses to Jesus and now, we claim, to Joseph Smith.

A widespread falling away from truth (apostasy) occurs.

People accept the truth (good choice).

People begin to turn away from the prophet's messages (not good) and distance themselves from God (even worse).

Scan this code to meet **Brandon McEuen** and watch the story of his decision to join The Church of Jesus Christ of Latter-day Saints through the influence of his on-the-field rival, but off-the-field friend, Teren Bingham.

MORMYTH: Because they believe their church is true, Mormons think that they are the only ones who will go to heaven and that other churches are bad.

Answer: False.

If that were the case, heaven would be a very lonely place indeed, considering that 99.98 percent of the world's population are not members of the LDS Church.

We firmly believe that God is a God of perfect justice and mercy and that no heavenly blessing will be given to one person that is not made available and offered to everyone (see chapter 4 to understand this concept more fully).

Additionally, although we humbly claim that The Church of Jesus Christ of Latter-day Saints is the Lord's official church, we honor the goodness and virtue of other churches and belief systems as well as their faithful and wonderful adherents. The LDS handbook of instructions for its local leaders says, "Much that is inspiring, noble, and worthy of the highest respect is found in many other faiths."[17] Perhaps LDS Church President Gordon B. Hinckley (1910–2008) stated our viewpoint best in 2002: "This [that the LDS Church is Jesus Christ's restored church] must be our great and singular message to the world. We do not offer it with boasting. We testify in humility but with gravity and absolute sincerity. We invite all, the whole earth, to listen to this account and take measure of its truth. . . . To [those of other faiths] we say in a spirit of love, bring with you all that you have of good and truth which you have received from whatever source, and come and let us see if we may add to it."[18]

3

Are Mormons Christian?

Latter-day Saints and the Gospel of Jesus Christ

Mislabels can cause problems.

Perhaps it's because of our "Mormon" nickname (officially we are The Church of Jesus Christ of Latter-day Saints), but Mormonism is sometimes mislabeled as a non-Christian religion. If being a "Christian" is defined by a love of Jesus Christ, believing in His saving divinity, and a desire to follow His teachings, then Latter-day Saints are most decidedly Christian. Obviously, the LDS Church has some theological differences about Jesus that make it distinct from most Protestant Christian denominations. However, as Mormonism's founding prophet, Joseph Smith, said, "The fundamental principles of our religion are . . . concerning Jesus Christ, that He died, was buried, and rose again the third day, and ascended into heaven; and all

Mislabels can cause problems.

other things which pertain to our religion are only appendages to [this]."[1] As Mormons, "We talk of Christ, we rejoice in Christ, we preach of Christ, we prophesy of Christ, and we write according to our prophecies, that our children may know to what source they may look for a remission of their sins" (2 Nephi 25:26).

Here's a little about how Mormons view the Savior of the world, even Jesus the Christ.

The question is not "Are Mormons Christian?" The real question is "Are Mormons the original Christians?" See chapter 2 to understand this point more fully.

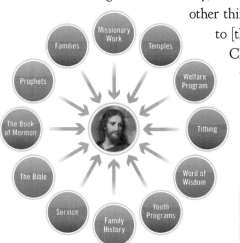

". . . all other things which pertain to our religion are only appendages to [Jesus Christ]."—Joseph Smith

Which of These Paintings Is Good Art?

Most people today would say that both of these paintings are good pieces of art. As a matter of fact, many people could probably name the artist who painted the lilies quicker than they could name the artist who painted the classical piece. But if we had been living in France in the mid-1800s, almost none of us would have considered the impressionist piece as "art," let alone *good* art. The impressionists (like Monet, Degas, and Renoir) expanded on the classical definition of art and its purpose, and it turned out wonderfully. But how did traditional painters and the French salons respond to the impressionists' paintings? (Note: the following line must be read with a snooty, nineteenth-century French accent.) "Quoi? This is not true aaaaahhhhrt. Theees is le Ugly!"

If we had been living in France in the mid-1800s, almost none of us would have considered the impressionist piece as "art," let alone good art.

So what does art history have to do with Mormons and Jesus? Simply that, just as the impressionists were still artists even though their art expanded on classicism, Mormons are still "Christian," even though our theological painting of Jesus takes a slightly different style from that of "classical" Christianity. (Hey, is that a Van Gogh print in your kitchen?)

Who Do Mormons Believe Jesus Was and Is?

Here are a few titles Latter-day Saints give Jesus of Nazareth:

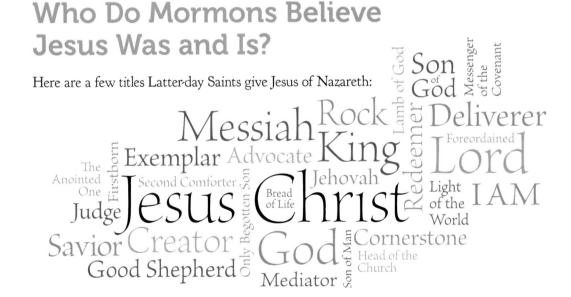

Latter-day Saints believe that Jesus Christ . . .

Every talk, every prayer, every blessing, and every ordinance in Mormonism is done *in the name of Jesus Christ.*

- is the **"firstborn"** spirit of Heavenly Father in the premortal life (see Romans 8:29; Doctrine and Covenants 93:21).

- is a **God** and one **member of the Godhead** (i.e., God the Father, Jesus Christ, and the Holy Ghost) (see 2 Nephi 31:21; Doctrine and Covenants 20:28).

- is a **distinct** and **separate individual** from God the Father, although He is **one in purpose** with His Father (see 1 Corinthians 8:6; 1 Timothy 2:5; 2 Nephi 31:21; Mosiah 15:4; Doctrine and Covenants 20:28).

- is the **"only begotten"** of God in the flesh (see John 1:14; 3:16; Alma 5:48).

- is the **creator** of the world (see John 1:3; Mosiah 3:8).

- is the **Great Jehovah** of the Old Testament and the God of Israel; the great "I AM" (see Exodus 3:14; Isaiah 12:2; John 8:57–58).

- is **perfect** and **sinless** (see Doctrine and Covenants 45:4), although He was tempted like all of us (see Luke 22:28; Hebrews 4:15).

- is the **master teacher** (see John 3:2), and His ways are the path to happiness in this life (see Mosiah 2:41).

- **suffered** for the sins of the world and overcame death for all through His crucifixion and subsequent resurrection (see Matthew 20:28; 2 Nephi 2:7; Alma 7:11–14).

- experienced and **overcame all** the physical, emotional, mental, and spiritual pains of all of mankind in the Garden of Gethsemane (see Luke 22:41–44; Alma 7:11–14).

- is our perfect **exemplar** (see John 13:15; 2 Nephi 31:16; 3 Nephi 27:27).

- has the power to **forgive** sins (see Matthew 9:6; Doctrine and Covenants 61:2).

- is the **Savior** of the world (see 1 John 4:14; 1 Nephi 13:40; Doctrine and Covenants 43:34).

- is **resurrected** with a tangible body of flesh and bone (see Luke 24:36–39; 3 Nephi 11:14–17).

- is the **living head** of The Church of Jesus Christ of Latter-day Saints (see Colossians 1:18; Mosiah 26:22; Doctrine and Covenants 1:1).

- is our **advocate** with the Father and our **mediator** at the final judgment (see 1 Timothy 2:5; 1 John 2:1; Doctrine and Covenants 45:3).

- will **come again** to the earth and reign personally upon it as its king (see Matthew 24:3).

- will **save** all those who believe on His name (see John 1:12; 2 Nephi 25:13).

Scan this QR code to read an official declaration published in 2000 by the LDS First Presidency and Quorum of the Twelve Apostles: "**The Living Christ: The Testimony of the Apostles.**"

Mary—The Mother of Jesus

Although our worship and faith is centered in Jesus Christ, we revere Mary as the mortal mother of God's son and believe that—as one of the noblest of all God's spirit children—she was chosen before she was born to become the mother of the Son of God (see 1 Nephi 11:15). About 125 years before Jesus was born, a Book of Mormon prophet testified: "And he shall be called Jesus Christ, the Son of God, the Father of heaven and earth, the Creator of all things from the beginning; and his mother shall be called Mary" (Mosiah 3:8).

Jesus and God the Father

This is one point of distinction between LDS theology and some other religions that also believe in the divinity of Jesus Christ. Most Christians believe that God the Father and Jesus Christ are the same person in different forms. However, Mormons believe that God the Father and Jesus Christ are two separate and distinct individuals.

Joseph Smith wrote, "I saw two Personages, whose brightness and glory defy all description, standing above me in the air" (Joseph Smith—History 1:17).

When LDS prophet Joseph Smith saw his First Vision in 1820, he "saw two Personages, whose brightness and glory defy all description, standing above me in the air. One of them spake unto me, calling me by name and said, pointing to the other—*This is My Beloved Son. Hear Him!*" (Joseph Smith—History 1:17; emphasis in original). For Latter-day Saints, this is consistent with Biblical passages such as when the disciple Stephen saw the resurrected "Jesus standing on the right hand of God" (Acts 7:55). Mormons believe that the "oneness" of God the Father and Jesus Christ spoken of in the scriptures comes through a unity of shared purpose, similar to the oneness and unity among the twelve separate apostles that Jesus prayed for: "that they [the apostles] may be one, even as we [God the Father and Jesus] are one" (John 17:22).

The Atonement of Jesus Christ

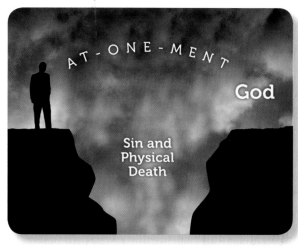

Mormons believe that because of the fall of Adam and Eve, all mankind has become subject to both physical death and spiritual death (sin). Sin and physical death stop us from becoming like our Heavenly Father and returning to His presence. Jesus Christ's Atonement overcame the effects of sin and death for all mankind and made us "at one" with God again (thus, *at-one-ment*, or Atonement). Because of Jesus Christ, we will all be resurrected and live forever

Jesus Christ's Atonement overcame the effects of sin and death for all mankind and enabled us to be "at one" with God again.

(see John 5:29), and by submitting ourselves to Jesus' teachings (such as developing faith in Jesus Christ and repenting of our mistakes) and Jesus' ordinances (such as baptism), we can be cleansed from the effects of our sins and made worthy to live in our Heavenly Father's presence. The Book of Mormon summarizes it this way: "Behold, [God] created Adam, and by Adam came the fall of man. And because of the fall of man came Jesus Christ . . . ; and because of Jesus Christ came the redemption of man" (Mormon 9:12).

We believe that, in the Garden of Gethsemane, Jesus Christ "stood in our place and suffered the penalty for our sins."[2]

We believe that Jesus voluntarily gave His life on the cross and that, as God's Son, He had the power to take His life again, becoming an immortal being of flesh and bone (see Luke 24:36–39; 3 Nephi 11:14–17). Because Jesus has power over death, we believe that all

We believe that Jesus voluntarily gave His life on the cross.

mankind can and will be resurrected and live forever (see 1 Corinthians 15:22; Alma 11:41; Mormon 9:13).

As God's Son, Jesus Christ had the power to take His life again, becoming an immortal being of flesh and bone.

Nobody Knows How I Feel . . . Except Jesus

We believe that Jesus has experienced every physical, emotional, spiritual, and mental challenge ever faced by humanity. Not only has He experienced them, He has overcome them. Because He has overcome them, we believe that Jesus is able to help us, guide us, and strengthen us to meet and overcome any challenge we may face in our lives (see Alma 7:11–14).

We believe that Jesus has experienced every physical, emotional, spiritual, and mental challenge ever faced by humanity.

"How Great Thou Art!"

A favorite hymn that Mormons often sing in our church meetings is "How Great Thou Art." The words of the hymn describe many of the great and glorious things we believe Jesus has done. We feel that our theology exalts and expands our understanding of Jesus and His divine role. For example, Mormons don't think that people began exercising faith in Jesus Christ and being baptized in His name beginning in A.D. 30, but we believe that Jesus has been the central feature of God's plan since the days of Adam[3] and that "all the prophets who have prophesied ever since the world began" have declared that Jesus is the Christ (Mosiah 13:33; see also John 8:56–58). We even believe we were worshipping Jesus before we were born.[4] We also believe that Jesus didn't limit His presence to only those living near Jerusalem at the time of His mortal ministry, but that He visited His people in the Americas shortly after His resurrection (see 3 Nephi 11), as well as visiting others.[5]

We declare that Jesus is not only the creator of this world, but that "worlds without number" (Moses 1:33) have been and continue to be created by Jesus Christ.

We declare that Jesus is not only the creator of this world, but that "worlds without number" (Moses 1:33) have been and continue to be created by Jesus Christ.[6] We believe that not only did Jesus speak to prophets in the past, but that He continues to reveal Himself and speak to prophets today. These are just some reasons why Mormons sing to Jesus, "How Great Thou Art."

What Is the "Gospel of Jesus Christ"?

The gospel of Jesus Christ is this:

1. Faith in the Lord Jesus Christ,
2. Repentance,
3. Baptism by immersion by one holding the proper priesthood authority,
4. Reception of the Holy Ghost (see Articles of Faith 1:4).

In the Book of Mormon, Jesus defines the gospel this way: "Repent, all ye ends of the earth, and come unto me and be baptized in my name, that ye may be sanctified by the reception of the Holy Ghost, that ye may stand spotless before me at the last day. Verily, verily, I say unto you, this is my gospel" (3 Nephi 27:20–21).

Little Children and Jesus' Atonement

We believe that Jesus' atonement freely saves all children who die before the age of accountability (eight years old) because "little children need no repentance, neither baptism" (Moroni 8:11). Because of Jesus' atonement, "all children who die before they arrive at the years of accountability are saved in the celestial kingdom of heaven" (Doctrine and Covenants 137:10).

MORMYTH:
Mormons don't believe in being "saved by grace."

Hear it loud and clear: The answer to this question is FALSE! (Amen! Hallelujah!)

If you ever hear someone answer "no" to whether Mormons believe they will be saved by Jesus' grace, then they simply don't understand our doctrine. The Book of Mormon is wonderfully rich on the doctrine of grace and teaches that "there is no flesh that can dwell in the presence of God, save it be through the merits, and mercy, and grace of the Holy Messiah" (2 Nephi 2:8). In all, there are more than twenty-eight references to "grace" in the Book of Mormon, and the concluding message of the Book of Mormon is this: "Yea, come unto Christ, and be perfected in him, and deny yourselves of all ungodliness; and if ye shall deny yourselves of all ungodliness, and love God with all your might, mind and strength, then is his grace sufficient for you, that by his grace ye may be perfect in Christ" (Moroni 10:32).

In all, there are more than twenty-eight references to "grace" in the Book of Mormon.

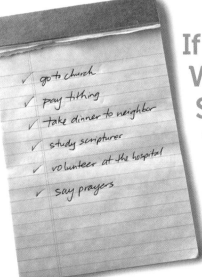

✓ go to church
✓ pay tithing
✓ take dinner to neighbor
✓ study scriptures
✓ volunteer at the hospital
✓ say prayers

If Jesus Saves, Then Why Do Mormons Place Such Emphasis on Their "Works"?

Nice job, but we don't believe any of these works will save us.

This is a fair question, because, although we know it is Jesus who saves us and not ourselves, we do place a lot of importance on whether or not we live the gospel. **However, the idea that Mormons believe in salvation by works is not true.**

Mormons try to do good works for a few primary reasons: (1) because we love Jesus and therefore worship Him by striving to follow His teachings and example (see John 14:15); (2) as we do good works, we become more receptive to and influenced by God's Spirit, which produces increased joy, love, and happiness (see Galatians 5:22–25); and (3) because we want to be worthy to make covenants (or sacred agreements) with God that will bind us to Christ (see the "Joined with Jesus" section below).

However, even if as Mormons we fed all the world's hungry, clothed all the naked, provided for all the poor, prayed ten times daily, and studied the scriptures until our retinas were burnt, we still don't think *those works* would save us. After all, it is Jesus' grace that inspires and helps us to do good works in the first place, and it is only through Jesus' grace that our sins are remitted and that we will be resurrected. Thus, we believe that it is only through the grace of Jesus that we will be saved.

Joined with Jesus—the Covenant

For you math geniuses out there, what is the answer to this equation?

$$\infty + 30 =$$

The answer, of course, is infinity, because something that is infinite cannot be added to nor taken away from.[7]

The Book of Mormon describes Jesus' atonement as "an infinite atonement" (Alma 34:12; see also 2 Nephi 25:16). This means that Jesus has paid the price for all sin, for all people, for all time. There is no end to Jesus' ability to save. But how do we become connected to Christ and His infinite ability to save? How do we become joined with Jesus? How do we get access to His saving grace?

The answer to that question is through *covenant*, which is a sacred agreement between God and man. Our good works (like the "30" in the infinity equation) simply prepare us to make covenants with God. The key to the equation is the plus symbol—the thing that joins the number (representing us) to infinity (representing Jesus).

Consider the covenant of marriage[8]—we covenant and promise to join ourselves with our partner, to be faithful, to be true, and to give all that we have and are to this person. In return, our spouse makes the same promises to us. We witness this exchange through a marriage *covenant*.

Similarly, when we make covenants with God, we give all that we are to Christ, and He, in return, gives all that He has and is to us. His perfection becomes our perfection; His purity, our purity. Thus, through honoring our covenant connection with Jesus, we are made clean and able to return worthy to God's presence. We make covenants with God through necessary outward ordinances like baptism (see Mark 16:16). Thus, as a metaphor, Jesus tells us to "take my yoke upon you" (Matthew 11:29). A yoke is something that *joins* two things together. It is through joining (+) yourself (30)

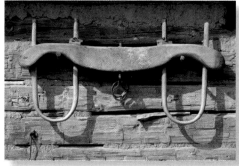

Jesus tells us to "take my yoke upon you" (Matthew 11:29). A yoke is something that joins two things together and is a metaphor for a covenant.

with the infinite Christ (∞) by covenant that "ye shall find rest unto your souls" (Matthew 11:29) (=) in heaven. (See chapter 5 for more on the role of priesthood authority in making covenants.)

If Mormons Believe in Jesus, Why Don't They Have Crosses on Their Buildings?

LDS prophet and Church President Gordon B. Hinckley (1910–2008) once said: "I do not wish to give offense to any of my Christian brethren who use the cross on the steeples of their cathedrals and at the altars of their chapels, who wear it on their vestments and imprint it on their books and other literature. But for us, the cross is the symbol of the dying Christ, while our message is a declaration of the living Christ."[9]

Some have said that the symbol of Mormonism is our temples, or even the angel on top of our temples.[10] Others have said our symbol has

"I do not wish to give offense to any of my Christian brethren. . . . But for us, the cross is the symbol of the dying Christ, while our message is a declaration of the living Christ."—President Gordon B. Hinckley

become our missionaries,[11] or the unique way that we Mormons live our lives.[12] **While all of these may be true, they all point to the true symbol and head of our Church—the risen Lord Jesus Christ.** All Mormon temples have the name of Jesus Christ on them, all Mormon missionaries wear a tag each day that bears the Lord's name on it, and each member of the LDS Church makes a promise to "take upon [them] the name of Christ, by baptism" (2 Nephi 31:13). Jesus Christ is the greatest symbol of our Church, and all other symbols in Mormonism point to and declare His living reality.

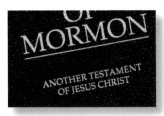

The Savior's name is also in the subtitle of the Book of Mormon.

All Mormon temples have the name of Jesus Christ on them.

What? Jesus and Satan Are Brothers?

Sometimes people hear that Mormons teach that Satan and Jesus are "brothers," implying through this statement an elevated view of Satan or a degraded view of Jesus. This idea stems from the LDS doctrine that all spirits—including Jesus' and Satan's—were created by God in an innocent premortal state. However, some of these spirits, led by Satan (or Lucifer, as the scriptures name him), rebelled against God and were cast out of God's presence to the earth as disembodied spirits (see Revelation 12:7–11).

Other than the common spiritual parentage with God the Father that we all share, nowhere in LDS doctrine do we teach that Jesus and Satan are "brothers" or alike in any way. Rather, we adhere to Jesus' teaching that "whosoever shall do the will of my Father which is in heaven, the same is my brother, and sister" (Matthew 12:50). Therefore, in that spiritual sense, LDS doctrine confirms that Satan is in no way closely related to Jesus.

Scan this QR code to read about how other Mormons respond to the question, **"Are Mormons Christian?"**

4 What Is the Purpose of Life?

Perhaps no more important questions are asked than the ones centered on the meaning of life: "What is life's purpose?" "Who am I?" "Where did I come from?" "What happens when I die?" Mormons believe we have answers to these questions and that there is more to life than just a person's day-to-day mortal existence. Latter-day Saints believe that everyone's life has a divine meaning and purpose. We believe that within each person on this earth there is something divine. We believe that each life has infinite worth. We believe that this life is part of a heavenly plan.

And we are not alone. Guess what?

85%

of Americans believe that "God is a caring God who has a plan for us."[1]

"For behold, this is my work and my glory—to bring to pass the immortality and eternal life of man" (Moses 1:39).

God's Plan of Salvation

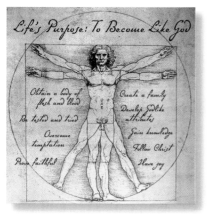

The *plan of salvation* is the term used to describe God's eternal purpose for all mankind. We believe that God's purposes are best summarized in this LDS scripture: "For behold, this is my work and my glory—to bring to pass the immortality and eternal life of man" (Moses 1:39). The plan of salvation includes our premortal birth in God's presence as His spirit children, the creation of the world as a place for us to inhabit, the Fall of Adam and Eve, which brought about physical death and sin, and the atonement of Jesus Christ, which reconciles our fallen condition. The plan of salvation also includes all the teachings of Jesus Christ. Because of this plan, mankind can receive a fullness of joy and happiness, have family relationships that last eternally, be made perfect by Jesus' Atonement, and eventually become like God and live eternally in His presence.

How old do you think this person is? Maybe 6,000,000 years old? Keep reading.

When Did My Life Begin? The Premortal Life

Whoever you are reading this book, you are probably not the age you think you are—at least your spirit isn't. And sorry to all of you who are thinking, "Of course I'm not my age. I'm younger in spirit!" Leave it to the Mormons to give you a downer: You are actually *older* in spirit—probably thousands and thousands of years older. (Hey, turning fifty suddenly doesn't seem so bad!)

Mormons believe that life on earth begins when a person's spirit enters its mortal body and that each individual spirit came into existence long before he or she was ever born on earth. We believe that God the Father created each individual spirit and that we all are *literally* the spirit sons and daughters of God. We are His offspring. We believe that all people lived with God in a premortal condition as His spirit children before they were born. Although Mormonism is one of the few belief systems that formally teaches this concept, **fully 28% of Americans believe they "lived with God before coming to earth."**[2]

In this premortal life, God taught all of us about His purposes and His plans—including His desire to enact a plan for all His children to eventually become like Him.

There we learned, developed talents, progressed, developed our identity, and—having been endowed with the freedom to choose for ourselves—we were able to choose obedience or disobedience to God's plan. We believe that in this premortal life mankind was prepared to come to earth and continue to progress.

> Joseph Smith taught about the premortal life: "God himself, finding he was in the midst of spirits and glory, because he was more intelligent, saw proper to institute laws whereby the rest could have a privilege to advance like himself."[3]

A 2007 Gallup poll indicates that **70 percent** of Americans believe in the devil.[4]

Latter-day Saints believe that in the premortal life one of God's spirit sons, Lucifer, used his agency and chose to rebel against God and His plan of salvation. Because of this open rebellion, God cast Lucifer and those who followed him out of heaven to the earth, where they were denied the opportunity to obtain a mortal body or ever go to heaven. Lucifer became known as "Satan" and has continued to fight against God and His purposes ever since (see Revelation 12:7–9).

Who Am I?

GOD the Father

Latter-day Saint children sing a song that contains perhaps the most important knowledge available to mankind in understanding a person's true identity: "I am a child of God, and he has sent me here."[5] So many of us are searching to find ourselves, yet on our spiritual ancestry we need look back no further than one generation: We believe all mankind are literally **sons and daughters of God**.

We believe all mankind are literally sons and daughters of God.

Your identity is not whether you are male or female, black or white, short or tall, white-collar or blue-collar, rich or poor, Jew or Gentile, Christian or Muslim. You are a child of God.

"If Children, Then Heirs": Our Divine Potential

The Apostle Paul wrote a scripture loaded with divine potential: "The Spirit itself beareth witness with our spirit, that we are the children of God: and if children, then heirs; heirs of God, and joint-heirs with Christ" (Romans 8:16–17). For Latter-day Saints, since we believe all mankind are literally the children of God, then logically **all mankind has inherited divine potential.** We believe every individual has the innate capacity to eventually become like God. Just as an oak seed can eventually become a mighty oak tree, we believe that, as God's seed, each person has the potential to eventually become like our Mighty Parent in the next life.

Just as an oak seed can eventually become a mighty oak tree, we believe that, as God's seed, we have the potential to become like our Mighty Parent in the next life.

Quotes on Divine Potential: Gods in Embryo

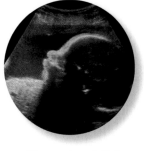

- The Old Testament Psalmist: "I have said, Ye are gods; and all of you are children of the most High" (Psalm 82:6).

- Jesus in the New Testament: "Is it not written in your law, I said, Ye are gods?" (John 10:34).

"Ye are gods; and all of you are children of the most High" (Psalm 82:6).

- The LDS Doctrine and Covenants: Those who go to heaven "are gods, even the sons of God" (Doctrine and Covenants 76:58).

- Writer and Christian theologian C. S. Lewis proposed that we are all potential gods and goddesses in embryo, writing: "It is a serious thing to live in a society of possible gods and goddesses, to remember that the dullest and most uninteresting person you can talk to may one day be a creature which, if you [saw] it now, you would be strongly tempted to worship. . . . There are no *ordinary* people. You have never talked to a mere mortal."[6]

Why Am I Here? The Purpose of Life

"In the premortal existence, Heavenly Father prepared a plan to *enable us to become like Him* and receive a fulness of joy."[7]

We believe that the purpose of life can be summarized into five words: **TO BECOME MORE LIKE GOD.**

If we each are here to become more like God, the logical follow-up is the question: **What is God like?** Latter-day Saints believe that

- **God is perfect** (see Matthew 5:48). Connected to His perfection is the fact that God is perfectly holy—meaning He is perfectly clean from sin and wrongdoing (see 2 Nephi 9:20; Moses 6:57).

- **God has divine attributes** such as kindness, love, patience, gentleness, mercy, and empathy (see 1 John 4:8; Alma 26:35; Moroni 8:3).

Although not discussed overtly in official statements of LDS doctrine, we believe all of mankind are the spiritual offspring of heavenly parents—an Eternal Father and an Eternal Mother—who are joined in a celestial, eternal marriage. (See chapter 19 for more on the LDS doctrine pertaining to a Heavenly Mother.)

- **God is omniscient.** The Book of Mormon teaches that "for [God] knoweth all things, and there is not anything save he knows it" (2 Nephi 9:20).

- **God is the Father** of everyone's spirit (see Romans 8:16), and all are children of "heavenly parents."[8]

Joseph Smith taught: "If you were to see [God] today, you would see him like a man in form—like yourselves in all the person, image, and very form as a man."[9]

There are those who point to Biblical verses about "the invisible God" (Colossians 1:15) or that "God is a Spirit" (John 4:24) to reject LDS theology on the corporal nature of God, and although we respect that interpretation, we kindly disagree. We believe that God is invisible to those who are not in harmony with His will and that God does have a spirit, as well as a body, as do we.

Aside from Genesis 1:26–27, which speaks of man being created in God's corporal image, there are numerous Biblical references that refer to God's bodily nature. The scriptures speak of God's face (see Genesis 32:30; Exodus 33:11), his feet (see Exodus 24:10), his finger (see Exodus 31:18), his back (see Exodus 33:23), his mouth (see Numbers 12:8), and his body (see Philippians 3:21).

The resurrected Christ had His disciples touch His hands and feet, and He told them, "a spirit hath not flesh and bones, as ye see me have" (Luke 24:39). We believe that whosoever has seen Christ "hath seen the Father" (John 14:9) and that similarly God the Father is indeed a tangible being with an actual body of flesh and bone (see Doctrine and Covenants 130:22).

- **God has an immortal, physical body** "of flesh and bones as tangible as man's" (Doctrine and Covenants 130:22). We believe that when "God created man in his own image" (Genesis 1:27), that is exactly what it means. God has a body, head, hands, arms, and legs—and humanity is patterned after His likeness.

So if mankind is here to learn to become more like God, and if knowing the nature of God gives necessary direction to life's purpose, then some of the main reasons we are here on earth are to

- **Receive a body.** Not only are we here to receive a body, but we are also here to learn to control its appetites and passions within the boundaries God has set for us. We believe much of life's purpose revolves around treating the body with dignity and respect, as it is the instrument of the spirit. Additionally, because we receive a mortal body, we are all destined to die, but—through Christ's merciful atonement—we will all eventually be resurrected and have an *immortal* body, which is a necessary component to becoming like God. (See chapter 10 for more on this concept.)

We believe if a person harms the body, they harm the spirit, and therefore the soul.

"Know ye not that ye are the temple of God, and that the Spirit of God dwelleth in you? If any man defile the temple of God, him shall God destroy; for the temple of God is holy, which temple ye are."—1 Corinthians 3:16–17

"And the spirit and the body are the soul of man."—Doctrine and Covenants 88:15

■ **Gain intelligence and knowledge.** Can you imagine a God who doesn't know everything—including history, science, art, and math? Mormon doctrine declares that "the glory of God is intelligence, or, in other words, light and truth" (Doctrine and Covenants 93:36). If God is intelligent, then to become like Him, a person needs to try to be intelligent as well. Knowing that God is intelligent is one reason why Mormons "consider the obtaining of an education to be a religious responsibility."[10]

■ **Develop Godlike attributes.** Developing kindness, selflessness, charity, empathy, patience, purity, humility, and a host of other godly attributes is another purpose of life. For many of us, these attributes do not come easily and often come only as a result of character refinement through difficulty and trial.

■ **Create an eternal family.** We believe that marriage is necessary to become like God and that "Marriage between man and woman is essential to [God's] eternal plan."[12] It makes logical sense that to become more like our heavenly parents that it is necessary to become earthly parents, joined together with a spouse for eternity in a loving marriage. That

To become more like our Heavenly Parents, it is necessary to become earthly parents.

is why LDS scriptures teach that being "sealed" (or joined together forever) to a spouse by the proper authority in the temple is necessary for exaltation and to become like God (see Doctrine and Covenants 131:1–4; 132:18–21). (See page 49).

■ **Become perfected and holy through coming unto Christ.** The commandment to be perfect like God (see Matthew 5:48) is impossible to fulfill during mortality. The fact is that each person on earth who is capable of sin is unholy to one degree or another and therefore not like God or able to live in His purified presence (see Romans 3:23).

But if God is perfect, and mankind is not, then how do we become so?

The answer, like all such answers, is found in Jesus Christ. **We believe that through the atonement of Jesus Christ all of mankind can overcome the effects of sin** (see chapter 3). However, Mormons believe that becoming cleansed from sin through Jesus' suffering is conditional upon a person's acceptance of Jesus as his Redeemer and upon his commitment to strive to follow Jesus' ways as one of His disciples. Therefore, Latter-day Saints believe that one of the fundamental purposes of this life is to come unto Christ, exercise faith and repent in His name, witness that we are willing to become His disciples through the covenant of baptism, and thereafter be led by His Spirit and strive to do His will.

If We All Lived with God Before, Then Why Didn't We Just Stay There?

Latter-day Saints believe that although we all lived in God's presence before birth, coming to this earth was a necessary step to fulfill God's plan in helping His children become more like Him. There was only so far a person could progress in a premortal condition. It's like a single forty-year-old guy who still lives in his parents' basement—move on, man, move on. We believe that it was necessary to come to earth to receive a mortal body, learn to control its inherent appetites and passions, be more fully tested and tried, and create families. Those things were either limited or not fully available in our premortal condition. Therefore, **it was necessary for each of us to "move out" of our premortal childhood home and come to earth as part of our eternal progression.**

Agency and Accountability

One doctrine related to the plan of salvation that Latter-day Saints hold dear is the doctrine of agency. **Agency means the power of independent action, or the ability to choose between good and evil, right and wrong.** We believe this divine gift of agency has been with each person since their premortal life. We believe God gives people the power and strength to choose righteousness and happiness, no matter what their circumstances.[13] We don't believe that Satan has power over a person, except for what that person permits him to have.

Agency is "the ability to choose and to act for yourself" and "is essential in the plan of salvation."[14]

God does not force a soul to heaven, nor a soul to hell. This gift of agency is a necessary element in the plan of salvation and allows all mankind to be held accountable for their own actions at the final judgment.

> Joseph Smith taught, "All beings who have bodies have power over those who have not. The devil has no power over us only as we permit him."[15]

Why Does God Allow Temptation and Sin?

Do you remember back in the day when shopping sprees were popular? Someone won the opportunity to run through a store and grab all the stuff they wanted within a set amount of time. Being presented with a bunch of options in limited time forces people to pick what they truly desire. (You're grabbing cleaning supplies? Really? Go over to the electronics or sporting goods section, man!) When people checked out from the shopping spree, the items in their cart reflected what they desired and wanted.

Being presented with a bunch of options in limited time forces people to pick what they truly desire.

Part of the purpose of this life is to prove to God what we desire or want, and whether each of us will choose to follow His ways, even when a lot of different choices are made available. **It is by allowing both good and evil that God enables all of us to act for ourselves and purposely choose Him or not.** The Book of Mormon teaches that "God gave unto man that he should act for himself. Wherefore, man could not act for himself save it should be that he was enticed by the one or the other" (2 Nephi 2:16). We believe that at the final checkout (final judgment) God wants people with a cart full of righteous selections, even though sin was right there in front of them to choose.

If God Is Loving, Then Why Does He Allow Bad Things to Happen to Good People?

Latter-day Saints believe that God's plan for His children is not necessarily a plan of ease and comfort; it is a plan of salvation. In order for God to get us from where we are to where He wants us to be, we each must be stretched and given opportunities to grow. And, as we all know, growth often entails some discomfort and pain. If we are to develop Godlike attributes such as forgiveness, then God must allow us to occasionally be hurt by others. If we are to learn humility, then some disappointment is usually necessary. If we are to learn compassion and empathy, then we must suffer as others do. **If God were to take away life's challenges, He would be taking away our greatest friends and benefactors, as these challenges are the mold that forges divine character.**

As LDS Apostle Orson F. Whitney said so eloquently: "No pain that we suffer, no trial that we experience is wasted. It ministers to our education, to the development of such qualities as patience, faith, fortitude and humility. All that we suffer and all that we endure, especially when we endure it patiently, builds up our characters, purifies our hearts, expands our souls, and makes us more tender and charitable, more worthy to be called the children of God . . . and it is through sorrow and suffering, toil and tribulation, that we gain the education that we come here to acquire."[16]

MORMYTH:

Mormons believe that the Fall of Adam and Eve was a good thing.

Answer: True.

We don't think Adam and Eve were wicked people who messed up the good thing God had going in Eden. On the contrary, we believe that Adam and Eve were among the most noble and choice spirit sons and daughters of God. We believe that **Adam and Eve consciously and selflessly made the choice to partake of the forbidden fruit so that God's plan for His children could move forward** by their becoming mortal and enabling them to have children. We believe that God made provisions for a Savior—Jesus Christ—to redeem Adam and Eve and all their posterity from their fallen condition. Latter-day

Saint scripture says that after the Fall, "Eve . . . was glad, saying: Were it not for our transgression we never should have had seed, and never should have known good and evil, and the joy of our redemption, and the eternal life which God giveth unto all the obedient" (Moses 5:11).

MEET a Mormon

Scan this QR code to meet **Helmut**, a Latter-day Saint concert manager in Austria, and learn about how being a Mormon, and a father, gives him perspective on the purpose and meaning of life.

Man Is That He Might Have Joy!

Even with all this serious talk about the purpose of life, Latter-day Saints also believe mankind is here to experience happiness and joy. The Mormon ideal is not *American Gothic*, it is more like *American Frolic*. (Where's Grant Wood to paint that one?) One of our fundamental scriptures on the plan of salvation says, "Adam fell that men might be; and men are, that they might have joy" (2 Nephi 2:25).

Joseph Smith taught that **"Happiness is the object and design of our existence."**[17] We believe that God sent people to earth not only for a serious purpose, but also to enjoy the experience of it all. The scriptures tell us that one reason God created the world was aesthetic—"to please the eye and to gladden the heart" (Doctrine and Covenants 59:18). So enjoy life:

- read a book

- look at some beautiful art

- take in the fresh smell after it rains

- go for a run

- turn up the radio in your car loud enough that you think you sound good when you sing along

- eat a good meal (just no alcohol ☺)

- play a fun game

- stay up late having an enlightened and lively conversation with someone you love

- love your family

- tickle a toddler until he giggles uncontrollably

Enjoy a good book.

In other words, **have joy**. Ultimately, if each of us chooses to follow God's "plan of happiness" (Alma 42:8), not only will we experience joy in this life, but we will have a "fulness of joy" (Doctrine and Covenants 138:17) in the life to come.

Tickle a toddler.

Joseph Smith taught that the commandments of God are "calculated in [their] nature to promote that happiness which He has designed."[18]

5 LDS Priesthood Authority and Ordinances

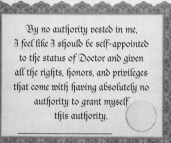

By no authority vested in me, I feel like I should be self-appointed to the status of Doctor and given all the rights, honors, and privileges that come with having absolutely no authority to grant myself this authority.

Sign on this line here and you are a self-appointed doctor!

"The priesthood cannot be conferred like a diploma. It cannot be handed to you as a certificate. It cannot be delivered to you as a message or sent to you in a letter. It comes only by proper ordination. An authorized holder of the priesthood has to be there. He must place his hands upon your head and ordain you."—LDS Apostle Boyd K. Packer (1924–)[1]

So you want to be a medical doctor? Oh, don't worry about qualifying, just go ahead and give yourself the title. Congratulations! Make sure you celebrate!

Oh, you want to be the governor of your state now? No need for an election, just make a self-appointment. Always fancied yourself an attorney-at-law? What are you waiting for? Slap a sign in the office window and start offering legal counsel tomorrow! Not enough police help in your city? Then put down this book and head on over to yonder superstore and get a badge and a gun—now you're official!

Well, actually, you're not.

It's pretty clear what societal problems and confusion would result if people assumed these important titles and positions without going through legitimate channels to gain the proper authority. But what about gaining authority to officially act in the things of eternity?

When it comes to religion, there are many today who feel they can simply assume heavenly authorization. A quick search on the Internet, a few clicks of a mouse, and, no questions asked, a person can obtain a certificate to begin baptizing and confirming people, offering sacred sacraments and spiritual ceremonies without any celestial sanction. This problematic claim to heavenly authority is not new, as is evident in a telling rhyme by Charles Wesley, directed toward his more famous brother and eighteenth-century religious reformer, John Wesley:

> "How easily are bishops made
> By man or woman's whim:
> Wesley his hands on Coke hath laid,
> But who laid hands on him?"[2]

Mormon doctrine provides a logical answer to Wesley's question. Latter-day Saints believe **there is order and structure to who can claim heavenly authority, how it is received and passed on, and why it is necessary.**

Here's a little bit about what Mormons believe about priesthood authority and ordinances.

"Man Must Be Called of God"

For Mormons, the priesthood is "the power and authority that God gives to man to act in all things necessary for the salvation of God's children."[3] The Prophet Joseph Smith said this of conferring priesthood power: "We believe that a man must be called of God, by prophecy, and by the laying on of hands by those who are in authority, to preach the Gospel and administer in the ordinances thereof" (Articles of Faith 1:5).

Jesus was teaching in the temple when He was twelve. We expect our twelve-year-olds to carry some responsibility.

The Aaronic and Melchizedek Priesthoods and Offices

The New Testament speaks of two priesthoods: "the order of Melchisedec" and "the order of Aaron" (Hebrews 7:11). The Aaronic Priesthood was named after Moses' brother, Aaron, and the Melchizedek Priesthood was named after the king of Jerusalem and great high priest, Melchizedek (see Doctrine and Covenants 107:2). The Bible tells us that Jesus Himself was "an high priest . . . after the order of Melchisedec" (Hebrews 5:5–6). Similarly, in Jesus' reestablished Church today, there are the same two priesthood divisions.

The Aaronic Priesthood is the lesser, preparatory priesthood, and Latter-day Saints who hold the Aaronic Priesthood are usually young men between the ages of twelve and eighteen. Yes, *twelve* years old. (Jesus was teaching in the temple when He was twelve—why can't we expect our twelve-year-olds to carry some responsibility too?) Generally, when a worthy young man is sixteen years old, he is able to advance in the

Aaronic Priesthood and be ordained to the office of a priest and is given the authority to baptize and to administer the sacrament of the Lord's supper. (Yes, *sixteen*. How amazing is it that the Lord gives sixteen-year-old boys sacred power to perform ordinances and responsibilities of service? And you thought a driver's license shows trust!)

The higher priesthood in the LDS Church is the Melchizedek Priesthood. This priesthood "holds the right of presidency, and has power and authority over all the offices in the church in all ages of the world, to administer in spiritual things" (Doctrine and Covenants 107:8). A worthy man may be ordained to the Melchizedek Priesthood when he is eighteen years old by making a covenant promise with God that he will faithfully serve Him in righteousness (see Doctrine and Covenants 84:33–44). Within the Melchizedek Priesthood there are different offices depending upon how you are asked to serve in the LDS Church, including the priesthood offices of elder, high priest, patriarch, seventy, and apostle. Through the authority of the Melchizedek Priesthood, LDS Church leaders guide and direct the Church on the local and general levels.

Scan this QR code to meet **Spencer Zimmerman**, a thirteen-year-old deacons quorum president, and learn how he served his fellow priesthood quorum member **Dayton Hayward**, who suffers from cerebral palsy, by carrying him during a triathlon.

LDS Priesthood Offices

The following are the offices and principal duties of each LDS priesthood office:

Melchizedek Priesthood (greater priesthood)

Elder	High Priest	Patriarch	Seventy	Apostle

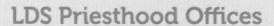

LEVEL OF RESPONSIBILITY

Deacon	Teacher	Priest	Bishop

Aaronic Priesthood (lesser priesthood)

Aaronic Priesthood

Deacon—Passes the sacrament to the congregation and helps collect offerings made for the poor.

Priest—They "teach, . . . and baptize, and administer the sacrament, and visit the house of each member" (Doctrine and Covenants 20:46–47).

Teacher—Prepares the sacrament and helps "watch over the church" (Doctrine and Covenants 20:53) by visiting members' homes with a senior companion from the Melchizedek Priesthood.

Bishop—Presides over all the members of a congregation, known as a ward, and helps determine a person's worthiness and preparedness to participate in gospel ordinances. Though a bishop is an office in the Aaronic Priesthood, a high priest in the Melchizedek Priesthood normally fills the position (see Doctrine and Covenants 107:17).

Melchizedek Priesthood

Elder—Confirms those who have been baptized as new members and confers the gift of the Holy Ghost. Elders also bless those who are sick and afflicted through the laying on of hands.

High Priest—Administers "in spiritual things" (Doctrine and Covenants 107:12) and oversees the administration of local LDS congregations. Men are usually "ordained high priests when they are called to a stake presidency, high council, or bishopric [the congregational bishop and his two counselors]."[4]

Patriarch—Gives patriarchal blessings to members of the Church. These blessings declare a person's lineage and tribe in the house of Israel as well as give lifelong counsel and promised blessings.

Apostle—Is a "special [witness] of the name of Christ in all the world" (Doctrine and Covenants 107:23) and is responsible to oversee the global preaching of the gospel.

Elder David A. Bednar was ordained as an Apostle in 2004.

Seventy—Preaches the gospel to the whole world and acts under the direction of the Quorum of the Twelve Apostles.

Where Did the LDS Church Get Its Priesthood Authority?

We believe that the New Testament Church of Jesus Christ fell into eventual apostasy and that the priesthood authority given by Jesus to His New Testament apostles was not passed on through the laying on of hands to subsequent successors. (See chapter 2.) Therefore, to reestablish His Church on the earth and to provide the priesthood authority to perform necessary ordinances for salvation (like baptism),

John the Baptist restored the authority of the Aaronic Priesthood.

in 1829 the Lord sent His resurrected disciples John the Baptist, Peter, James, and John to Joseph Smith, who conferred on him, by the laying on of hands, the priesthood authority they had likewise received from Jesus (see Doctrine and Covenants 13:1; 27:12).

As an authorized servant of Jesus Christ through the laying on of hands by those already in authority, Joseph Smith then laid his hands on others and gave them priesthood authority, who in turn laid their hands on others, and others, down to today. Therefore, every single Latter-day Saint who holds the priesthood can trace his authority to perform gospel ordinances directly back to Jesus Christ. Here is a real example of a Latter-day Saint's line of authority:

In 1829, the Lord sent Peter, James, and John to restore the authority of the Melchizedek Priesthood.

Anthony Sweat was ordained an elder on 9/7/1994 by

Dennis Sweat, who was ordained at elder on 6/2/1968 by

Harold Ranquist Jr., who was ordained an elder on 8/23/1953 by

Cornelious Williams, who was ordained an elder on 10/17/1937 by

Albern Bingham, who was ordained a high priest on 9/10/1905 by

Joseph F. Smith, who was ordained an apostle on 7/1/1866 by

Brigham Young, who was ordained an apostle on 2/14/1835 by

Oliver Cowdery/David Whitmer/Martin Harris, who were given authority on 2/14/1835 to ordain the original LDS Twelve Apostles by

Joseph Smith Jr., who was ordained an apostle in 1829 by

Peter, James, and John, who were ordained as apostles by

Jesus Christ

The Laying On of Hands

It is evident in the scriptures that priesthood authority was conferred by the laying on of hands (placing your hands on someone's head) by those in authority. Moses was told to put the "honour" of his priesthood call on Joshua, "and he laid his hands upon him, and gave him a charge" (Numbers 27:20, 23). Saul and Barnabas were ordained by the apostles having "laid their hands on them" (Acts 13:3). Similarly, Latter-day Saints who hold priesthood authority today lay their hands on the head of a worthy candidate to confer the priesthood upon him and ordain him to priesthood offices.

Why Is Organized Religion and Priesthood Authority Even Necessary in Order to Worship God?

Some people believe that organized religion is not necessary and that people can get close to God in their own way, such as through experiencing nature or through personal study and meditation or prayer, without any need for systematic religion or priesthood authority. Mormons agree that God can indeed be found through personal worship, but we believe that organized religion *is* necessary because of two simple words: "ordinances" and "covenants."

Latter-day Saints believe that there are certain gospel ordinances—sacred, physical acts with symbolic religious meaning, such as baptism and the conferral of the Holy Ghost—that are necessary for salvation and that these ordinances are always received by virtue of a binding covenant between God and man. We believe that it is only by ordinances and covenants that we have full access to Jesus' grace and saving power. Thus **Latter-day Saints are a covenant-making people. Those covenants require ordinances, which require priesthood authority, which requires an organized religion to oversee the conferral and use of that authority.**

The Doctrine and Covenants says, "Therefore, in the ordinances thereof, the power of godliness is manifest" (Doctrine and Covenants 84:20). We believe organization and authority are necessary because we believe covenants and ordinances are necessary.

God might be found in nature, but we believe an organized Church with authority is neccessary because we believe covenants and ordinances are neccessary.

Who Are LDS Priesthood Holders and How Are They Called?

If you know any LDS man, then you probably know an LDS priesthood holder. Yes, the butcher, the baker, and the candlestick maker are all potential LDS priesthood holders. Similar to how Jesus called common fishermen and tax collectors to be His disciples and servants, Latter-day Saint priesthood holders are common men with regular vocations and families.

LDS priesthood holders are young and old, rich and poor, educated and uneducated, from all nationalities of the world and walks of life. They are both recent converts and lifelong members. In plain words, they are plain people.

When LDS men are called and ordained to the priesthood, they continue in their professional careers and family life, working in a lay priesthood and voluntarily sacrificing their time to serve others through their priesthood calling. Mormon lay priesthood holders do not receive any formal academic training to qualify them for the work, nor do they receive any monetary compensation for their priesthood position or services. They do not appoint themselves to priesthood positions through their own inspiration, determination, or scholarly qualification.

Those already in LDS priesthood positions of authority (like a Mormon bishop) identify and approve others to be called to priesthood service, following the pattern laid out by God repeatedly in scriptures and articulated by Jesus to His Apostles: **"Ye have not chosen me, but I have chosen you, and ordained you"** (John 15:16). Although LDS priesthood holders continue their ordinary work in their professional vocations, they strive to be "men of honest report, full of the Holy Ghost and wisdom" (Acts 6:3) in their extraordinary work of voluntary priesthood service.

No Self-Selection

One pattern that is repeated in scriptures is that God's servants did not choose themselves; they were chosen. The Lord called Moses (Exodus 3:10), Jeremiah (Jeremiah 1:5), the Twelve (Luke 6:13), the Seventy (Luke 10:1), and others. After Jesus' resurrection and ascension, those who were left in authority (the Apostles) called others by inspiration, such as Matthias (Acts 1:23–26) and Saul (Acts 13:1–3). Similarly, Latter-day Saints believe that a man can't call himself to the priesthood; he must be called of God by those who are in authority.

What Do LDS Priesthood Holders Do?

Priesthood holders are primarily called to serve God's children by overseeing and performing gospel ordinances for people, and to serve and watch over the members. Here are some of the main ordinances that LDS priesthood holders perform:

Baptism: Latter-day Saints believe that baptism by immersion is for the remission of sins, and thus we do not baptize people until they are old enough to be accountable for their own actions, which we believe is eight years old (see Doctrine and Covenants 68:27). At baptism, we make a covenant with God that we will be disciples of Christ and strive to follow His teachings. We believe baptism to be a necessary ordinance to enter the celestial kingdom of heaven (see Mark 16:16; 3 Nephi 11:33; Mormon 9:23; Doctrine and Covenants 18:22).

We are baptized when we are eight years old.

Conferral of the Gift of the Holy Ghost: The New Testament teaches that the gift of the Holy Ghost was given by the laying on of hands by those in authority (see Acts 8:14–18). After a person is baptized by immersion, Melchizedek Priesthood holders lay their hands on the baptized person's head and confirm him or her a member of The Church of Jesus Christ of Latter-day Saints and confer upon him or her the gift of the Holy Ghost, with the injunction to "receive the Holy Ghost" (Doctrine and Covenants 84:64). We believe that a person must "be born of water and of the Spirit" (John 3:5) to enter God's kingdom. We believe that the reception of the Holy Ghost is important for a person to receive a remission of his or her sins and be born again. The confirmation and conferral of the Holy Ghost completes a person's baptism in the LDS Church.[5]

We believe that only through the reception of the Holy Ghost can a person receive a remission of his or her sins and be born again.

Blessings on the Sick and Afflicted: We believe that another reason God gave priesthood authority to men was to bless His children in their times of sickness and affliction. The Biblical apostle James says, "Is any sick among you? let him call for the elders of the church; and let them pray over him, anointing him with oil in the name of the Lord: and the prayer of faith shall save the sick, and the Lord shall raise him up" (James 5:14–15). Melchizedek Priesthood holders do exactly that, and lay their hands on people's heads, anointing them with holy, consecrated olive oil (which is symbolic of the healing power of Jesus' Atonement), and bless them in the name of Christ.

Consecrated olive oil is symbolic of the healing power of Jesus' Atonement.

Mormons believe that the sacrament is a renewal of the covenants of Christian discipleship we made with God at baptism.

The Sacrament: Aaronic Priesthood holders in the LDS Church offer the sacrament to Church members once each week during Sunday services. (See chapter 22 for more about Sunday worship service.) Mormons believe that the sacrament is a renewal of the covenants of Christian discipleship we made with God at baptism and that through the ordinance of the sacrament we can receive the Holy Ghost and have the cleansing effect of our baptism renewed.[6]

Conferring the Priesthood and Ordaining Others to Priesthood Offices: With approval from their local congregational leader, priesthood holders can also lay their hands on the heads of other worthy males and confer the same priesthood authority they hold upon others, ordaining them to different offices within that priesthood.

Aside from providing these ordinances, Mormon priesthood holders are also called to voluntarily serve in various priesthood leadership positions within the LDS Church and oversee the spiritual work of the Lord. (See chapter 21.)

Priesthood "Keys"

PETRUS

Mormons talk a lot about priesthood "keys." They aren't literal keys that open or lock doors, but their purpose is much the same: they unlock the flow of power and authority to direct and control the priesthood and the kingdom of God on the earth.[7] To His New Testament apostles, Jesus said, "I will give unto thee *the keys of the kingdom* of heaven" (Matthew 16:19; emphasis added), which we interpret to mean that Peter was to be in charge of directing the affairs of the New Testament Church. There is even a great statue by the Danish sculptor Bertel Thorvaldsen that shows Peter holding those keys promised to him by Jesus.

We believe that the same keys given to Peter to direct Jesus' kingdom on the earth were also given to Joseph Smith by angelic visitors (including Peter), giving him, and subsequent LDS Church leaders, the keys of authority to direct the kingdom of God on the earth in the latter days.

Priesthood Power Is Different from Priesthood Ordination

Although any worthy LDS male can be ordained to priesthood offices and called to service positions, we believe that "the rights of the priesthood are inseparably connected with the powers of heaven, and that the powers of heaven cannot be controlled nor handled only upon the principles of righteousness" (Doctrine and Covenants 121:36). In order to have heavenly power to bless other people's lives, LDS priesthood holders must strive to live Christlike lives of goodness and purity, because "no power

Holding the LDS priesthood is a great blessing in the life of a man, because it requires him to be faithful, humble, and selfless.

or influence can or ought to be maintained by virtue of the priesthood, only by persuasion, by long-suffering, by gentleness and meekness, and by love unfeigned" (Doctrine and Covenants 121:41). **We believe that although our priesthood authority comes by way of our ordination, our priesthood power comes by how we live our lives.**[8] Holding the LDS priesthood is a great blessing in the life of a man, not because it gives him rank, makes him powerful or superior, or puts him in charge, but because it requires him to be faithful, humble, selfless, and to offer service to God's children.

Holding the priesthood doesn't create masters—it creates servants.

If an LDS man tries to abuse his priesthood power by displaying pride, exercising unrighteous dominion, force, control, or compulsion, or undertaking to cover up his sins, "the heavens withdraw themselves; the Spirit of the Lord is grieved; and when it is withdrawn, Amen to the priesthood or the authority of that man" (Doctrine and Covenants 121:37). If an LDS man acts unfaithfully and violates his covenants, not only does he lose his priesthood power, but he may also lose the priesthood itself.

Aren't Women Left Out Because They Don't Hold the Priesthood?

Although LDS women are not ordained to priesthood offices, the blessings and power of the LDS priesthood are available to all who receive the gospel of Jesus Christ, both male and female. All the ordinances necessary to enter into heaven are available equally to both men and women in the LDS Church. Priesthood is not compatible with self-aggrandizement—for pride, power, position, or prestige—but it is strictly designed as a means to serve others.

Women are called to serve in organizational leadership roles in the LDS Church from the general Church level down to the congregational level, and they work hand-in-hand and side-by-side with male priesthood holders to serve God's children together.

There is no priesthood "ladder" that is necessary to climb in the LDS Church to reach heaven; only priesthood ordinances are necessary for salvation, and they are available to all.

MORMYTH:

Mormons of black African descent couldn't be ordained to priesthood offices until 1978.

Answer: True.

Although from its very beginning, the LDS Church has always had an open *membership* policy for people of all races,[9] during the leadership of Brigham Young the Church adopted the position that members of black African descent could not be ordained to priesthood offices or receive the ordinances of the LDS temple.

There is no official doctrinal reason or revelation as to why this policy was implemented, and various speculative statements have been given over the years by some LDS Church leaders and members seeking to explain the restriction.[10]

For decades, LDS Church prophets foretold that the day would come when the policy would be changed, but repeatedly felt the right time had not arrived.[11] Then, in June 1978, President Spencer W. Kimball, the current prophet, received a revelation reversing this policy and lifting the priesthood restriction from those of black African ancestry. In President Kimball's words, "We have pleaded long and earnestly in behalf of these, our faithful brethren. . . . [The Lord] has heard our prayers, and by revelation has confirmed that the long-promised day has come when every faithful, worthy man in the Church may receive the holy priesthood" (Doctrine and Covenants, Official Declaration 2).

Since that time forward, worthy Mormons of *all* races have been given the priesthood, been ordained to priesthood offices, received the blessings of the LDS temple, and served in local and general priesthood leadership positions within the LDS Church. We believe that the Lord works with "the children of men line upon line, precept upon precept" (2 Nephi 28:30), and based on the conditions of His people and society He gives less or more of His word.[12] The LDS Church leadership, its members, and the world have grown in knowledge, understanding, and preparedness, and thus, in 1978, the Lord gave us more of His word, which we have happily received.

It is estimated that about 5 percent of the LDS Church—or about 700,000 members today— are black, found mostly in Mormon congregations in Africa, Brazil, and the Caribbean.[13] Black membership continues to grow significantly, especially in West Africa, where two LDS temples were recently built.

6 Mormons and Marriage

To quote the clergyman from the film *The Princess Bride:* "Mawwi-age is what bwings us togethaw today." Well, it's at least what brings us together for this chapter. Marriage is a topic closely connected to Mormonism—from our doctrine on eternal marriage to our stance on same-gender marriage to our past history of plural marriage. Here, then, is a little bit about Mormons and that "bwessed awwangement, that dweam within a dweam": MARRIAGE.

Latter-day Saints believe that marriage between a man and a woman is ordained of God and is essential to God's plan of happiness for His children.

Marriage Is Ordained of God and Can Be Eternal

Latter-day Saints believe that marriage between a man and a woman is ordained of God and is essential to God's plan of happiness for His children. Beginning with Adam and Eve,[1] God has desired that a man and a woman become one in a marriage covenant (see Genesis 2:21–25), and today Latter-day Saints seek to do the same. We believe that the divine nature of male and female spirits complement and complete each other.[2]

Mormons believe that the principles of our religion help us maintain happy marriages.

We also believe that life's greatest fulfillment and purpose is accomplished through principles found in marriage and family. Those reasons might explain why a higher percentage of Latter-day Saints are married, why fewer Mormons are divorced or single, and why we tend to marry earlier in life in comparison to non-LDS peer groups.[3] But perhaps the greatest reason why Latter-day Saints strive to establish a happy marriage as one of our life goals is that we believe marriage to be central to God's plan of happiness and necessary to fulfill some of the fundamental purposes of life.

What Is "Eternal" Marriage?

Perhaps one of the greatest truths that God has reestablished through The Church of Jesus Christ of Latter-day Saints is that a man and a woman can be married for time and all eternity. Central to our theology on marriage is that to become exalted in the highest heaven, a man and a woman "must enter into . . . the new and everlasting covenant of [eternal] marriage" (Doctrine and Covenants 131:2). We believe that a man cannot fulfill his ultimate divine potential without a woman, nor a woman without a man, and thus "neither is the man without the woman, neither the woman without the man, in the Lord" (1 Corinthians 11:11).

We believe that a man and a woman can be married for time and all eternity.

Jesus told His ancient apostle Peter, "Whatsoever ye shall bind on earth shall be bound in heaven" (Matthew 18:18), and we believe that this same sealing power was given by Jesus to Peter, and then to Joseph Smith, and since then to subsequent LDS prophets. By that same power and authority, **a man and a woman can be "sealed," or joined together, for time and all eternity in an LDS temple marriage ceremony.** As long as they keep their covenants of faithfulness and righteousness, their marriage relationship will continue forever, beyond "until death do us part" and extending into the eternities.

> We believe that not only are there three degrees of heaven (celestial, terrestrial, and telestial), but that within the celestial kingdom itself there are "three heavens or degrees" (Doctrine and Covenants 131:1). To attain the highest part of the celestial kingdom is what Mormons call "exaltation," and an eternal marriage is necessary for exaltation.

Many of us wonder how heaven could possibly be heaven without the husband or wife we have spent a lifetime loving and serving and with whom we've become "one flesh" (Genesis 2:24). Mormons believe that the Lord has made unending love both possible and eternally purposeful. (See chapter 4 and chapter 8.)

What About Those Who Didn't Have the Chance for Eternal Marriage but Want It?

We believe that no eternal blessing will be offered to one person that is not offered to all people. We believe God will compensate anyone whose circumstances denied him or her the opportunity for eternal marriage here in mortality.[4] Each person will have the opportunity to have an eternal marriage and family if he or she desires, whether in this life or the next.

Can Mormons Marry Non-Mormons?

The answer is yes, we can. However, most Mormons tend to marry other Mormons. A 2007 Pew Study found that **Mormons are second only to Hindus in marrying within their faith,** with 83 percent of Latter-day Saints marrying another Latter-day Saint.[5]

It is not forbidden for a Mormon to marry someone of another faith, but most Mormons tend to marry other Mormons.

Because Latter-day Saints believe that eternal marriage is necessary for heavenly exaltation and that an eternal marriage takes place in an LDS temple, where only faithful members of the LDS Church can enter, then the intra-faith marriage statistic makes sense.

A study of students at LDS-owned Brigham Young University indicated that 93 percent of men and 97 percent of women surveyed have an LDS temple marriage as one of their important life goals,[6] and thus they will probably marry another Latter-day Saint. However, **this does not mean that it is forbidden for a Mormon to marry someone of another faith,** nor does it mean that a Mormon who does marry someone from another faith cannot be a fully faithful and practicing Mormon.

Do Mormons Have Arranged or Forced Marriages?

Mormons find their spouses the same way most people in America do: at school, at work, through regular dating experiences, and through life's experiences and encounters. Latter-day Saint marriages aren't arranged by fathers or mothers, and LDS bishops don't tell people who to marry either. A Mormon doesn't have to marry anyone he or she doesn't voluntarily choose to marry. All marriage decisions remain with the individual Latter-day Saint, as we believe the right to act and choose for ourselves (agency) to be a fundamental doctrine of Mormonism.

Dating and Marriage

Mormons view dating as a preparation for marriage, and we have some fairly common dating standards. We are taught by Church leaders not to start dating until we are sixteen years old and to date only those with high moral standards. While in our teens, we are encouraged to date socially and in groups, and we are advised to refrain from steady dating (or seriously pairing off as a couple) until we are at an age when we begin thinking of marriage.[7]

Most Latter-day Saint young men will not seriously consider marriage until after returning from missionary service, usually around the age of twenty-one. (See chapter 23 for more about missionary service.) But even with those conservative dating standards, Mormons tend to marry younger than the rest of the nation. Roughly 60 percent of the state of Utah is Mormon, and a US census report released in 2005 showed that Utah had the lowest average age of a first marriage (21.9 for women and 23.9 for men), which is about three years younger than the national average.[8]

What Is the LDS Position on Divorce?

Speaking of marriage, Jesus said, "What therefore God hath joined together, let not man put asunder" (Matthew 19:6). When the Pharisees questioned this position, saying that Moses allowed divorce, Jesus answered, "Moses because of the hardness of your hearts suffered you to put away your wives: but from the beginning it was not so" (Matthew 19:8).

LDS Church leaders have repeatedly spoken out against the common practice of divorce.

The LDS Church disapproves of divorce, and LDS Church leaders have repeatedly spoken out against its common practice and warned of the dangers of the disintegration of the family.[9] Latter-day Saints who are having marital problems are encouraged to seek to reconcile differences by applying the teachings of Jesus Christ—such as repentance, humility, forgiveness, kindness, selflessness, respect, and service. However, if the marriage proves irreconcilable (especially in cases of adultery, abuse, and neglect), Latter-day Saints may consider and obtain a divorce if necessary and still retain their standing in the Church.

Do Mormons Really Have Lower Divorce Rates than Average?

Although results have varied, multiple studies have found notable differences in divorce rates between LDS temple marriages and the national average.[10] A recent study estimates the lifetime LDS temple marriage divorce rate to be about 2.5 times less than the national lifetime divorce rate.[11]

2.5x LESS LIKELY TO DIVORCE

The lifetime LDS temple marriage divorce rate is about 2.5 times less than the national lifetime divorce rate.

Scan this QR code to meet **Rose Yvette**, a talented artist who finds meaning and purpose not only in her art, but also through her marriage and family.

Mormons believe that the principles of our religion—all of which are centered on the teachings of Jesus Christ—help us maintain happy marriages. LDS Church President Gordon B. Hinckley said that "the greatest factor in a happy marriage is an anxious concern for the comfort and well-being of one's companion. In most cases selfishness is the leading factor that causes argument, separation, divorce, and broken hearts."[12]

Our religion teaches us to serve our spouses and respect them. We should pray and worship together as husband and wife. We are taught to be morally clean, to abstain from alcohol, to reject pornography, and to avoid other sins that so often destroy marriages. We believe that both men and women—husbands and wives—have divine roles, and we honor and support each other in those roles as coequals. We strive not to center our lives on money or the accumulation of worldly goods.

We believe that the top titles in life are not "Dr.," "President," "CEO," or "Professor," but "son of God," "daughter of God," "husband," "wife," "mother," and "father." Marriage has a divine purpose that provides eternal perspective to life's daily challenges, so when we hit our fifth wedding anniversary, or our fiftieth, we know we are still just getting started. ("One more year down; eternity to go!")

We believe that all of these factors, and many more, help Latter-day Saints have stable and happy marriages.

What About Single, Divorced, or Widowed People in the LDS Church?

Although all Latter-day Saints are encouraged to strive for the ideal family,[13] adults who have never married, are divorced or widowed, or are single parents make up a significant part of the faithful and active membership of the LDS Church. Unmarried Latter-day Saints are involved in many areas of LDS Church leadership and activities. **Although we are a marriage- and family-centered Church, we are first and foremost a Christ-centered Church.** All people—no matter their marital status—are welcomed and wanted to worship God the Father and His Son Jesus Christ equally in the LDS Church along with other, married, Latter-day Saints.

For a complete reading on the LDS Church's stance on same-gender marriage, see "The Divine Institution of Marriage."[14]

What Is the LDS Church's Position on Same-Gender Marriage?

Anything that is inconsistent with God's plan of salvation for His children is not endorsed by the LDS Church. (See chapter 4 for more on God's plan of salvation.) We believe that we are all the spirit children of "heavenly parents"[15]—an eternal *Father and Mother* in heaven.[16] The primary purpose of God's plan is for us to become more like them. Therefore, The Church of Jesus Christ of Latter-day Saints "affirms that marriage between a man and a woman is essential to the Creator's plan for the eternal destiny of His children."[17]

A same-gender marriage is inconsistent with LDS doctrine on eternal marriage and its purpose.

A same-gender marriage is inconsistent with LDS doctrine on eternal marriage and its purpose and is inconsistent with our teachings of the purposes of human sexuality, which we believe are closely tied to the biological powers and responsibilities of creating and raising children. (See chapter 18.) Therefore, **the LDS Church does not sanction or support same-gender marriages, and "affirms defining marriage as the legal and lawful union between a man and a woman."**[18]

The LDS Church works closely with many other "churches, organizations, and individuals"[19] who oppose same-gender marriage, both for its religious and social implications. However, it should be noted that the LDS Church "does not object to rights . . . regarding hospitalization and medical care, fair housing and employment rights, or probate rights"[20] of same-gender couples, as long as those rights don't infringe on the right to practice religion free from governmental interference. In 2009, the LDS Church supported a pair of civil rights laws in Salt Lake City, Utah, that forbade local landlords and employers from discriminating against those in same-gender relationships.[21]

Additionally, as stated in the LDS Church's 2008 press release related to same-gender marriage: "Protecting marriage between a man and a woman does not affect Church members' Christian obligations of love, kindness and humanity toward all people. . . . The [LDS] Church does not condone abusive treatment of others and encourages its members to treat all people with respect."[22] Jesus loved people, even when He did not support or authorize their behavior, such as the woman taken in adultery (see John 8:3–11). Latter-day Saints strive to do the same with issues regarding homosexuality and same-gender marriage, and we are encouraged to reach out with understanding and respect to individuals who have same-gender attraction.

MORMYTH: Mormons practice polygamy.

Answer: False today, but true in the late 1800s.

Although Latter-day Saints haven't practiced plural marriage in more than a century, "polygamy" is still the top free-word-association connected to Mormonism.[23] To clarify, **we believe God's standard law on marriage is one man to one woman.**

The Book of Mormon plainly teaches that a man should "have save it be one wife" (Jacob 2:27). However, the Book of Mormon also indicates that *the Lord* can make an exception to this rule, and if God commands His people, plural marriage can be practiced (see Jacob 2:30). This apparently was the case in the Bible, when prophets such as Abraham, Jacob, and Moses had plural wives, and for a brief period of time, it was also the case for some Latter-day Saints in the early days of the Church. Between about 1840 and 1890, 20 percent to 25 percent[24] of married Latter-day Saints practiced polygamy, where a man married more than one woman at a time (technically polygyny).

Of the LDS men who were invited to participate in plural marriages, most married only one additional wife.[25] Those Latter-day Saint men and women were following a revelation from their prophet to begin practicing plural marriage,[26] and they followed a revelation from their prophet to end its practice.[27]

Although Mormons are not ashamed of our polygamist past, **it is against the standards and teachings of the Latter-day Saints to practice plural marriage today.** Anyone who is currently practicing polygamy is not a faithful Mormon and is excluded from membership in the LDS Church, even if the laws of their country allow it.

In 1998, President Gordon B. Hinckley (1910–2008) made the following statement about the LDS Church's position on plural marriage:

"This Church has nothing whatever to do with those practicing polygamy. They are not members of this Church. . . .

"If any of our members are found to be practicing plural marriage, they are excommunicated, the most serious penalty the Church can impose. Not only are those so involved in direct violation of the civil law, they are in violation of the law of this Church."[28]

7 Mormons and Family

During the commercial break of your favorite show, right between the car and clothing ads, a thirty-second commercial might pop on. Looking like a movie trailer, the ad shows a father and his son swashbuckling against make-believe musketeers, trying to rescue a princess. The voice-over at the end of the ad says the familiar words, "Imagine what a little time can do for your family. From The Church of Jesus Christ of Latter-day Saints. Family: Isn't it about . . . time?"

Our ads were created to turn people's minds and hearts to their families.

These Mormon public service ads have been running on TV and radio stations around the world for nearly thirty years. They have garnered Emmy Awards and Cannes Film Festival honors and won commercial of the year awards by the American Advertising Federation.[1] But the ads weren't created to win awards; they were created to turn people's minds and hearts to their families and help people know that Mormonism is a family-centered religion. In fact, in a national survey on what Americans like about Mormonism, the most frequently mentioned phrase was "family-oriented."[2]

Latter-day Saints believe that the family is the most important and fundamental social unit on earth and in eternity. Here is a little bit more about why the family is so central to Mormon theology and how we try to apply our message of the fundamental importance of families to our own families.

The Family Is Central to God's Plan

Modern-day LDS apostles have formally proclaimed that "the family is central to the Creator's plan for the eternal destiny of His children."[3] Mormons believe that God has established families to help bring us happiness, to help us learn correct principles in a loving environment, and to prepare us for eternal life with God. We believe that the family home, under the direction of a loving father and mother who are united in marriage, is the best place to teach children to learn and implement the teachings of Jesus Christ, to love and serve others, and to be productive members of society. We believe that a family exists for more than just to provide food, clothing, and shelter. We believe that **a family is the organization of God,** established by Him to efficiently and effectively fulfill His plan to help us progress and learn to become more like Him.

Mormons and Eternal Families

Not only do Latter-day Saints believe we can be married to our spouses for eternity (see chapter 6), but we also believe that **a family can be joined together forever.** We believe that through sacred ordinances available in LDS temples, a father and a mother can be united with their children for eternity. That means family relationships can and will continue beyond the grave, and "that same sociality which exists among us here will exist among us there, only it will be coupled with eternal glory" (Doctrine and Covenants 130:2). We believe that through these sacred ordinances, and our faithfulness to our covenants, our family relationships as parents and children, brothers and sisters, and husbands and wives will continue hereafter.

Latter-day Saints believe that a family can be joined together forever.

What Do Mormons Believe Is the Secret to Family Success?

There is no one sure way to raise a child, or else everyone would do it. As the seventeenth-century English poet John Wilmot once said: "Before I got married I had six theories about bringing up children; now I have six children and no theories."[4]

Working with our kids helps them learn and develop skills, encourages family unity, and provides ideal teaching moments.

Mormons don't pretend to have all the answers when it comes to raising kids, but we do believe that **"happiness in family life is most likely to be achieved when founded upon the teachings of the Lord Jesus Christ."**[5] Think of how much more successful families across the world could become if parents and children applied Jesus' teachings of kindness, compassion, selflessness, love, forgiveness, respect, obedience, and honor.

We also try to work and play together as families as often as possible. Working with our kids helps them learn and develop skills, encourages family unity, and provides ideal teaching moments. (Plus, hey, free labor!) Not only will all work and no play make Jack a dull boy, but it can also make home a dull place. Parents and children should plan time to do fun things together often,[6] like going on vacations, on camping trips, to the movies, or on a hike. (No, not telling your kids to take a hike, but actually going with them.) We feel that these three components—learning and applying the teachings of Jesus Christ, working together, and playing together—help create a happy and healthy family environment for raising successful children and families.

When, in the Course of Human Events, It Becomes Necessary to Declare the Doctrine of the Family . . .

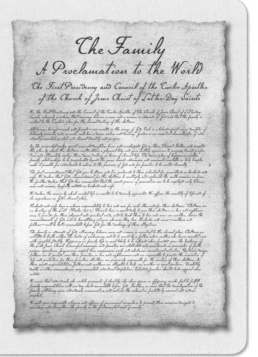

In 1995, the leadership of the LDS Church—the First Presidency and Quorum of the Twelve Apostles— issued the Church's definitive statement on the family, entitled **"The Family: A Proclamation to the World."** This document sets forth the standard LDS beliefs on the divine purpose of the family. This inspired proclamation is as foundational to LDS families as the Declaration of Independence is to American freedom.

Scan this QR code to read the full document.

What Is Family Home Evening?

For almost a century, LDS Church leaders have instructed Latter-day Saint parents to set aside one night a week as a "family home evening." The evening is reserved as a time for the family to learn together, counsel together, and do activities together that strengthen the family and help foster family unity and love. Since the 1970s, Monday night has been the evening designated by the LDS Church for family home evening, although some Latter-day Saints hold their family night on a different day depending on their schedules.

Monday night is akin to a family Sabbath,[7] where the evening is reserved solely for family: no late nights at the office, no church meetings or activities, no going out on the town with friends. A typical Latter-day Saint family home evening often begins with the family singing a hymn and having a prayer, followed by a short lesson that is given by a family member on a gospel topic. After the lesson, it's fairly common to conclude with a prayer and then enjoy a fun family activity together (i.e., playing a board game, playing catch, etc.) and refreshments.

Family nights are usually pretty relaxed and not very formal; it's up to the parents to decide what to teach and do and how best to approach it. In the hustle and bustle of the modern world, Latter-day Saints feel that family home evening is a God-sent tradition to help us strengthen, unify, and teach our family members in the home.

Family Prayer and Family Scripture Study

We believe that studying the scriptures each day helps us maintain an eternal perspective.

Latter-day Saint parents focus a lot of effort and energy to hold regular family scripture study and daily family prayer. As families become busier and schedules divide family members among the four winds, we believe that gathering together briefly each day to study from the scriptures and unite in family prayer helps us maintain an eternal perspective, remember Christ, and foster feelings of family unity and love. Additionally, we believe that parents have a divine responsibility to teach their children to have faith in Christ and to follow Him (see Doctrine and Covenants 68:25). These moments of family worship provide ideal settings for children to learn the doctrines and principles of Jesus Christ's gospel in a family environment with their parents and siblings.

MORMYTH:
LDS husbands are more important than LDS wives.

Answer: False.

Although husbands and wives have different roles within the family organization, Latter-day Saints don't believe that either the husband or the wife is superior or inferior to the other. A husband and his wife serve their family together as coequals. While it is true that the husband is designated as the spiritual leader of his family (or "presides" in LDS terminology), that does not mean he is more important or influential than his wife. It simply means that he has a divine duty to ultimately oversee the direction of his family. A husband and wife walk hand-in-hand, side-by-side, in a joint family partnership. They may have different assignments, but they share a joint goal to help bring their family to Christ.

The Apostle Paul said that the "husband is the head . . . even as Christ is the head of the Church" (Ephesians 5:23). Mormons believe this means that the husband should love and selflessly serve his wife and family, "even as Christ also loved the church" (Ephesians 5:25). We believe it is contrary to the order of heaven—and offensive to the Spirit of God—for a father to exercise unrighteous dominion, control, or compulsion over his wife or family. A father's leadership should be "by long-suffering, by gentleness and meekness, and by love unfeigned" (Doctrine and Covenants 121:41).

The Father

"By divine design, fathers are to preside over their families in love and righteousness and are responsible to provide the necessities of life and protection for their families."[8] An LDS husband should lead his "family in regular prayer, scripture study, and family home evening."[9]

The Mother

"Mothers are primarily responsible for the nurture of their children."[10] Latter-day Saints hold motherhood as one of the highest and holiest works that can be performed among mankind, and women as "instruments in the hands of Providence to guide the destinies of nations."[11] (See chapter 19 for more about Mormon women.)

LDS fathers and mothers work together as equal partners in helping one another fulfill these responsibilities, and adapt in their roles according to individual circumstances.

Scan this QR code to meet **Nadja Pettitt**, a free-lance translator who speaks half a dozen languages, but who also raises half a dozen children (seven to be exact). Hear Nadja's perspective on raising a happy family.

Sanctuary! The LDS Home

Latter-day Saints believe that second to LDS temples, home is the most sacred place on earth.[12] It is more than a suburban boardinghouse or a bed-and-breakfast; our homes are places where the work of God (raising children and teaching them truth) takes place. Latter-day Saint scripture teaches us to "establish a house, even a house of prayer, a house of fasting, a house of faith, a house of learning, a house of glory, a house of order, a house of God" (Doctrine and Covenants 88:119); such instruction applies not only to our holy temples, but also to our own homes. As such, **we try to make our homes places where the Spirit of God may be present.**

Regardless of the size or quality of the house, we try to make our homes beautiful, neat, and well-kept. ("Try" is the key word there. Having children often makes this goal a paradox!) We try to fill our homes with beautiful artwork, great books, wholesome entertainment, and uplifting music. Above all, we try to fill our homes with love, peace, and laughter and to establish them as a place where our children can thrive spiritually, mentally, emotionally, and physically.

Why Do Mormons Have Such Big Families?

Minivan makers must love Mormons. The 2007 US Census indicated that Utah (which is 60 percent Latter-day Saint) had the highest birthrate in the nation at 20.8 births per 1,000 women, nearly 45 percent higher than the average US birthrate (14.3 births per 1,000 women).

Latter-day Saint couples often have more children than the average couple.

Although LDS birthrates rise and fall along with general birthrates that are influenced by societal conditions, Latter-day Saint couples nevertheless have more children than the average.[13]

American Latter-day Saints average about three children per family, about three times more than the US average of .90 children per family.[14]

US Average: .90   LDS Average: 3.0

Part of the reason why Latter-day Saints want, and often have, many children is that we believe that "God's commandment for His children to multiply and replenish the earth remains in force."[15] Because of our doctrine of a premortal life, we believe there are spirit children of God currently living in

His presence who are ready to come to earth and begin their mortal lives. **We believe that we have a divine responsibility to assist in God's work by providing physical bodies for God's spirit children, and then to rear, nurture, and teach those children in a loving family environment as best we can.**

If couples cannot have children of their own and they choose to adopt, their adopted children may be sealed to them in the temple. And yes, we assume the responsibility of *parenting* children, not just having them. Contrary to societal trends, higher-income Mormon professional families have and care for significantly more children than non-professional, low-income Latter-day Saint families.[16] That being said, we don't believe that there is some greater heavenly reward for the Mormon family who raises ten kids ("Whoa, they're driving that ten-seater Econoline van right into heaven") as compared to the Mormon family who raises one child.

The LDS Church does not dictate to its members how many children to have nor when to have them. Those decisions are made privately between a husband and wife based on their individual circumstances and revelation from the Lord.

> The LDS handbook of instructions says: "The decision as to how many children to have and when to have them is extremely intimate and private and should be left between the couple and the Lord. Church members should not judge one another in this matter."[17]

Yes, Mormons Believe Children Are *Entitled* . . .

Although the 2007 US Census showed that Utah (with its high Latter-day Saint population) had the highest birthrate in the nation, it also showed that the state had the lowest out-of-wedlock birthrate in the nation, nearly 50 percent lower than the US average.[18]

"The Family: A Proclamation to the World" states that "children are entitled to birth within the bonds of matrimony, and to be reared by a father and a mother who honor marital vows with complete fidelity."[19] We believe that the most ideal environment to raise children is one where both a father and a mother are joined in a loyal and loving marriage.

This is not to imply that single, divorced, widowed, or other parental guardians cannot raise excellent, wonderful, and successful children and families. Obviously, they can and do, and for various circumstances—such as death, divorce, and separation—many faithful Latter-day Saints find themselves as part of single-parent families. But we believe that having both a father and a mother, united in marriage, provides the *ideal* environment for raising a child.

In 2007 Utah had the highest birthrate and lowest out-of-wedlock birthrate in the nation.

Thus, the LDS Church does not support single-parent adoption or artificial insemination for single women.[20] Additionally, the LDS Church encourages its teenage or single expectant mothers (if marriage to the father is unlikely) to place the child for adoption through a reputable agency to allow the child the opportunity to be raised by a father and a mother in a loving family.[21]

No Other Success . . .

When many people hear the word "success," they think of bling-bling and ka-ching. Not Mormons. For us, "success" is more about wedding rings and offspring. LDS Church President David O. McKay (1873–1970) famously quoted J. E. McCullough, who said, "No other success can compensate for failure in the home."[22] Because the family has eternal consequence in LDS theology, nothing temporal can outweigh it in importance. Worldly titles, honors, money, power, good looks, and the like are all fleeting and will be gone soon enough. But **the titles of husband, wife, father, and mother can and will be eternal,** and thus we are taught to give our family our highest priority over any other accomplishment or accolades. We believe our careers, our pleasures, and even our friends should all play second fiddle to our family.

We are taught to give our family our highest priority over any other accomplishment or accolades.

The Family Filter

Every decision a faithful Latter-day Saint makes ideally runs through a family filter (and no, that's not a piece of computer software), where we ask ourselves: How will this affect my family? Will it bless it, or hurt it?

We believe that keeping family first helps us keep our priorities straight and ultimately helps us keep God first in our lives (see Exodus 20:3).

HOW DOES THIS AFFECT MY FAMILY?

Exercising and eating right
Reading that website
Flirting with my coworker
Watching that movie
Taking a new job offer
Buying a new car
FAMILY
Going to church
Playing on the neighborhood basketball team
Going back to school to get my degree
Going to Vegas for the weekend with my friends

We believe that the family is ordained of God and that family relationships help us become more like God. The LDS handbook says, "Latter-day Saint husbands and wives . . . establish their marriage as the first priority in their lives."[23] A letter from the LDS First Presidency dated February 11, 1999, says, "We counsel parents and children to give highest priority to family prayer, family home evening, gospel study and instruction, and wholesome family activities."[24]

Why Are Mormons So Big on Family History?

It is interesting for all of us to know our roots and that our uncle's third cousin twice removed is related to the Queen of England. But that isn't necessarily why Latter-day Saints have the largest collection of genealogical records in the world[25] or why we do so much family history.

Our focus on family history is related to our belief in eternal families and our desire to link parents to children throughout generations in the gospel. Our genealogy work is also related to our belief that **all mankind has the right to receive the ordinances of the gospel,** but that uncounted numbers of our ancestors and friends have lived and died without that opportunity.

Therefore, we search out their names, and when we find them, we submit their vital information to an LDS temple so that gospel ordinances such as baptism and eternal marriage can be performed in their behalf. (See chapter 8 for more about ordinance work for the dead.) We believe our ancestors are taught the gospel in the spirit world (where our eternal spirits continue to live after death), where they have the choice to accept or decline the gospel ordinances performed for them in temples.

Latter-day Saints believe that we have a responsibility toward our ancestors to help provide them the necessary gospel ordinances they missed out on due to their life circumstances. Motivated by love, we try to provide a link

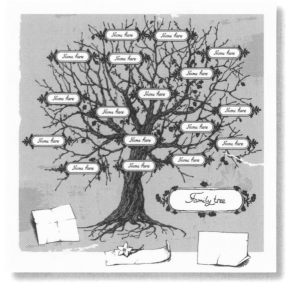

It's interesting to find out you have royalty in your bloodline, but the real reason we do family history work is to link families eternally.

through the generations, sealing parents to children through successive generations of our family history. That is the real reason why Mormons search high and low to find their roots. Knowing that you have royalty in your bloodline or that your seventh-great-grandpa was a pirate are just side benefits.

We try to provide a link through the generations, sealing parents to children through successive generations of our family history.

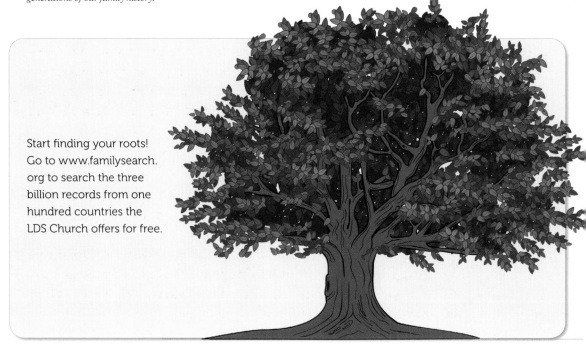

Start finding your roots! Go to www.familysearch.org to search the three billion records from one hundred countries the LDS Church offers for free.

8 What Happens inside LDS Temples?

One of the most distinct and peculiar practices of Latter-day Saints is our temple worship. Most people who have seen an LDS temple would agree that they are unique and magnificent edifices. Although the outside of the buildings is remarkable, people are more curious about what is happening inside of them. Before we go on, though, the reader must understand that to Latter-day Saints a temple is the most holy place on earth. The temple is to Mormons what Mecca is to Muslims and the Bodh Gaya is to Buddhists.

The temple is literally the house of the Lord and figuratively the place where heaven meets earth. Entering the temple and receiving its ordinances is the pinnacle of Mormon activity. Therefore, although this book is published to a general audience, the things that are discussed in this section are mentioned with reverence and we hope that they are received in that way. Because, to Mormons, when we enter the temple, like Moses at the burning bush, we feel that we are walking on holy ground (see Exodus 3:5).

Tabernacles and Temples

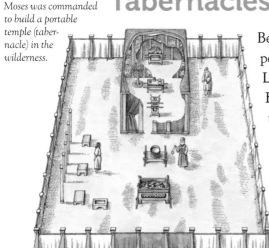

Moses was commanded to build a portable temple (tabernacle) in the wilderness.

Beginning in Old Testament times, God told His people to build temples—sacred places where the Lord could meet with, teach, bless, and make known His will to His people. We believe that temples and temple worship have always been vital to God's plan for His children.

Moses was commanded to build a portable temple (tabernacle) in the wilderness where he could commune with God (see Exodus 26–27), and when the children of Israel camped, the temple was at the center of the camp (see Numbers 2). When they arrived in the promised land, Israel's

King David planned for a temple, which was built by his son King Solomon (see 1 Kings 6). Later rebuilt by Zerubbabel (see Ezra 3:8), and then by Herod, the temple became central to the worship of the house of Israel and was a place where Jesus was often found during His ministry (see Matthew 21:12; 26:55; Mark 11:11; Luke 2:46; John 7:14). In the Book of Mormon, God's people, upon arriving in the Americas, built a temple (see 2 Nephi 5: 16).

So it should come as little surprise that today, as part of the reestablishment of Christ's church, the Lord has again commanded Latter-day Saints to build temples and for temples to be the center of our worship. In fact, the LDS Church was barely three years old when Joseph Smith and the early Latter-day Saints were commanded to build a temple (see Doctrine and Covenants 95). **Everywhere God's people were in the past, they built temples, and everywhere Mormons go today, they build temples too.**

It's Not Just the Salt Lake Temple— There Are Mormon Temples All over the World

Although the Salt Lake Temple in Utah is probably the most well-known and historic LDS temple, it isn't the only Mormon temple in the world. As of early 2012, there are 136 operating Latter-day Saint temples across the world, with 15 more under construction, and 15 more announced and awaiting construction. Because temple worship is central to our theology, the LDS Church tries to build temples in close proximity to its many congregations around the world. Currently, 85 percent of Mormons live within 200 miles of a temple.[1] There are five LDS temples in Africa, nine in Asia, five in Australia, fourteen

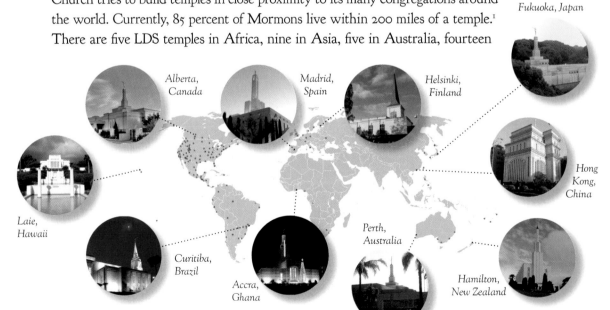

Fukuoka, Japan

Alberta, Canada

Madrid, Spain

Helsinki, Finland

Laie, Hawaii

Hong Kong, China

Curitiba, Brazil

Perth, Australia

Accra, Ghana

Hamilton, New Zealand

in Europe, twenty in South America, one hundred eight in North and Central America, and five scattered in the Pacific Islands.[2] The red dots on the previous page are LDS temples in operation worldwide, and the blue dots are temples that have been announced or are under construction (as of 2010).

What's the Difference between a Mormon Chapel and a Mormon Temple?

Temples are different from normal Mormon meeting-houses, such as a chapel where Mormons meet each Sunday for public worship. Mormon chapels are open to all visitors—members and nonmembers alike. On Sundays, we sing, pray, teach each other, take the sacrament, and conduct business for our local congregations (see chapter 21); and on selected weekdays, we have youth and social activities at our chapels. We also baptize new members in our church buildings. But **temples are reserved for our most holy ordinances** (such as performing sealings for eternal marriages), and only practicing Mormons who are prepared and have been found worthy by their ecclesiastical leaders can enter the temple.

Chapels (above) are for public worship services and weekday activities. Temples, such as the Mount Timpanogos Temple (below), are reserved for our most holy ordinances, including eternal marriages.

What Goes on inside a Mormon Temple?

In the temple we learn about God's plan for His children and make covenants with God to be obedient and to dedicate our life to Him. **Much of the work that goes on inside LDS temples is related to families.** We believe that the ordinances performed in the temple help us to fulfill the fundamental purposes of life, which are centered on forming an eternal family. Latter-day Saint Apostle President Boyd K. Packer (1924–) summarized what happens inside Mormon temples this way: "There, in a sacred ceremony, an individual may be washed and anointed and instructed and endowed and sealed. And when we have received these blessings for ourselves, we may officiate for those who have died without having had the same opportunity."[3] Here is a brief explanation of what each of those activities means:

- **Washing and anointing.** Before being instructed in the temple endowment, Latter-day Saints are symbolically washed and anointed, a ceremony reminiscent of how Aaron and his sons were washed and anointed before they performed their temple service (see Exodus 40:12–13).

- **Endowment.** An "endowment" is a gift or bestowal. When Mormons go to the temple, we receive many gifts—gifts of knowledge, understanding, covenants, ordinances, and blessings. These combined gifts are the temple "endowment." The official LDS publication *True to the Faith* summarizes the LDS temple endowment in these words: "The ordinance consists of a series of instructions and includes covenants we make to live righteously and comply with the requirements of the gospel. The endowment helps us focus on the Savior, His role in our Heavenly Father's plan, and our commitment to follow Him."[4]

When Mormons go to the temple, we receive many gifts—gifts of knowledge, understanding, covenants, ordinances, and blessings.

- **Sealing.** Most commonly referred to as "temple marriage" or "eternal marriage," this ordinance is where a man and a woman kneel across an altar and are married in the temple by priesthood authority for time and all eternity. We believe that the same sealing power given to Peter, stating that "whatsoever thou shalt bind on earth shall be bound in heaven" (Matthew 16:19), was restored to Joseph Smith and given to subsequent LDS prophets and that it is by this power that a man and a woman and their children can be sealed together for eternity (see chapter 5 for more about priesthood authority and ordinances). This is not only *extremely* romantic (who doesn't dream and sing of eternal love?) but, theologically, it is also the key ordinance that fulfills the purpose of life (see chapter 6 for more about eternal marriage).

Eternal marriages (sealings) are performed in temples.

- **Ordinances for the dead.** Latter-day Saints perform gospel ordinances (such as baptism, washing and anointing, endowment, and sealing) in behalf of their deceased family and friends in order to provide them with the opportunity to voluntarily accept gospel ordinances they may not have been able to receive in their mortal lifetime.

Aside from performing these ordinances, Latter-day Saints also go to the temple to pray for themselves and others, to ponder and focus on eternal things, and to take a breather from the hustle of daily life. Because of the sacred work that is done there, the temple is a place where we can easily feel of God's influence and love, receive inspiration, and feel spiritually strengthened to meet and overcome trials we may be facing in life. The temple is a quiet and reverent place where we can focus on the things of eternity and recommit to following Christ.

A Place of Covenants

Latter-day Saints go to the temple to make covenants of faithfulness to God and the gospel of Jesus Christ. A covenant is a binding agreement between God and man, where God sets the conditions and promises blessings for our faithfulness to the covenant. Former LDS Church President Gordon B. Hinckley (1910–2008) summarized the temple covenants this way: "We take upon ourselves covenants and obligations regarding lives of purity and virtue and goodness and truth and unselfishness to others."[5] The LDS Church's official booklet *Preparing to Enter the Holy Temple* says, "We covenant to give of our resources in time and money and talent—all we are and all we possess—to the interest of the kingdom of God upon the earth."[6]

Baptisms for the Dead

One of the ordinances we perform in LDS temples is called baptisms for the dead. But don't worry—we don't actually baptize dead people. As a labor of love, we perform baptisms in temples as a proxy for and in behalf of our deceased family and friends who died without the opportunity to be baptized. Why do we do this? Because Latter-day Saints believe that baptism is necessary for salvation (see Mark 16:16; John 3:5; 3 Nephi 11:33–34). **The problem is that uncounted millions of people, through no fault of their own, have lived and died without the opportunity to be baptized by those holding the proper authority.** Therefore, a just and merciful God has provided a way for **everyone** to accept the ordinance of baptism. We believe that when we are baptized in behalf of those who have died, the deceased person (whose spirit is still alive in the world of spirits awaiting the resurrection) has the opportunity to voluntarily accept or reject the temple baptism that was performed in their behalf. In this way, all mankind may receive baptism if they desire.

The *Population Reference Bureau* estimates that there have been about 106 billion people that have ever been born on earth.[7] If, as Jesus said, "He that believeth and is baptized shall be saved" (Mark 16:16), how many of those 106 billion people have had the fair chance to believe and be baptized by proper authority? Mormons believe that all 106 billion people should have the chance to be baptized and receive all other essential gospel ordinances if they desire.

The Bible suggests that baptisms for the dead were being performed and apparently were common knowledge in the Apostle Paul's day, as he made the following passing reference to it: "Else what shall they do which are baptized for the dead, if the dead rise not at all? why are they then baptized for the dead?" (1 Corinthians 15:29). The concept of vicarious work to help others be saved should not be strange or new to modern believers in Jesus Christ: The Savior's atonement was itself a vicarious work—He did something for us that we couldn't do for ourselves to help us get to heaven.

What Does a Temple Look like Inside?

All temples are different in appearance, both on the outside and on the inside. However, because temples share the same purpose, they all have similar rooms inside them, such as ordinance rooms, sealing rooms, a font for baptisms for the dead, and a celestial room to symbolize heaven. Recently, at Temple Square in Salt Lake City, the Church created a detailed replica of the Salt Lake Temple, with cutaway sides so everyone could see some of these rooms. Here are some pictures of the replica that show the beauty that is inside this specific temple:

This replica found on Temple Square in Salt Lake City shows many of the rooms inside the Salt Lake Temple.

In each temple is a celestial room. It represents the perfect, peaceful, and exalted state of heaven that exists in the presence of our Heavenly Father and His Son, Jesus Christ.

The beautiful celestial room represents heaven.

In the temple, there are also sealing rooms where a bride and groom kneel across an altar and are married not only for this life, but also for eternity. In these rooms, children can also be sealed to their parents as part of an eternal family.

The bride and groom kneel across an altar like this one.

The baptismal font rests on the backs of twelve oxen.

There is also a baptismal font that sits on the back of twelve oxen that represent the twelve tribes of Israel. This is where baptisms are performed in behalf of those who died without the opportunity to be baptized during their mortal life.

There are ordinance rooms where we learn about God's plan for His children—specifically the central and saving role of Jesus Christ—and where we make sacred promises (covenants) of faithfulness to the gospel of Jesus Christ.

These are ordinance rooms where we learn about God's plan for His children.

MEET
a
Mormon

Scan this QR code to meet some Mormons discussing the blessings of the temple and to see video of LDS temple exteriors and interiors.

The Law of Sacrifice

Some of our Jewish friends might be surprised when they come to a Mormon temple and see only nice trees, flowers, and shrubbery instead of sacrificial lambs and oxen wandering on the grounds. Although in the days of the Old Testament, God's children offered animal sacrifices at the temple, there are no sacrifices of burnt offerings at modern LDS temples. We believe that Jesus Christ offered the great and last sacrifice for sin and, because of that, animal sacrifice is no longer necessary (see 3 Nephi 9:19; Hebrews 7:27). Instead, Christ commands us to "offer for a sacrifice unto me a broken heart and a contrite spirit" (3 Nephi 9:20). When we enter the temple, we make promises to God that we will obey His commandments, live pure and virtuous lives, and serve our fellow man. In that sense, the spirit of sacrifice is alive and well in modern-day LDS temples.

What Are the Undergarments that Mormons Wear?

After Mormons receive the temple endowment, they wear a special undergarment that reminds them of the covenant promises they have made in the temple. These undergarments look very similar to many common T-shirt style and boxer-brief type underwear for men. **The garment is a visual and tactile reminder to the wearer of the covenants of faithfulness he or she has made in the temple,** and as such it helps spiritually strengthen Latter-day Saints to resist sin and to live good, clean, honorable lives. The Mormon garment is similar in its purpose to a priestly collar or clothing of a clerical minister: It serves to remind the wearer of his or her dedication to God. The only difference is that Mormons wear their garments under their clothing instead of outside it.

The Mormon garment is similar in its purpose to a priestly collar. It serves to remind the wearer of his or her dedication to God.

What Do Mormons Wear inside Temples?

If you've ever seen a Mormon entering or exiting a temple, odds are they were carrying a little shoulder bag or suitcase. These bags contain our temple clothing that we change into during certain temple ordinances. After entering the temple, everyone changes into white clothing in private locker rooms. Some of the ordinances of the temple require priestly robes, similar to the ones you can read about in the Old Testament (see Exodus 28) that the sons of Aaron wore while officiating in the tabernacle or temple.

Like many religions that have special clothing as part of their worship (think of the different ceremonial or religious clothing associated with Catholics, Jews, Muslims, and Buddhists, for example), the clothing we wear in the temple is symbolic and very meaningful and is meant to tangibly teach spiritual things.

Orthodox Jew   *Muslim woman*   *Catholic priest*

Many religious people wear special clothing as part of their worship.

Can I Go inside a Temple?

Yes, you can. Before temples are dedicated for official Church use, they are opened for several weeks so the general public can go in and see what these beautiful temples look like inside. Recently, nearly 685,000 people toured a new temple before it was dedicated.[8] But after the temple is dedicated, a person must be a worthy Latter-day Saint in order to enter and participate in temple ordinances.

Some people wonder why there are certain qualifications to enter a temple. Remember prerequisites in school? Addition comes before division. Division comes before algebra. Algebra before trig. We can relate to that.

Similarly, there are certain prerequisites (such as the ordinance of baptism) that must be met before someone can enter an LDS temple and receive additional ordinances. A person must be a member of the LDS Church for at least one year, be at least twelve years old, and be found worthy to hold a current temple recommend.[9] To determine if a person is ready to enter the temple, our local LDS minister conducts a private interview and asks certain questions about our faithfulness. If we have complied with those requirements, then we are granted a recommend to enter the temple and participate in its ordinances. Anyone who is prepared and found worthy is welcome and wanted in a temple.

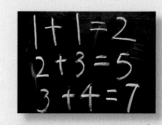

This ↑ comes before this. ↓

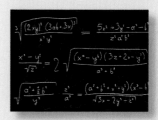

What Are Mormons Asked in the Temple Recommend Interview?

LDS Apostle President Boyd K. Packer (1924–) wrote: "Here [in the interview with their local LDS minister] the member is asked searching questions about his or her personal conduct, worthiness, and loyalty to the Church and its officers. The person must certify that he or she is morally clean and is keeping the Word of Wisdom [see page 146], paying a full tithing, living in harmony with the teachings of the Church, and not maintaining any affiliation or sympathy with apostate groups."[10]

Who Is That Gold Statue on Top of Your Temples?

Most Mormon temples have a gold-leafed statue of an angel crowning the top of the temple—the angel Moroni. Moroni was the last of the authors of the Book of Mormon and, as a resurrected being, he appeared to Joseph Smith in the early 1800s and showed him where he had buried the golden plates (see Joseph Smith—History 1:27–54; see also chapter 13 for more about the Book of Mormon).

The angel Moroni with his trumpet is a symbol that the gospel of Jesus Christ has been restored on earth.

The angel Moroni with his trumpet is a symbol that the gospel of Jesus Christ has been restored on earth (see Revelation 14:7) and proclaims to the world that the Lord has sent "his angels with a great sound of a trumpet" (Matthew 24:31) to tell the world to prepare for Christ's return to the earth for His Second Coming. The golden figure of the angel Moroni has become an iconic symbol of Mormonism throughout the world.

MORMYTH: What happens inside the Mormon temple is "secret."

Answer: False.

It's not secret. It's sacred—and there is a difference. If something were secret then it implies that we don't want other people to know about it. On the contrary, Mormons would love everyone to gain the knowledge and blessings available in the temple. But because what happens and is taught in temples is sacred, then we are careful not to discuss it with those who might not understand or appreciate its significance.

Jesus Himself often told His followers not to publicly discuss certain sacred experiences, such as what happened with Peter, James, and John on the Mount of Transfiguration, charging them to "tell no man" (Mark 9:9; see also Matthew 8:4; 16:20). Most everyone has had a special or personal experience that they wouldn't share or discuss with just anybody, fearing that sharing something near to their heart with someone unappreciative wouldn't be understood or would be taken lightly. Similarly, Latter-day Saints are instructed to discuss certain aspects of the temple only within the safety of the sacred setting of the temple.

9 LDS Scriptures and Sources of Truth

Just prior to Jesus' crucifixion, Pilate asked Him, **"What is truth?"** (John 18:38). Philosophers for ages have debated that same question, and the debate continues today. There are some who argue that there are no absolute truths and that truth is relative based upon personal experiences and the cultural socialization of individuals.

> The problem with relying only on relative truth is that it is subjective and points in all different directions. Eternal truth, however, crosses time and culture, always pointing in the same direction and to the same source.

We Believe There Is Eternal, Unchanging Truth

While "little t"—relative truth—exists, Latter-day Saints firmly believe that there is also "capital-T Truth"—eternal, unchanging truths that govern existence and form the foundation of God's plan for His children. Ultimately, we believe that Jesus—His teachings and Atonement—is "the way, the truth" (John 14:6). We believe that part of the reason we are here on earth is to learn these truths and put their principles into practice in our everyday lives.

So where do Mormons go to discover eternal truths?

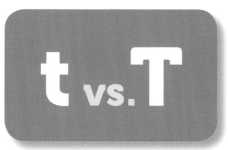

Latter-day Saints firmly believe in "capital-T Truth"—eternal and unchanging.

Latter-day Saint Scriptures

Our scriptures—the Bible, the Book of Mormon, the Doctrine and Covenants, and the Pearl of Great Price—are our foundational source of eternal truth and doctrine. Here is a brief summary of each book of scripture:

■ **The Book of Mormon.** The Book of Mormon is a record of God's dealings with some of His prophets and people who lived on the American continent between about 600 B.C. and A.D. 400. We believe this ancient record was given to Joseph Smith and that he translated it by the gift and power of God. The Book of Mormon is the central book of the LDS faith and contains the teachings of Christ's gospel as given to His ancient American prophets. We believe, as the Prophet Joseph Smith said, that a person can "get nearer to God by abiding by its precepts, than by any other book."[1] (See chapter 13 for more about the Book of Mormon.)

■ **The Old Testament, the New Testament, and the Joseph Smith Translation of the Bible.** Latter-day Saints love and routinely study the Bible in Church classes and at home. For English-speaking Latter-day Saints, the LDS Church publishes and recommends studying the King James Version of the Bible (the Reina Valera translation for Spanish-speaking Saints). Regarding the Bible, one of our Articles of Faith says, "We believe the Bible to be the word of God as far as it is translated correctly" (Articles of Faith 1:8). We believe there are some biblical passages that, over the years and through repeated translations, have lost some of their original meaning. Thus,

Latter-day Saints love and routinely study the Bible in Church classes and at home.

after Joseph Smith finished translating the Book of Mormon, he, through divine inspiration, restored the original meaning of some important verses in the Bible; we call this the Joseph Smith Translation of the Bible. To aid in our study, many verses of the Joseph Smith Translation are included as footnotes in the Latter-day Saint edition of the King James Version of the Bible.

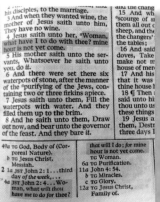

When Jesus' mother, Mary, asks Him for help at the wedding in Cana, the King James Version of the Bible records Jesus' response as, "Woman, what have I to do with thee?" (John 2:4), implying that Mary's worries were perhaps of little concern to Jesus. The Joseph Smith Translation restores the original response of Jesus as, "Woman, what wilt thou have me to do for thee?" which suggests just the opposite: that Jesus honored His mother and was willing to serve and help her.

- **The Doctrine and Covenants.** The Doctrine and Covenants is, first of all, a collection of many of the revelations received by LDS founder, the Prophet Joseph Smith, as he was reestablishing Jesus Christ's Church on the earth.[2] Just as the Quran is a record of Muhammad's revelations over a period of years, the Doctrine and Covenants is a compilation of many of Joseph Smith's revelations over a twenty-one-year period of time (from 1823 to 1844). However, although Muslims believe the Quran to be the final revelation from God, Latter-day Saints do not believe that God has ceased to speak or that Joseph Smith's revelations are the last. We believe that God "will yet reveal many great and important things pertaining to the Kingdom of God" (Articles of Faith 1:9).

  Therefore, the Doctrine and Covenants is an *open* book of scripture, so to speak, and significant revelations of Church doctrine or direction that have been received by modern LDS prophets can be officially canonized and added to it. The last time this happened was the addition of the 1978 revelation to LDS prophet Spencer W. Kimball extending the opportunity for all worthy males to hold the LDS priesthood (see chapter 5 for more on this revelation). There is no "The End" on the last page of the Doctrine and Covenants for a reason.

- **The Pearl of Great Price.** The Pearl of Great Price is "a small selection from the revelations, translations, and narrations of Joseph Smith" (Pearl of Great Price, title page). It includes five books:

To Latter-day Saints, this book of scripture is like the "pearl of great price" (Matthew 13:46) Jesus compared the kingdom of heaven with.

  1. *Selections from the Book of Moses.* This is Joseph Smith's translation of Genesis 1–6 from the Bible, restoring through divine inspiration much of what was lost in Moses' original account of the creation down to Noah.

  2. *The Book of Abraham.* This is Joseph Smith's translation of an ancient papyrus that was discovered in Egypt and brought to Joseph Smith in 1835. Joseph Smith explained that the papyrus contains "the writings of Abraham while he was in Egypt" (introduction to the Book of Abraham).

  3. *Joseph Smith—Matthew.* This is an extract from Joseph Smith's translation of Matthew 23–24 of the Bible.

  4. *Joseph Smith—History.* This short history, written by Joseph Smith in 1838, details the beginning of The Church of Jesus Christ of Latter-day Saints and describes the First Vision he experienced as a fourteen-year-old boy, his experience receiving the Book of Mormon and translating it, and his receiving priesthood authority from John the Baptist.

  5. *The Articles of Faith.* These thirteen fundamental Latter-day Saint beliefs were written by Joseph Smith and include such statements as "We believe that through the Atonement of Christ, all mankind may be saved, by obedience to the laws and ordinances of the Gospel" (Articles of Faith 1:3).

Each of these four books—the Book of Mormon, the Bible, the Doctrine and Covenants, and the Pearl of Great Price—are considered holy scripture by Latter-day Saints. We are encouraged to regularly read, study, and apply the teachings of each of these books of scripture in our search for eternal truth.

Living Prophets

All four of the Latter-day Saint books of scripture are intricately cross-referenced between one another to help those who study them find statements of truth from multiple scriptural sources.

Although our canonized scriptures form the foundation of our doctrine and sources of truth, they are not more important to Latter-day Saints than the living prophets are. The Church of Jesus Christ of Latter-day Saints is governed by fifteen prophets, seers, and revelators—three in the First Presidency (the highest governing body of the Church) and twelve in the Quorum of the Twelve Apostles (the second-highest governing body). We believe these men to be God's authorized, living prophets, who speak the mind and will of the Lord, just as Isaiah or Peter did in Biblical times. **These living prophets are more important to living Latter-day Saints than past prophets because we believe they reveal God's will for his children today.**[3] The revelations of Adam didn't tell Noah how to build his ark, and Noah's revelations didn't tell Moses how to lead the children of Israel to freedom. Adam, Noah, and Moses each needed their own, current direction from God, and Mormons believe that we do too. Therefore, Latter-day Saints look to the words of our living prophets as one of the most important sources of truth and direction for us today. We believe this to be a "living church" (Doctrine and Covenants 1:30), and that implies growth and change and continued revelation through living prophets.

When the LDS First Presidency and the Quorum of the Twelve Apostles speak unanimously on a doctrine, principle, or practice, Latter-day Saints believe their declarations "shall be the will of the Lord, shall be the mind of the Lord, shall

Former LDS prophet John Taylor (1808–1887) said that God gave "new revelations [to former prophets], adapted to the peculiar circumstances in which the churches or individuals were placed. . . . These all had revelations for themselves, and so had Isaiah, Jeremiah, Ezekiel, Jesus, Peter, Paul, John, and Joseph. And so must we, or we shall make a shipwreck."[4]

be the word of the Lord, shall be the voice of the Lord, and the power of God unto salvation" (Doctrine and Covenants 68:4). The prophets and other general LDS Church authorities speak to the entire Church twice a year in a general conference that is held at the LDS Conference Center in Salt Lake City, Utah, and is broadcast to Church members all over the world. They also publish monthly messages in the LDS Church's official magazines: the *Ensign*, the *Liahona*, the *New Era*, and the *Friend*. From these addresses, Latter-day Saints receive direction, counsel, insight, and inspiration.

Air Jordans Are the Best! Official LDS Doctrine?

Not everything spoken by LDS prophets and apostles represents official Church doctrine or position. Doctrine and Covenants 107:27 specifically mentions the need for unanimity among the First Presidency and Quorum of the Twelve Apostles, stating that "every decision made by either of these quorums must be by the unanimous voice of the same; that is, every member in each quorum must be agreed to its decisions." Thus, **formal declarations written or approved by the united body of the LDS First Presidency and the Quorum of the Twelve Apostles are considered official doctrine for the LDS Church and its members.** (Recent examples include the 2010 *Handbook 2: Administering the Church* for local LDS Church leaders and the missionary guidebook *Preach My Gospel*.) However, as the LDS Church's public affairs department stated: "Not every statement made by a Church leader, past or present, necessarily constitutes doctrine. A single statement made by a single leader on a single occasion often represents a personal, though well-considered, opinion, but is not meant to be officially binding for the whole Church."[5]

NOT *the official shoe of the LDS Church!*

Thus—using an extreme example to prove a point—if an apostle says that "Air Jordans are the best!" it doesn't mean Air Jordans become the official sponsored shoe of the LDS Church or that its members are required to buy them. The same applies if an LDS General Authority expresses his ideas on a doctrinal matter—like where the lost ten tribes of Israel are. His words don't make it an official position for the Church. For something to be a binding statement of official LDS position or doctrine, it must be presented by the united voice of the LDS First Presidency and the Quorum of the Twelve Apostles.

For the past fifty years, the LDS Church has translated and broadcast all over the world its general conference proceedings from Salt Lake City. Here are some statistics on how a worldwide Church translates the words of its prophets across the globe:[6]

- Portions of LDS general conference are interpreted into ninety-two different languages.
- Forty-four languages are interpreted during conference itself in the Conference Center and broadcast via satellite.
- Eight hundred people work together to translate general conference.
- There are fifty-eight interpretation booths in the LDS Conference Center in Salt Lake City.

Personal Inspiration

We believe that God not only speaks to His living prophets, but He also speaks to all His children who seek Him. Latter-day Saints believe that we can receive inspiration from God, or "personal revelation," as it is often referred to in the LDS Church.

There is perhaps no more oft-repeated promise in the scriptures than this: "Ask, and it shall be given you" (Matthew 7:7). Any communication from God to man—such as an individual asking God in prayer and receiving an answer—can be considered "revelation," and thus it is our belief that anyone can receive personal revelation.

We believe that God inspires and speaks to people through the invisible influence of the Holy Ghost, sometimes referred to in the scriptures as the "Spirit of God" or "the Holy Spirit." Latter-day Saint scripture states, "[God] will tell you in your mind and in your heart, by the Holy Ghost" (Doctrine and Covenants 8:2). The Holy Ghost speaks to a person's mind in the form of enlightened thoughts, ideas, memories, or clarified understanding. His spiritual influence can also come through uplifting feelings such as peace, comfort, confidence, love, and joy. Sometimes He warns and restrains us through foreboding feelings such as uneasiness or doubt. Through the Holy Ghost, individuals can also have visions, revelations, inspired dreams, and other experiences where God communicates knowledge and truth to him or her.

We believe that to the degree we faithfully seek and try to live the teachings of Jesus Christ, God can inspire us through the Holy Ghost to know for ourselves the truthfulness of the gospel, independent of any other person, for "by the power of the Holy Ghost [a person] may know the truth of all things" (Moroni 10:5).

The Light of Christ

The Light of Christ is the internal source of truth that informs our basic ability to distinguish right from wrong.

Aside from the Holy Ghost, Mormons believe there is a universal influence found in all people called the Light of Christ, which enables us to judge good from evil. Some people call it a conscience, a gut feeling, intuition—even your own personal Jiminy Cricket. The Light of Christ is the internal source of truth that informs our basic ability to distinguish right from wrong and allows mankind to know that murder, rape, abuse, and other evils are inherently immoral. It is the influence that makes children seek fairness and love. It is the power that naturally invites human beings to care for one another and give of themselves to help each other. We believe this Light of Christ is another source of truth for all mankind.

General Religious, Moral, Philosophical, and Scientific Truths

Since the earliest days of the Church, LDS leaders have placed high emphasis on learning and education. We believe educating our minds and gaining knowledge is part of the purpose of life as we strive to become more like God, for "the glory of God is intelligence" (Doctrine and Covenants 93:36). Latter-day Saint scripture tells us to "seek learning" (Doctrine and Covenants 88:118) and that we should learn a variety of subjects, "of things both in heaven and in the earth" (Doctrine and Covenants 88:79).

We believe educating our minds and gaining knowledge is part of the purpose of life as we strive to become more like God.

One of the first things Joseph Smith did when founding the city of Nauvoo, Illinois, was to establish a university. And just a few short years after bringing the exiled LDS Church into the Salt Lake Valley, Brigham Young began the University of Deseret (now the University of Utah). While we humbly believe that the heavenly authority and ordinances necessary for salvation are found only in The Church of Jesus Christ of Latter-day Saints, we don't believe that our religion has the corner on the market of all truth.[7] We believe God is the author of knowledge[8] and that He inspires and reveals truths to many people from all religious backgrounds, walks of life, and fields of study. Latter-day Saints are encouraged to learn and accept any religious, moral, philosophical, or scientific truths that are designed to benefit mankind, as we believe the gospel of Jesus Christ ultimately embraces every correct and true principle into one great whole.

Truth

Scriptures

The Holy Ghost

Science

Prophets

The Light of Christ

Philosophy

"The religion of Jesus Christ embraces every true and perfect principle, every correct science, every principle of philosophy—that is, every true principle, and is calculated to benefit mankind in every way."—LDS President George Albert Smith (1870–1951)[9]

How Do Mormons "Know" What They Believe Is True?

Gaining knowledge of spiritual and eternal things is very different from gaining knowledge of secular or tangible things. Spiritual truths can be understood and communicated only by the Spirit of God. The Apostle Paul taught, "For what man knoweth the things of a man, save the spirit of man which is in him? even so the things of God knoweth no man, but the Spirit of God" (1 Corinthians 2:11). **We believe that the more a person brings his or her life into harmony with God's will, the more clearly he or she will comprehend and "know" intangible spiritual truths.**

The following is a hypothetical example of how we believe someone might be able to "know" the truthfulness of an eternal, intangible, spiritual principle—in this case, the principle of selflessly serving others.

1. You **learn** that Jesus taught us to care for and serve others.
↓
2. You find yourself **thinking and pondering, and even praying,** about Jesus' teaching; you desire to know its merits.
↓
3. **Enlightened thoughts** along the lines of "I should be more concerned about others' needs and try to serve and help more often" or "It is a good thing to give of yourself for the benefit of others" come to your mind as you ponder.
↓
4. Edifying **feelings inside your heart** accompany these thoughts, indicating that the idea to serve others is inspired and should be followed through on.
↓
5. You decide to **act in faith** on your thoughts and feelings and provide service, when the opportunity arises, to your neighbor who is in need.
↓
6. You **notice the positive "evidence"** that results from this service—perhaps increased friendship, a sense of brotherhood or sisterhood, feelings of self-worth, a desire to act more nobly, or increased joy. These positive outcomes are what the scriptures call the "fruit[s] of the Spirit" (Galatians 5:22).
↓
7. You make a preliminary **conclusion** that serving others is a correct or true principle, as it produced positive thoughts, feelings, and outcomes in your life and in the life of others.
↓
8. You **seek God in prayer**, asking Him in faith to confirm your conclusions (see James 1:5).
↓
9. You **repeat** this process.

(Note: These items don't necessarily have to happen in this order.)

Through this process, little by little, thought by thought, feeling by feeling, action by action, and evidence by evidence, we can increase our belief, until we move to the point where our repeated experiences cause us to say, "I *know* this is good, right, and true." We believe this is why Jesus said, "If any man will do [God's] will, he shall know of the doctrine" (John 7:17).

The Book of Mormon tells us to "experiment" on the teachings of the gospel, and that "because ye have tried the experiment, and planted the seed [the word of truth], . . . ye must needs know that the seed is good" (Alma 32:33). **The same process applies to any spiritual principle, whether it is to know that God exists and loves His children, the reality of Jesus' divinity, or the truthfulness of the Book of Mormon.**

Like a three-legged stool, these three things—edifying thoughts, feelings, and outcomes—provide Latter-day Saints with a foundation we call a "testimony," upon which we can stand and say that we know an intangible, spiritual principle is true based on our own personal experiences.

Truth Squared

When a person comes to a conclusion about a truth, he or she can "square it" with the following to help assess its truthfulness:

- How does it square with various passages found in the holy scriptures?

- How does it square with the teachings of the living prophets?

- How does it square with personal evidence (outcomes) received by the Holy Ghost?

- How does it square with knowledge and findings from various fields of learning?

If the idea squares with each of these sides, then it is probably in harmony with Truth. However, if the conclusion isn't in line with one side, something may be amiss and ought to be reconsidered.

Scan this QR code to meet **Sergio Sanchez**, a man of science and a man of faith, to learn about how he searches for and learns both scientific and spiritual truths.

MORMYTH:
Latter-day Saints are blind followers.

Answer: False. (We're actually told *not* to be blind followers.)

It is important to know that although faithful Mormons revere the holy scriptures and the living prophets of God, we are counseled "to independently strive to receive [our] own spiritual confirmation of the truthfulness of Church doctrine"[10] and to gain our own testimony of the truthfulness of doctrinal teachings as explained by Mormon prophets.

We are taught to seek our own spiritual conclusions, use our own agency (our independent ability to choose), and do our own thinking. Additionally, we are urged by our scriptures and our Church leaders to "seek learning" (Doctrine and Covenants 88:118) and gain all the education we can, both spiritual and secular.

Latter-day Saints take that injunction to seek learning seriously. **Multiple studies have found that active Latter-day Saints "have significantly more education than the general public"[11]** and that higher activity and religiosity in the LDS Church is related to higher educational attainment. One study found that 40 percent of LDS young men and women who had served LDS missions had received college degrees, compared to 18 percent of the general American population, and that 25 percent of LDS returned missionaries had completed graduate or professional school, compared to 8 percent of the national average.[12] Another study found that the LDS community produced more scientists per capita than most religious groups in twentieth-century America.[13]

As a whole, Latter-day Saints cannot be fairly characterized as uneducated, close-minded, or brainwashed people who blindly follow their faith, nor do the modern LDS prophets want them to be. Most Mormons are above-average-educated independent seekers of truth who simply believe through personal experience that they have found Truth in The Church of Jesus Christ of Latter-day Saints.

10 The Mormon View of the Afterlife

Is how you picture heaven?

When most people think of heaven, they probably think choirs and harps, robes and clouds (cumulonimbuses?), eternal rest, and lots and lots of singing. Not Mormons. When we think of heaven, we think of a glorified physical earth; we think of tangible, resurrected people of flesh and bone. We think of a place where there is continued learning and eternal progression. And while there might be lots and lots of singing, there will also be lots and lots of families. Although some of these specific ideas about heaven may seem unique, the idea of heaven and an afterlife is not unique to Mormons: **Over 80 percent of Americans believe in heaven,**[1] **and 82 percent believe there is life after death.**[2]

The following is a little bit about how Latter-day Saints view the afterlife.

Where Do We Go When We Die?

> "The spirit and the body are the soul of man."
> —Doctrine and Covenants 88:15

We believe that each person has an immortal spirit and that a spirit together with a mortal body makes a living soul. Death is the separation of the spirit from the mortal body. When a person dies, although their body is buried, **their eternal spirit continues to live on in what Latter-day Saints call the spirit world.**

When people enter the spirit world, they are still the same person they were on earth—death doesn't change their identity, personality, or desires. In the spirit world, those who obeyed the teachings of Jesus Christ are received into a state of paradise where they live in "a state of rest, a state of peace, where they shall rest from all their troubles and from all care, and sorrow" (Alma 40:12).

Those who have "died in their sins, without a knowledge of the truth, or in transgression, having rejected the prophets" (Doctrine

> "That same spirit which doth possess your bodies at the time that ye go out of this life, that same spirit will have power to possess your body in that eternal world."—Alma 34:34

and Covenants 138:32) are also in the spirit world, but exist in a state described in the scriptures as "darkness" (Doctrine and Covenants 138:22) or "prison" (1 Peter 3:19; Doctrine and Covenants 76:73). LDS teachings state that "the spirits in prison are 'taught faith in God, repentance from sin, vicarious baptism for the remission of sins, the gift of the Holy Ghost by the laying on of hands, and all other principles of the gospel that [are] necessary for them to know' (Doctrine and Covenants 138:33–34). If they accept the principles of the gospel, repent of their sins, and accept ordinances performed in their behalf in [Latter-day Saint] temples, they will be welcome into paradise"[3] and become "heirs of salvation" (Doctrine and Covenants 138:59). We believe that the spirit remains in the spirit world until the time of the resurrection (see Alma 40:14), which for most of mankind will occur after Jesus Christ returns to the earth for His Second Coming.

> We believe that during the interim between Jesus Christ's death and resurrection, He organized the teaching of the gospel to those in spirit prison. Peter tells us that Christ "went and preached unto the spirits in prison" after being "put to death in the flesh" (1 Peter 3:19, 18). For a complete reading on the subject of preaching the gospel to those who are in the spirit world, see Doctrine and Covenants 138.

> Doctrine and Covenants 88:95–101, along with other scriptures (1 Corinthians 15:23; Alma 40:8), indicates that people will come forth from the resurrection at different times after the Second Coming of Jesus, depending on their righteousness (sooner) or wickedness (later).

Who Will Be Resurrected?

Latter-day Saints believe that everyone who has ever been born on earth will be resurrected[4] (see John 5:29) and receive an immortal body of flesh and bone. The scriptures teach, "For as in Adam all die, even so in Christ shall all be made alive" (1 Corinthians 15:22). **Because of Jesus Christ, you—and all those who have died—will receive the free gift of resurrection.**

The resurrection is the reuniting of the spirit with an immortal body, never again to be separated (see Doctrine and Covenants 138:17). As resurrected beings, mankind will live

> John 5:29 also suggests a universal resurrection: "And shall come forth; they that have done good, unto the resurrection of life; and they that have done evil, unto the resurrection of damnation."

forever in a glorified and immortal condition, free from the pains and challenges of the mortal body. Additionally, we believe that all will be restored to a perfect form in the resurrection (see Alma 40:23): no bodily flaws, no disabilities, no injuries, and no defects. (In Matthew 10:30 Jesus said the very hairs of our head are numbered. Bald men everywhere, rejoice!)

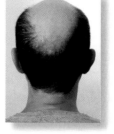
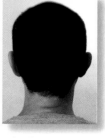

Before the resurrection. *After the resurrection.*

All will "be restored to their proper and perfect frame."—Alma 40:23

We believe that having a resurrected body will not only enable us to have "a fulness of joy" (Doctrine and Covenants 93:33) in the afterlife, but that a resurrected body is also necessary to become like God.

MEET a Mormon

Scan this QR code to meet **Jenny**, a wife and mother of five, and hear her story of how her faith in the eternal nature of our spirits and in the resurrection has helped her deal with the tragic death of her four-year-old son, Russell.

"Mortal eye cannot see nor mind comprehend the beauty, glory, and majesty of a righteous woman made perfect in the celestial kingdom of God."
—LDS Apostle James E. Talmage (1862–1933)[5]

There Are Three Heavens or Degrees of Glory

Latter-day Saints believe that there are three degrees, or levels, of heaven: the celestial (highest), the terrestrial (middle), and the telestial (lowest) kingdoms of heaven. **The Bible also speaks of three heavens in the resurrection:** "There is one glory of the sun, and another glory of the moon, and another glory of the stars: for one star differeth from another star in glory. So also is the resurrection of the dead" (1 Corinthians 15:41–42). The Apostle Paul spoke of being "caught up to the third heaven" (2 Corinthians 12:2) in a vision. And the Prophet Joseph Smith had a remarkable vision where he saw each heaven and the characteristics of its inhabitants (see Doctrine and Covenants 76).

Please note: **they are all a heaven.** Even the lowest kingdom—the telestial—is still a kingdom of glory "which surpasses all understanding" (Doctrine and Covenants 76:89).

Because of the mercy and grace of Jesus Christ and His atoning sacrifice, **we believe that all mankind born on earth, excepting those few who go to outer darkness, will inherit a degree of heaven that is better than anything we can relate to on earth.** Mormons believe that God's plan really is a plan of salvation and that God truly "saves *all* the works of his hands" (Doctrine and Covenants 76:43; emphasis added).

> "Because of the Atonement of Jesus Christ, all spirits blessed by birth will ultimately be resurrected . . . and inherit kingdoms of glory that are superior to our existence here on earth."—LDS Apostle Quentin L. Cook (1940–)[6]

The celestial kingdom is compared to the brightness and glory of the sun.

The Celestial Kingdom: The celestial kingdom is the highest degree of heaven. In the scriptures, it is compared to the brightness and glory of the sun (see 1 Corinthians 15:40–41; Doctrine and Covenants 76:70). In the celestial kingdom, we live in the presence of God and Jesus Christ, we are eventually able to become like them, we can live together forever with those of our family who qualify, and we will receive a fullness of joy. All those who have exercised faith in Jesus Christ, repented of their sins, received baptism and the Holy Ghost by those in proper authority, and continued in faithfulness in the gospel will attain celestial glory.

The terrestrial kingdom is compared to the brightness and glory of the moon.

The Terrestrial Kingdom: The terrestrial kingdom is the middle heaven. In the scriptures, it is compared with the brightness and glory of the moon (see 1 Corinthians 15:40–41; Doctrine and Covenants 76:97). In general, we believe that those who lived honorable lives on earth but who deliberately chose not to accept or fully live the gospel of Jesus Christ will go to the terrestrial kingdom (see Doctrine and Covenants 76:71–80).

The telestial kingdom is compared to the brightness and glory of the stars.

The Telestial Kingdom: In the scriptures, the telestial kingdom is likened to the glory of the stars (see 1 Corinthians 15:40–41; Doctrine and Covenants 76:81). Those who never accept the gospel of Jesus Christ, either in this life or in the spirit world (see Doctrine and Covenants 76:82, 101), and who do not repent but continue in rebellion and major sin will receive the telestial kingdom, or the lowest kingdom of heaven. We believe that the people who go here will have to wait in the spirit world for a thousand years after the Second Coming of Christ before they will be resurrected and receive their telestial glory (see Revelation 20:5; Doctrine and Covenants 76:106).

The telestial kingdom is for those who are not honorable people and who are the unrepentant "liars" and "adulterers" and "whoremongers" of the earth

(Doctrine and Covenants 76:103). We believe that such people will still suffer for their sins and pay the price for their rebelliousness to the laws of God, but the difference is that we believe their suffering will eventually come to an end and they will receive a kingdom of glory.

MORMYTH:
Mormons think they will be the only ones in heaven.
Answer: False.

How many wonderful and noble people are on this earth—or who have been on this earth—of all walks of life and religious faith? Too many to number. In the Book of Mormon, we read that God "loveth his children" (1 Nephi 11:17). We believe that every single person on earth will have the chance to fully hear, understand, accept, and live the true gospel of Jesus Christ. All societal and environmental factors, all misinformation and superstition, all falsehoods and traditions, and any other obstacles that might impede someone from hearing, understanding, and obeying the fullness of the gospel of Jesus Christ will, at some point, be stripped away. We believe that things as they really are—the truth—will be made manifest to all, and each person will have a fully conscious choice to accept or reject that truth. The virtuous and the noble of all faiths and walks of life who accept the truth will be saved and exalted in the celestial kingdom of God.[7]

Do Mormons Believe in Hell?

If we're talking eternal flames and fire and weeping and wailing and gnashing of teeth, then, no, Latter-day Saints don't believe in eternal hell for mankind. We believe that the "eternal" suffering of the wicked that is spoken of in the scriptures is more figurative than literal and that the actual suffering that people endure for rebellion and sin comes to an end once the penalty for their transgressions has been paid and served its purpose.

Doctrine and Covenants 19:6–12 says that descriptions such as "endless torment" or "eternal damnation" are not literal, but are used to help us change our hearts. "Eternal" and "Endless" are names for God, and thus in the scriptures when it speaks of "eternal punishment" it simply means "God's punishment" that will one day come to an end after the penalty for sin has been paid to justice.

LDS doctrine does speak of "outer darkness, where there is weeping, and wailing, and gnashing of teeth" (Doctrine and Covenants 101:91). **Outer darkness** is "hell," and Latter-day Saints believe that is where Satan and the third part of the host of heaven who rebelled against God in the premortal life will go, as well as a select few others of mankind. They are called "sons of perdition" (Doctrine and Covenants 76:43), and they are persons who committed the unforgivable sin against the Holy Ghost (see Matthew 12:31; Alma 39:6) and who are not saved in any kingdom of glory.

Sometimes the scriptures use the term "hell" to describe the temporary abode in the spirit world of those who were disobedient during mortality (Luke 16:23; 2 Nephi 26:10). However, Latter-day Saints believe that because Jesus Christ overcame death, "hell must deliver up its captive spirits" (2 Nephi 9:12) from the spirit world and that all mankind will eventually be resurrected and inherit a degree of heaven. Even the lowest degree of heaven reserved for the wicked and rebellious is a degree of glory incomparable to anything we know on earth. **Thus, Mormons believe that hell (in this sense) will have an end, and God's mercy and love will indeed win out.**

> "Hell, as thus defined, will have an end, when all the captive spirits have paid the price of their sins and enter into a degree of glory after their resurrection."—Bible Dictionary[8]

What Do Mormons Think the Final Judgment Will Be Like?

The Final Judgment will not be an evaluation of good acts versus bad acts . . .

. . . it will be an evaluation of who we have become.

Latter-day Saints believe everyone will be resurrected, and we also believe that everyone will be brought back to God's presence to stand before Him and be judged. We believe that God "will judge all men according to their works, according to the desire of their hearts" (Doctrine and Covenants 137:9; see also Alma 41:3). Those who have come unto Christ in faith, repented of their mistakes, and made covenants with God will receive mercy and be spared from the suffering their sins require (see Doctrine and Covenants 19:16–19; 45:3–5), "while he that exercises no faith unto repentance is exposed to the whole law of the demands of justice" (Alma 34:16) and is required to pay the penalty.

As the purpose of life is to become more like God, we believe that the "Final Judgment is not just an evaluation of a sum total of good and evil acts—what we have *done*. It is an acknowledgment of the final effect of our acts and thoughts—what we have *become*."[9]

Eternal Progression

This is a very wonderful concept: We believe that by the grace of Jesus Christ those who go to the highest heaven in the celestial kingdom will enjoy eternal progression. What this means is that in the celestial kingdom we can continue to learn, grow, progress, and eventually become more like God, enabled by an eternal marriage made available by heavenly power and authority in LDS temples. Those who receive eternal marriage are promised they can have "a continuation of the seeds forever and ever" (Doctrine and Covenants 132:19), which means that the blessings of marriage and family continue with them through eternity.

Within the celestial kingdom "are three heavens or degrees" (Doctrine and Covenants 131:1). To obtain this highest degree of glory, a man and woman must have an eternal marriage (see Doctrine and Covenants 131:2), having been sealed together for eternity by the heavenly authority and power available in LDS temples and having been faithful to their covenants. See chapters 6 and 8 for more on the concepts of eternal marriage and eternal families.

We don't pretend to fully understand the details of how this works, but the idea rings true: To be "damned" means to be stopped in our progress, so nothing seems more rewarding than the thought that those who inherit the celestial kingdom and all that God has will be allowed to progress eternally and eventually become like Him (see chapter 4). While those who attain celestial exaltation will always continue to revere, honor, obey, and glorify God as their Heavenly Father, we believe they can and will become like God.

A New Heaven and a New Earth

In Matthew 5:5, we learn that the meek "shall inherit the earth." Latter-day Saints believe that when Jesus comes again this earth will be renewed and it will be "a new heaven and a new earth" (Revelation 21:1; Ether 13:9; Doctrine and Covenants 29:23). Mormons don't believe that those who go to heaven will travel through a wormhole to some other world or be lifted up into the clouds in the sky. We believe that if we go to the celestial kingdom, we actually won't *go* anywhere: the celestial kingdom of heaven is actually right here (see Doctrine and Covenants 88:17–20). **Our doctrine is that this earth will be renewed and receive a celestial glory, and the righteous will inherit it forever.**

Part 2:
Mormon History

Here's a thirty-second summary of how The Church of Jesus Christ of Latter-day Saints came into existence, settled in Utah, and became a worldwide faith. Ready?

Joseph Smith experienced visions, proclaimed he was the Lord's prophet, published a new book of scripture, and organized a church. Some people were suspicious, so they persecuted Joseph and his followers and pushed them out of—count 'em—four states. The governor of one of those states even officially ordered the Mormons to be "exterminated." Eventually, Joseph Smith was martyred by a mob of 150 men, an act which some supposed would end Mormonism. Instead, senior LDS Apostle Brigham Young was ordained as the prophet and he led the beleaguered Saints across America's wilderness in an epic exodus all the way to the Salt Lake Valley. There, alone in the middle of nowhere, the Mormon Church settled, gathered strength, sent out missionaries, grew, and eventually became the global faith it is today.

Wow! That was fast! For those of you who would like a little more detail, here is a more extensive timeline covering the history of The Church of Jesus Christ of Latter-day Saints.[1]

It all started here →

December 1805. Joseph Smith Jr. is born in Vermont. *(Sharon, Vermont)*

Winter 1846. The Latter-day Saint pioneers winter in Nebraska, where hundreds die of disease and exposure. *(Omaha, Nebraska)*

July 1847. The first company of LDS pioneers arrive in the Salt Lake Valley. Brigham Young says, "This is the right place,"[3] and establishes the headquarters and gathering place of the LDS Church in the great Salt Lake Valley and surrounding Utah territory. *(Salt Lake City, Utah)*

June 1844. Joseph Smith submits to an arrest on old charges of treason, and prophesies, "I am going like a lamb to the slaughter" (Doctrine and Covenants 135:4). *(Nauvoo, Illinois)*

June–November 1856. Thousands of LDS pioneers who can't obtain or afford wagon teams begin walking across the country to the Salt Lake Valley, pulling handcarts. Hundreds die due to exposure or disease. *(Mormon Trail)*

June 1844. Joseph Smith and his brother Hyrum are awaiting trial in Carthage Jail when they are murdered by a mob of 150 men. *(Carthage, Illinois)*

August 1844. As the president of the Quorum of the Twelve Apostles, Brigham Young assumes leadership of the LDS Church. *(Nauvoo, Illinois)*

February 1846. Under pressure from the Illinois state militia, the Latter-day Saints begin the great Mormon American exodus west, leaving behind their city and temple in Nauvoo, Illinois. *(Nauvoo, Illinois)*

1847 to Today. Brigham Young and the Latter-day Saint pioneers establish more than 500 settlements, communities, and cities in the American West, Mexico, and Canada. Mormon missionaries continue to travel around the world, preaching the message that Christ's Church has been reestablished, and LDS converts continue to gather to the Utah territory. Since the 1890s, Church leadership has encouraged Latter-day Saint converts to remain in their homelands instead of gathering to Utah. Today, the LDS Church has more than 28,000 congregations in 177 countries worldwide.[4]

Red dots indicate an organized LDS ward or congregation.

Church in Thirty Seconds

2 **B** **Spring 1820.** As a fourteen-year-old boy, Joseph Smith prays in a grove of trees, and God the Father and Jesus Christ appear to him and tell him that Christ's authorized Church is not found on the earth. *(Palmyra, New York)*

3 **B** **September 1823.** An angel named Moroni appears to seventeen-year-old Joseph Smith and tells him about an ancient record written on golden plates. The angel also says that God intends to use Joseph as an instrument to reestablish Christ's true Church on earth. *(Palmyra, New York)*

4 **B** **September 1827.** Joseph receives the golden plates—and the interpreters to translate them—from the angel Moroni. *(Palmyra, New York)*

5 **C** **May–June 1829.** Joseph Smith and Oliver Cowdery receive the priesthood—the power and authority to act in the name of God—by the laying on of hands from John the Baptist, and Peter, James, and John. *(Harmony, Pennsylvania)*

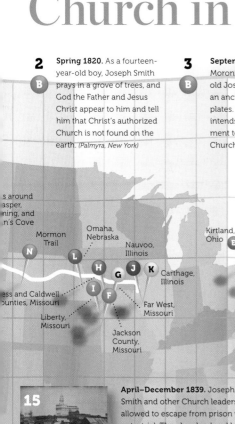

s around asper, ning, and n's Cove

Mormon Trail **N**

Omaha, Nebraska **L**

Nauvoo, Illinois

H **G** **J** **K** Carthage, Illinois

I **F**

ess and Caldwell bunties, Missouri

Liberty, Missouri

Far West, Missouri

Jackson County, Missouri

Sharon, Vermont **A**

Palmyra, New York **B** **D**

Kirtland, Ohio **E**

Fayette, New York

C Harmony, Pennsylvania

6 **B** **March 1830.** The Book of Mormon is published. *(Palmyra, New York)*

12 **G**

7 **D** **April 1830.** Joseph Smith officially organizes The Church of Jesus Christ of Latter-day Saints. *(Fayette, New York)*

January–March 1838. Joseph Smith and most Church members leave Kirtland, Ohio, due to persecution and widespread dissension. The Church and its headquarters eventually settle in Far West, Missouri. *(Far West, Missouri)*

8 **E** **February–June 1831.** Joseph Smith and his followers move from New York to Kirtland, Ohio, where many locals are joining the new Church due to missionary efforts. *(Kirtland, Ohio)*

15 **J** **April–December 1839.** Joseph Smith and other Church leaders are allowed to escape from prison without a trial. They buy land and begin building a city from a swamp—Nauvoo, Illinois. *(Nauvoo, Illinois)*

16 **J** **August 1839.** Many LDS apostles leave for Great Britain on a mission. There they baptize thousands who emigrate to America to join the Saints in Nauvoo and eventually travel to Salt Lake City. *(Nauvoo, Illinois)*

13 **H** **October 1838.** The "Extermination Order" is issued by Missouri Governor Lilburn W. Boggs, authorizing the extermination of any Mormon in Missouri by force.[2] Latter-day Saints are forced to flee Missouri and travel to Illinois in the dead of winter. *(Daviess and Caldwell Counties, Missouri)*

9 **F** **July 1831.** Joseph Smith receives a revelation designating Independence, Missouri, as the place to build the latter-day city of Zion spoken of in the scriptures. *(Jackson County, Missouri)*

17 **J** **March 1842.** Joseph Smith organizes the female Relief Society—an organization to care for the poor and the needy. *(Nauvoo, Illinois)*

14 **I**

December 1838–April 1839. Joseph Smith and a half dozen other LDS Church leaders are incarcerated for nearly five months in a stone prison awaiting trial on trumped-up charges of treason. *(Liberty, Missouri)*

18 **J** **May 1842.** Joseph Smith begins to administer LDS temple ordinances to the Saints. *(Nauvoo, Illinois)*

March–April 1836. The first LDS temple is finished and dedicated. The Lord Jesus Christ, as well as Moses, Elias, and Elijah, appear to Joseph Smith and Oliver Cowdery and give them additional heavenly power and authority, such as the power to perform eternal marriages and other LDS temple ordinances. *(Kirtland, Ohio)*

11 **E**

10 **E** **February 1835.** Joseph Smith calls and organizes the Quorum of the Twelve Apostles and the Quorum of the Seventy, two of the three overall governing bodies of the LDS Church. *(Kirtland, Ohio)*

12 The Joseph Smith Story

Joseph Smith accomplished what no other person had since Muhammad 1,400 years prior: He brought about the rise of a new world religion.

On a rainy May morning in 1844, a future mayor of Boston, Josiah Quincy Jr., and a grandson of US President John Adams, Charles Francis Adams, stopped in the Mormon city of Nauvoo, Illinois, and spent some time meeting and conversing with the Mormon prophet, Joseph Smith. Although skeptical of Joseph's prophetic claims, Josiah Quincy was immediately impressed by the founder of Mormonism, commenting on the "kingly faculty" with which Joseph Smith seemed naturally endowed.

Nearly forty years after the encounter, and long after Joseph Smith had been killed, Josiah Quincy was still fascinated by Joseph Smith. He wrote: "'It is by no means improbable that some future textbook for the use of generations yet unborn, will contain a question something like this: **What historical American of the nineteenth century has exerted the most powerful influence upon the destinies of his countrymen?** And it is by no means impossible that the answer to that interrogatory may be thus written: **Joseph Smith, the Mormon Prophet.** And the reply, absurd as it doubtless seems to most men now living, may be an obvious commonplace to their descendants.'"[1]

Beginning with Joseph Smith's First Vision in 1820 and ending with his martyrdom in 1844, Latter-day Saints believe that, in the short space of twenty-four years, Joseph Smith was an instrument in the hand of God to bring about the "marvellous work and a wonder" (Isaiah 29:14; 2 Nephi 25:17) of reestablishing Jesus Christ's church and kingdom in the latter days.

Born without the privilege of wealth, education, or family prominence, Joseph Smith accomplished what no other person had since Muhammad 1,400 years prior: He brought about the rise of a new world religion.[2]

For a timeline pertaining to some of the major events of Joseph Smith's life, see chapter 11, "The History of the LDS Church in Thirty Seconds."

Here is a little about Joseph Smith's calling, life, ministry, teachings, and why Latter-day Saints revere him as the great prophet of God in our day.

A Prophecy of Good and Evil Fulfilled

Iosephus Smith (Latin)
(Arabic) جوزيف سميث
斯密約瑟 (Chinese)
ג'וזף סמיט (Hebrew)
Джозеф Смит (Russian)
Ο Τζόζεφ Σμιθ (Greek)

Joseph Smith stated that, when he was only seventeen years old, an angel told him "that my name should be had for good and evil among all nations, kindreds, and tongues" (Joseph Smith—History 1:33). Whether you believe Joseph Smith is a true prophet, a religious genius, a frontier talent, or a duplicitous fraud and charlatan, the fact remains that that prophecy—spoken about an obscure, uneducated, poor, common farm boy with the homeliest of names—has most decidedly come true in our day.

Go to **www.joseph smith.net** to learn more about the life and teachings of Joseph Smith.

How Was Joseph Smith Called as a Prophet?

Joseph Smith didn't set out to be a prophet. As a fourteen-year-old boy in 1820, he set out to answer two questions that had been pressing on his mind: **How can my sins be forgiven?** and **Which church is right?**

Joseph lived in upstate New York, a place where "there was . . . an unusual excitement on the subject of religion" (Joseph Smith—History 1:5). His own family was divided on the issue of which church to join, and Joseph said that he felt that "there was no society or denomination that built upon the gospel of Jesus Christ as recorded in the new testament."[3] So, in the spring of 1820, after having read a profound passage in the New Testament—"If any of you lack wisdom, let him ask of God" (James 1:5)— Joseph determined to take his questions to God.

In the woods behind his home, Joseph Smith poured out his heart in prayer, and a marvelous vision burst upon him.

In the woods behind his home, he poured out his heart in prayer, and a marvelous vision burst upon him. He later wrote: "I saw a pillar of light exactly over my head, above the brightness of the sun, which descended gradually until it fell upon me. . . . When the light rested upon me **I saw two Personages, whose brightness and glory defy all description, standing above me in the air. One of them spake unto me, calling me by name and said, pointing to the other—This is My Beloved Son. Hear Him!"** (Joseph Smith—History 1:16–17).

Regaining his composure, Joseph asked his two questions to the persons before him, God the Father and Jesus Christ. Their answer to his first question was, "Joseph <my son> thy sins are forgiven thee"[4] and the answer to his second question of "which of all the sects was right" was somewhat unexpected: "I was answered that I must join none of them, for they were all wrong" (Joseph Smith—History 1:18–19). **Latter-day Saints call this vision of God the Father and Jesus Christ the "First Vision" because it was the beginning of the visions of Joseph Smith.** This vision marks what we believe to be the opening of a new era of Jesus reestablishing His authorized Church on the earth through Joseph Smith.

This vision also set Joseph Smith on a prophetic path from which he never turned back. Although his telling about his First Vision "was the cause of great persecution" (Joseph Smith—History 1:22) to the teenage Joseph, his sincerity and the reality of what happened to him—regardless of others' opinions and actions—are evident in his matter-of-fact and resolute conclusion of the whole experience: "I had actually seen a light, and in the midst of that light I saw two Personages, and they did in reality speak to me; and though I was hated and persecuted for saying that I had seen a vision, yet it was true; . . . I knew it, and I knew that God knew it, and I could not deny it" (Joseph Smith—History 1:25).

How Did Joseph Smith Acquire the Book of Mormon?

In 1823—three years after his First Vision—seventeen-year-old Joseph Smith again prayed to God "for forgiveness of all my sins and follies, and also for a manifestation to me, that I might know of my state and standing before him" (Joseph Smith—History 1:29). In answer to his prayer, he was visited in his room by an angel named Moroni, who told him "that God had a work for [Joseph] to do" (Joseph Smith—History 1:33).

In answer to his prayer, Joseph was visited in his room by an angel named Moroni, who told him "that God had a work for [Joseph] to do."

Moroni told Joseph about an ancient record on gold plates that was buried in a hill near Joseph's home. This record, of course, was the Book of Mormon. The angel Moroni also told Joseph **"that the time was at hand for the Gospel in all its fulness to be preached in power, unto all nations"** and that Joseph was **"to be an instrument in the hands of God"** in that work.[5]

The angel Moroni appeared to Joseph Smith four successive times during that night and the subsequent day, each time repeating the same message to him with some additional information. The next morning Joseph was told to tell his father about the visions (imagine that conversation!), to which his father replied "that it was of God, and [he] told me to go and do as commanded by the messenger" (Joseph Smith—History 1:50).

Joseph Smith was instructed by the angel to take the record home and translate it.

Joseph went to the nearby hill (the "Hill Cumorah" as it is commonly called) where he had been shown in vision the place where the gold plates were buried. There, the angel Moroni met him again and told him that the time had not yet arrived for Joseph to take the record, but that Joseph should meet him there once a year for the next four years on that same date. In the meantime, Joseph would be taught and instructed by the angel "respecting what the Lord was going to do, and how and in what manner his kingdom was to be conducted in the last days" (Joseph Smith—History 1:54).

After four years, when Joseph Smith was twenty-one, he was given permission and instructions by the angel to take the record home and translate it. (See chapter 13 for more on the translation process of the Book of Mormon and the witnesses of the gold plates.)

Joseph Smith's Life's Work and Mission

Near the end of his life, Joseph Smith said, "I don't blame any one for not believing my history. If I had not experienced what I have, I could not have believed it myself."[6]

Through revelation, Joseph learned that Jesus Christ was going to reestablish His authorized Church, set up the kingdom of God again, establish the city of Zion, gather the house of Israel, and preach the gospel to the whole world—and that Joseph was going to be God's prophet who would help move these events forward (see chapter 2). No small task, indeed!

After the Book of Mormon was published, Joseph Smith dedicated the remainder of his life to these divine purposes. We believe that through Joseph Smith the Lord restored "the dispensation of the fulness of times" as the scripture says, where Jesus "gather[ed] together in one all things in Christ" (Ephesians 1:10): things from both the Old Testament and the New Testament. Thus Joseph Smith not only brought back apostles and prophets (see Ephesians 4:11), but also patriarchs, temple worship, Old Testament priesthoods, and other ancient orders. He called missionaries and sent them to preach the gospel to all nations, and he called for a centralized gathering, for cities to be built, and for the founding of Zion.

Joseph Smith didn't set out to restore a mere church: he sought to reestablish God's kingdom and prepare the world for the return of Jesus Christ. He said: "Truly this is a day long to be remembered by the Saints of the last days,—a day in which the God of heaven has begun to restore the ancient order of His kingdom unto His servants and His people,—a day in which all things are concurring to bring about the completion of the fullness of the Gospel, a fullness of the dispensation of dispensations, even the fullness of times; a day in which . . . Jehovah has promised should be made known in His own due time unto His servants, to prepare the earth for the return of His glory."[7]

Did Joseph Smith Ever Have More Than One Wife?

Yes. Some people mistakenly assume that the LDS Church's now retired practice of plural marriage began with Brigham Young when the Saints came west, when in fact it began with Joseph Smith.

The Old Testament practice of plural marriage was revealed and restored to Joseph Smith perhaps as early as 1831[9] as part of the restoration of all things, including the marriage system of the ancient patriarchs such as Abraham, Isaac, Jacob, and Moses (see Doctrine and Covenants 132). To quote noted Mormon historian Richard Lyman Bushman, "Joseph [Smith] did not explain plural marriage as a love match or even a companionship. . . . He understood plural marriage as a religious principle."[10] Although estimates vary based on historical interpretations, most scholars agree that Joseph Smith was married or "sealed" to about thirty women during his lifetime.[11]

What Is Zion?

One of Joseph Smith's prophetic calls was to establish the city of Zion, or the New Jerusalem, that is spoken of in the scriptures (see Revelation 3:12, 21:2; Ether 13:3–10; Doctrine and Covenants 42:9). In the words of Joseph Smith, we believe "that Zion (the New Jerusalem) will be built upon the American continent" (Articles of Faith 1:10). **Zion will be a literal city in a literal place, a holy American city akin to Israel's Jerusalem, and a "land of promise"** (Doctrine and Covenants 57:2).

And no, the location of Zion is *not* Salt Lake City, Utah. Joseph Smith was told by revelation that Independence, Missouri, is the place for the city of Zion and "is the land which I [the Lord] have appointed and consecrated for the gathering of the saints" (Doctrine and Covenants 57:1). Those familiar with Mormonism's history and Joseph Smith's life know that accomplishing this objective remained unfulfilled, as the Mormons who originally gathered in Independence, Missouri, and founded the city of Zion were driven from the state by mob violence.

Joseph Smith and the Latter-day Saints eventually fled to Illinois, and after Joseph Smith's martyrdom, the Saints retreated west to the Great Salt Lake Valley, but their eyes always remained on establishing Zion. That's one reason why, if you visit Salt Lake City, you will see companies such as Zion's Bank and Zion Book Store and the Zion Lodge, and even Zion's Upholstering (those better be some celestial cushion covers).

After being driven out of Independence, Missouri, Joseph Smith was promised by the Lord that one day "Zion shall be redeemed" (Doctrine and Covenants 100:13). We still hold on to that promise. **Mormons believe that one day—when directed by the Lord through modern prophets—we will fulfill Joseph Smith's vision and "build a city, which shall be called the New Jerusalem"** (3 Nephi 21:23), **even the city of Zion.**

Did You Know . . .

Yes, Joseph Smith was the first Mormon. And no, David is not one of the four gospels.

A 2010 Pew Forum study on religious knowledge found that 51% of Americans know Joseph Smith was a Mormon. While that means that about half the country lacks basic information about Joseph Smith's life and mission as the founder of Mormonism, at least he was better known than the writers of the four gospels. Only 45% of those surveyed could name the four New Testament gospels of Matthew, Mark, Luke, and John.[12]

Joseph Smith's Persecution and Martyrdom

American linguist, philosopher, and MIT professor Noam Chomsky once observed: "The people who were honored in the Bible were the false prophets. It was the ones we call the prophets who were jailed and driven into the desert."[13]

Like so many prophets who came before him (see Matthew 5:11–12), Joseph Smith suffered immensely for his prophetic claims and teachings. From the time he was a fourteen-year-old boy, his revelations were "the cause of great persecution" (Joseph Smith—History 1:22) in his life. When he was twenty-six years old and the Church he had founded was in its infancy, he was dragged from his home

In the oxymoronically named Liberty Jail, Joseph Smith and a half dozen Mormon leaders spent five months during the winter of 1838 and 1839 in hellish conditions awaiting trial. (For defending the Saints against mob violence in Missouri, they had been falsely charged with treason.) The dungeon walls were four feet thick, and the interior measured only fourteen feet by fourteen feet, and just over six feet high. The prisoners suffered in cold, filthy conditions, with scanty food, no heat, and insufficient bedding. The only light came from two small barred windows, measuring about two feet wide by six inches high.[14]

in the middle of the night and tarred and feathered by a drunken mob of twenty-five anti-Mormons intent on killing him. **In his lifetime, Joseph Smith was arrested on various charges an estimated thirty times,** from trumped-up charges of treason to accusations of "being a disorderly person [by] setting the county in an uproar by preaching the Book of Mormon."[15] He was abused and insulted, chained and arrested, jailed and imprisoned. Toward the end of his life, Joseph admitted, "If I had not actually got into this work and been called of God, I would back out. But I cannot back out: I have no doubt of the truth."[16]

Joseph Smith eventually gave his life, at the young age of thirty-eight, for the cause he believed in. On the sultry afternoon of June 27, 1844, Joseph Smith and his brother Hyrum were shot and killed by a mob of about a hundred and fifty men who rushed

Joseph Smith and his brother Hyrum were shot and killed by a mob of about a hundred and fifty men.

the Carthage Jail where the Smith brothers were being held, along with two other men, awaiting trial. Joseph had previously prophesied to his friends "that 'he would not live to see forty years,'"[17] and there were indications from as early as 1829 that Joseph Smith knew that the price of his prophethood would be his own blood. (The Lord told the twenty-four-year-old Joseph Smith to "be firm in keeping the commandments . . . even if you should be slain" [Doctrine and Covenants 5:22]. See also Doctrine and Covenants 6:30; 3 Nephi 21:10.)

John Taylor, who was in the room with Joseph Smith when the Prophet was martyred, later memorialized Joseph Smith's suffering and death for his prophetic role in these words: "He lived great, and he died great in the eyes of God and his people; and like most of the Lord's anointed in ancient times, has sealed his mission and his works with his own blood" (Doctrine and Covenants 135:3).

Joseph Smith's Testimony of Jesus Christ

After seeing Jesus Christ in vision in 1832, Joseph Smith bore this witness of the Savior:

"And now, after the many testimonies which have been given of him, this is the testimony, last of all, which we give of him: "That he lives!

"For we saw him, even on the right hand of God; and we heard the voice bearing record that he is the Only Begotten of the Father—

"That by him, and through him, and of him, the worlds are and were created, and the inhabitants thereof are begotten sons and daughters unto God" (Doctrine and Covenants 76:22–24).

As a Prophet, Did Joseph Smith Ever Prophesy?

Repeatedly in the scriptures, prophets such as Isaiah and Jeremiah would prophesy of things to come. As a latter-day prophet, Joseph Smith was no different. It is estimated that the Doctrine and Covenants (a book of Joseph Smith's revelations) **"contains nearly eleven hundred statements about the future."**[18] Here are just a few samples of some of Joseph Smith's prophecies:

- In 1832, on the very day that Joseph Smith first met Brigham Young, the Prophet prophesied that "'the time will come when brother Brigham Young will preside over this Church.'"[19]

  Through numerous events unforeseeable to Joseph Smith, Brigham Young indeed succeeded Joseph Smith as the second president of the LDS Church.

  Brigham Young

- To a young judge named Stephen A. Douglas, who showed sympathy for the Mormons, Joseph prophesied: "Judge, you will aspire to the presidency of the United States," but, he warned, "if ever you turn your hand against me or the Latter-day Saints, you will feel the weight of the hand of Almighty upon you; and you will live to see and know that I have testified the truth to you."[20]

  Stephen A. Douglas later became a front-runner for the United States presidency, "but in a political speech in 1857, he viciously attacked the [LDS] Church as 'a loathsome, disgusting ulcer in the body politic.'"[21] The rest, as they say, is history. Stephen A. Douglas lost to a relatively unknown candidate named Abraham Lincoln, and a few months after the election, Stephen A. Douglas died in the prime of life.

- Joseph prophesied of his own death: "I am going like a lamb to the slaughter, but I am calm as a summer's morning. I have a conscience void of offense toward God and toward all men. If they take my life I shall die an innocent man, and my blood shall cry from the ground for vengeance, and it shall be said of me 'He was murdered in cold blood!'"[22]

  Joseph Smith's life was taken mere hours after he made that statement.

- In his journal, Joseph recorded this prophecy of the Latter-day Saint exodus to the Rocky Mountains: "I prophesied that the Saints would continue to suffer much affliction and would be driven to the Rocky Mountains, many would apostatize, others would be put to death by our persecutors or lose their lives in consequence of exposure or disease, and some of you will live to go and assist in making settlements and build cities and see the Saints become a mighty people in the midst of the Rocky Mountains."[23]

  Anyone familiar with LDS history knows this prophecy's historical accuracy.

■ In the early days of the Church, when there were still only a few members, the Prophet Joseph Smith said to a group of men: "You know no more concerning the destinies of this Church and kingdom than a babe upon its mother's lap. You don't comprehend it. . . . It is only a little handfull of Priesthood you see here tonight, but this Church will fill North and South America—it will fill the world."[24]

Currently there are fourteen million members of the LDS Church, in 177 countries, nations, and territories around the world.[25]

What Was Joseph Smith's Personality Like?

Joseph Smith prophesied that the LDS Church would fill the world.

An English convert wrote that Joseph was "no saintish long-faced fellow, but quite the reverse."[26] Joseph described himself as having a "native cheery temperament" (Joseph Smith—History 1:28), which surprised some people when they met him, as they had expected somebody who was a prophet to be a bit more somber and serious. One day, two ministers visited Joseph, trying to outwit him in the scriptures. After Joseph had proven himself superior to them in scriptural matters, they walked to the door where Joseph drew a line in the dirt, stopped, and jumped over the line, and then said to them, "Now gentlemen, you haven't bested me at the scriptures. See if you can best me at that."[27]

Another time a Methodist preacher met Joseph and somewhat mockingly asked, "Is it possible that I now flash my optics upon a Prophet?"

"Yes," Joseph replied and then playfully asked, "Would not you like to wrestle with me?"[28]

In terms of his physicality, Joseph Smith was described by one firsthand account as being "tall and well built, strong and active"[29] and by another person as "in stature and proportion a very large man; and his figure would probably be called a fine one. . . . His chest and shoulders are broad and muscular."[30]

Joseph loved to play sports, wrestle, and pull sticks against other men. He was vibrant and active, and he had a magnetic quality and greatness about him that caused others to instantly recognize him in a crowd although they had never seen him before.

"Strangers journeying to [Joseph Smith] from a distance, knew him the moment their eyes beheld his person. Men have crossed ocean and continent to meet him, and have selected him instantly from among a multitude."—LDS Apostle George Q. Cannon (1827–1901)[31]

More importantly, Joseph Smith's character exhibited the Christlike qualities you would expect from a prophet. He was kind, forgiving, generous, selfless, and loving. He once said, "I have no desire but to do all men good. I feel to pray for all men."[32] His missionary journal, written in his own hand, reveals two main themes and thoughts: Help the kingdom of God to be established, and "Lord, bless my family."[33] He loved his wife, Emma, and their children with his whole soul. As noted Joseph Smith biographer Truman G. Madsen summarized: "In Joseph Smith we have a man who physically, intellectually, emotionally, and spiritually was a living human multitude. He was many men in one, as it were. Many of his gifts were balanced with others, and all in all he was a superb instrument with whom the Lord could and did work."[34]

Joseph Smith loved his wife, Emma, and their children with his whole soul.

Joseph Smith for President!

No, Mitt Romney wasn't the first Mormon to run for president—it was actually Joseph Smith in the 1844 United States presidential campaign. In November 1839, Joseph Smith traveled to Washington, DC, to meet with President Martin Van Buren and to seek federal redress for the

wrongs committed against the Latter-day Saints in Missouri. President Van Buren replied: "Gentlemen, your cause is just, but I can do nothing for you. . . . If I take up for you I shall lose the vote of Missouri."[35] When the Latter-day Saints saw that no new presidential candidates would come out in support of them, they took matters into their own hands and nominated Joseph Smith for president. Joseph's brief presidential campaign was cut short when he was murdered in June 1844.

No, Mitt Romney wasn't the first Mormon to run for president—it was actually Joseph Smith in 1844.

MORMYTH:
Mormons worship Joseph Smith.

Answer: False.

We love and admire and respect Joseph Smith as the great prophet of the Lord in the latter days, but we don't believe our salvation comes through Joseph Smith, nor do we pray to Joseph Smith or perform ordinances in his name. We worship God the Father in the name of Jesus Christ, and we firmly believe what the Book of Mormon teaches: "There shall be no other name given nor any other way nor means whereby salvation can come unto the children of men, only in and through the name of Christ, the Lord Omnipotent" (Mosiah 3:17).

However, because of Joseph Smith's prophetic role in reestablishing Christ's Church, we humbly claim that he "has done more, save Jesus only, for the salvation of men in this world, than any other man that ever lived in it" (Doctrine and Covenants 135:3). Latter-day Saints sing a popular hymn called "Praise to the Man," set to the tune of a Scottish folk song:

> *Praise to the man who communed*
> *with Jehovah!*
> *Jesus anointed that Prophet and Seer.*
> *Blessed to open the last dispensation,*
> *Kings shall extol him, and nations*
> *revere.*[36]

Respect and honor? Yes. Worship? No.

Teachings from the Prophet Joseph Smith

Here are a few classic teachings from some of Joseph Smith's sermons and writings:

- "Love is one of the chief characteristics of Deity, and ought to be manifested by those who aspire to be the sons of God. A man filled with the love of God, is not content with blessing his family alone, but ranges through the whole world, anxious to bless the whole human race."[37]

- "Happiness is the object and design of our existence; and will be the end thereof, if we pursue the path that leads to it; and this path is virtue, uprightness, faithfulness, holiness, and keeping all the commandments of God."[38]

- "If you wish to go where God is, you must be like God, or possess the principles which God possesses. . . . Is not God good? Then you be good; if He is faithful, then you be faithful."[39]

- "We came to this earth that we might have a body and present it pure before God in the celestial kingdom. The great principle of happiness consists in having a body."[40]

- "The spirits of the just [who die] are exalted to a greater and more glorious work; hence they are blessed in their departure to the world of spirits. Enveloped in flaming fire, they are not far from us, and know and understand our thoughts, feelings, and motions."[41]

- "I want to reason more on the spirit of man. . . . I take my ring from my finger and liken it unto the mind of man—the immortal part, because it has no beginning. Suppose you cut it in two; then it has a beginning and an end; but join it again, and it continues one eternal round. So with the spirit of man."[42]

- "I made this my rule: when the Lord commands, do it."[43]

Praise from Outsiders

On September 4, 1843, a *New York Times* columnist wrote:

"**This Joe Smith must be set down as an extraordinary character, a prophet-hero**. . . . He is one of the great men of this age, and in future history will rank with those who, in one way or another, have stamped their impress strongly on society.

"'It is no small thing, in the blaze of the nineteenth century, to give to men a new revelation, found a new religion, establish new forms of worship, to build a city with new laws, institutions, and orders of architecture, to establish ecclesiastical, civil and military jurisdiction, found colleges, send out missionaries, and make proselytes on two hemispheres. Yet all this has been done by Joe Smith, and that against every sort of opposition, ridicule, and persecution.'

"In the short space of fifteen years, Joseph Smith, unschooled in the learning and the methods of the world, did all these important things. How was it possible? **Does not the only rational explanation lie in the claim that he was God-taught[?]** . . .

"Yes, Joseph Smith was able to confound the wise, to astonish the learned, and to outmarvel the great."[44]

Former Methodist minister and author George Wharton James said:

"'Let anyone, even a literary genius, after forty years of life, try to write a companion volume to the Book of Mormon, and then almost daily for a number of years give out "revelations" that internally harmonize one with another, at the same time formulate a system of doctrine for a Church, introduce many new principles, resuscitate extinct priesthoods, and formulate a system of Church government which has no superior upon earth . . . to deny such a man a wonderful power over the human heart and intellect is absurd. Only fanatical prejudice can ignore it. However, he may be accounted for by the reasoning mind, **Joseph Smith, the Mormon Prophet, was one of the wonders of his time.**'"[45]

Yale professor Harold Bloom said:

"**[Joseph] Smith was an authentic religious genius, unique in our national history.** . . .

" . . . I also do not find it possible to doubt that Joseph Smith was an authentic prophet. Where in all of American history can we find his match? . . .

" . . . If there is already in place any authentic version of the American Religion then . . . it must be Mormonism, whose future as yet may prove decisive for the nation, and for more than this nation alone."[46]

13 | The Book of Mormon

Joseph Smith not only announced that God had spoken to him and called him as a modern-day prophet, but he also offered the world tangible evidence of that calling. The evidence is in a book that has baffled, enlightened, angered, and inspired countless millions of people since it first appeared on the world's stage in 1830 under the title *The Book of Mormon*.

When a person first encounters the Book of Mormon, it is difficult to overlook or ignore the challenge it presents to account for its existence and content. After all, *somebody* wrote, "I, Nephi, having been born of goodly parents" (1 Nephi 1:1) and the subsequent 530 pages. The question is, who?

Some people claim that Joseph Smith simply made it up out of whole cloth. As Latter-day Saints, we claim that Joseph Smith translated it from gold plates.

Others claim Joseph Smith produced it in a flurry of literary inspiration.[1] Mormons believe Joseph Smith produced it in a flood of heavenly revelation.

Some suggest that Joseph Smith or his companions borrowed the words from others. We suggest that Joseph did, in fact, use someone else's words—the words of ancient American prophets named Nephi, Alma, and Moroni, among others.

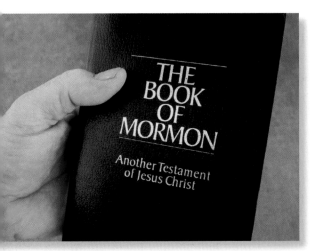

Some claim that Joseph Smith produced the book for profit. We claim that Joseph Smith produced it because he was a prophet.

Some people claim the book is a "Satanic wonder."[2] We claim it is "a marvellous work and a wonder" (Isaiah 29:14).

Here is a little more about the Book of Mormon and why Latter-day Saints consider it divine.

It is difficult to overlook or ignore the challenge the Book of Mormon presents to account for its existence and content.

What Is the Book of Mormon?

Similar to how the Bible is a record of God's dealings with some of His people in the areas surrounding the land of Israel, the Book of Mormon is a record of God's dealings with some of His people on the American continent. The main history of the Book of Mormon spans more than a thousand years, from roughly 600 B.C. to A.D. 400. During this time, various prophets in the Book of Mormon recorded their history, teachings, prophecies, and revelations. **A prophet named Mormon abridged these accounts onto gold metal plates and named the book the Book of Mormon.**

We believe the Book of Mormon is holy scripture and that it contains the fullness of Christ's everlasting gospel (see Doctrine and Covenants 20:9) as it was delivered to His people in the Americas. One of the book's primary purposes is to add a second witness, together with the Bible, that "Jesus is the Christ, the Eternal God, manifesting himself unto all nations" (Book of Mormon title page). The crowning moment of the Book of Mormon is Jesus Christ's appearance—shortly after His resurrection—to minister to and teach His people in the Americas.

Exactly Where Did the Book of Mormon Take Place?

The events described in the Book of Mormon took place *somewhere* in the Americas, but the exact locations are unknown. Theories have varied all over the map (literally and figuratively), and any declaration of actual geographic locations of the Book of Mormon history are only intelligent suppositions. The LDS Church has no official position on Book of Mormon locations.

Today, scholars support the notion that the Book of Mormon primarily deals with a clan of people living in the Americas rather than a coast-to-coast, hemispheric civilization. A leading researcher on Book of Mormon geography concludes that the events in the Book of Mormon probably took place in an area around five hundred miles long and two hundred miles wide.[3]

Why Do We Need the Book of Mormon If We Already Have the Bible?

The Book of Mormon has three main roles:

1. It serves as a second, independent witness to the Bible, a witness that Jesus—in all reality—is the Son of God and the Redeemer of the world. Jesus Himself declared "that in the mouth of two or three witnesses every word may be established" (Matthew 18:16).

2. It both confirms and clarifies many teachings in the Bible. People have been wrangling for centuries over the meaning of Biblical passages. Having two sources to establish the truth is helpful in resolving unclear doctrines.

3. It provides additional truths to questions that are not overtly discussed or clearly presented in the Bible. Here's just a smattering of topics the Book of Mormon covers in depth:

- Christ is the central feature of worship since the days of Adam (see 2 Nephi 11; Mosiah 15).

- Why there is a need for opposition (i.e., good and evil), and our ability to choose between them (see 2 Nephi 2).

- The infinite nature of Christ's atonement and His suffering (see 2 Nephi 9; Alma 7).

- The relationship between God's justice and mercy (see Alma 42).

- The nature and timing of the resurrection (see Alma 40).

- How to administer the Lord's supper (see Moroni 4–5).

MORMYTH:
Mormons replaced the Bible with the Book of Mormon

Answer: False.

Mormons love the Bible. We study the Bible. We believe in the Bible. As a matter of fact, we study the Old Testament for an entire year in our Sunday Schools. (What's that? The *Old* Testament? Yes!) And we study the New Testament for another entire year. That means that Mormon youth study the Bible for two of the four years they participate in their weekday LDS seminary study.

Latter-day Saints' study of the Bible shows. Findings from a 2010 Pew Study on US Religious Knowledge reported that **Mormons knew more about the Bible than any other religious group surveyed,** including Protestants, Evangelicals, and Catholics.[4] One of our Articles of Faith even states: "We believe the Bible to be the word of God as far as it is translated correctly"[5] (Articles of Faith 1:8).

The Book of Mormon does not replace the Bible, but it serves side-by-side in support of the Bible (see Mormon 7:9) and enhances our study of it. As evidence, the LDS Church publishes the King James Version of the Bible *together* with the Book of Mormon as a single bound book and has devised an amazing cross-referencing system to help people study their divine messages together. (See chapter 9 for more information on LDS scriptures.)

The Keystone of Our Religion: The Book of Mormon

Joseph Smith once said that the Book of Mormon is the "keystone of our religion,"[6] meaning that the LDS faith rests its teachings and beliefs on the truthfulness of the Book of Mormon. If the Book of Mormon is true, then, by association,

- Jesus is the Christ.

- Joseph Smith is a prophet.

- The Church of Jesus Christ of Latter-day Saints is the Lord's authorized, reestablished Church.

To us, the Book of Mormon confirms "that God does inspire men and call them to his holy work in this age and generation, as well as in generations of old" (Doctrine and Covenants 20:11). That is why, on another occasion, Joseph Smith said, "Take away the Book of Mormon and the revelations, and where is our religion? We have none."[7]

▲

The Book of Mormon is the keystone of our religion, meaning that the LDS faith rests its teachings and beliefs on the truthfulness of the Book of Mormon.

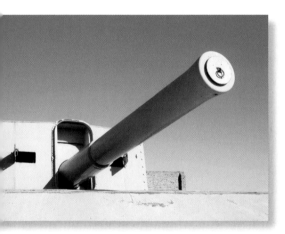

When people say that the canon is closed, they aren't talking artillery. They're talking scripture. Mormons believe God is still speaking to His prophets.

A Closed Canon?

When people say that the canon is closed, they aren't talking artillery. They're talking scripture. Mormons believe, however, that there are many unknown words God has spoken to His prophets; many of those sacred writings are even mentioned in the Bible, but have since been lost or excluded.

Wouldn't we be excited if archeologists discovered Moses' "book of the covenant" (Exodus 24:7) or the "book of Nathan the prophet" (2 Chronicles 9:29)? What if we found the writings of someone who recorded the "many other things which Jesus did" (John 21:25) mentioned by John? Wouldn't we be excited to have *more* of the word of God? Latter-day Saints believe that God's words "never cease" (Moses 1:4) and that it is a blessing, not a problem, to have additional scripture to help us learn eternal truths.

How Did Joseph Smith Get the Book of Mormon and Translate It?

When the ancient American prophet Mormon finished compiling the Book of Mormon record in about A.D. 400, he gave it to his son, Moroni, who concealed it just prior to his death.

In 1823, Moroni appeared as a resurrected angel to seventeen-year-old Joseph Smith and showed him where the golden plates (on which the Book of Mormon record was written) were hidden, buried in a stone box in a hillside near Joseph's home in upstate New York. (See chapter 12 for more about the life of Joseph Smith.)

As Latter-day Saints, we aren't alone in our belief of heavenly messengers like the angel Moroni. A 2007 Gallup poll indicated that **75 percent of Americans believe in angels**.[8]

Although practically laughable to most Americans in the 1800s when the Book of Mormon was published, the idea of records inscribed on metal plates seems not so absurd to people today. Not only does preserving a record by inscribing it on metal plates make practical sense, but since Joseph Smith told the world about the golden plates, there have been repeated discoveries of other ancient writings on metal plates found buried in stone boxes. Perhaps the best examples are the gold and silver plates of Darius II discovered in 1961 in Persia. Those plates date to the fourth century B.C.; the Book of Mormon begins in the sixth century B.C. Latter-day Saint scholar Hugh Nibley reported more than one hundred instances of discovered ancient records preserved on metal plates.[9]

Eventually, the angel Moroni allowed Joseph to take the golden plates home to translate them into English. However, Joseph Smith was completely unschooled and unlearned. Joseph's newlywed wife, Emma, said that "Joseph Smith could neither write nor dictate a coherent and well worded letter"[10] at the time he produced the Book of Mormon. So how did he take a record written in "reformed Egyptian" (Mormon 9:32) and translate it into English? According to Joseph Smith, God provided him with some interpreters, or "two stones in silver bows" called the "Urim and Thummim . . . for the purpose of translating the book" (Joseph Smith—History 1:35).

Metal tablet, Ankara, Turkey

The Urim and Thummim

With the Urim and Thummin, Joseph Smith was able to translate the lines of text inscribed on the plates. Some people, especially in Joseph Smith's day, might think that unbelievable. But recently, inventors have produced similar electronic devices that scan text and translate it. If mankind can create a device that translates text from one language to another, perhaps it's not too difficult to believe that God provided Joseph Smith with a tool that could do the same.

The Urim and Thummim are mentioned repeatedly in the Old Testament in connection with the office of the priest (see Exodus 28:30; Leviticus 8:8; Ezra 2:63), and also in relationship to revelation (see 1 Samuel 28:6). Many people connected with Joseph Smith handled or saw the Urim and Thummim. Oliver Cowdery and Martin Harris both acknowledged that they saw and held the interpreters. Joseph's mother, Lucy Mack Smith, and his brother William both testified that they handled the Urim and Thummim and "'found that it consisted of two smooth three-cornered diamonds set in glass, and the glasses were set in silver bows connected with each other in much the same way that old-fashioned spectacles are made.'"[11]

For a time, Joseph's wife, Emma, was his scribe while he translated. She said: "When [I was] acting as his scribe, [Joseph] would dictate to me hour after hour; and when returning after meals, or after interruptions, he would at once begin where he had left off, without either seeing the manuscript or having any portion of it read to him."[12]

Oliver Cowdery transcribed most of the Book of Mormon as Joseph Smith translated it. He said, "Day after day I continued, uninterrupted, to write from his mouth, as he translated with the Urim and Thummim . . . 'The Book of Mormon.'"[13]

The manuscript pages of the Book of Mormon show a steady stream of dictation—no revisions, no scribbles in the margin, no paragraphs crossed out.

The manuscript pages of the Book of Mormon show a steady stream of dictation—no revisions, no scribbles in the margin, no paragraphs crossed out. And—horror of horrors to English teachers and editors far and wide!—not even a single mark of punctuation. It is estimated that Joseph Smith translated about eight pages of the Book of Mormon per day,[14] and that it took him only about sixty-five working days[15] to produce the entire 531 pages of the Book of Mormon.

Admittedly, accounts of buried golden plates, seer stones, and resurrected angels might be difficult for some people to swallow. But it's equally difficult to ignore the fact that an **unlearned twenty-one-year-old farm boy—with no schooling or research libraries available—produced a 500-page book of literary complexity, internal self-consistency, Middle Eastern linguistics, and spiritual profundity in one draft within a few months' time.**

The Most Correct Book?

When Joseph Smith said that the Book of Mormon was the "most correct book,"[16] he wasn't talking about syntax or grammar. That statement refers to the idea that the Book of Mormon has a purity of *truth* in it, not that it was error-free in sentence structure. Punctuation was added to the translated manuscript by the original printer, and since then, hundreds of grammatical errors have been caught and changed for subsequent printings of the Book of Mormon.[17] When compared to the translated manuscript and previous printings, some words were discovered to have been written in error and other words have been changed for clarification. The prophet Mormon even anticipated a few minor errors, reminding today's reader, "And now, if there are faults they are the mistakes of men; wherefore, condemn not the things of God" (Book of Mormon title page).

To quote modern-day LDS Apostle Jeffrey R. Holland (1940–), "If Joseph Smith—or anyone else, for that matter—created the Book of Mormon out of whole cloth, that, to me, is a *far* greater miracle than the proposition that he translated it from an ancient record by an endowment of divine power."[18]

Did Anyone Else See the Golden Plates?

Although Joseph Smith was under direct instructions from God to keep the golden plates concealed from others, he was told that eleven others would be authorized to see the plates and testify of the reality of the Book of Mormon record. Three of Joseph's friends who helped in the translation process were visited by the angel Moroni and shown the plates. They testified "with words of soberness, that an angel of God came down from heaven, and he brought and laid before our eyes, that we beheld and saw the plates, and the engravings thereon" (Book of Mormon, the Testimony of Three Witnesses). They testified that they heard God's voice speak that the translation was true.

Shortly thereafter, a group of eight men was selected to also be witnesses of the golden plates. These men didn't see an angel, and they didn't hear a voice from heaven. Joseph Smith simply showed them the ancient record. Members of the group picked up the plates, handled them, looked them over, and examined them. Their sworn testimony was that they "bear record with words

Chiasmus

One example of Hebrew linguistic evidence in the Book of Mormon is called chiasmus, which is a reverse pyramid form of structuring.

idea A
  idea B
    idea C
    idea C
  idea B
idea A

Chiastic structures are found repeatedly in the Book of Mormon. A wonderful and unusually extended chiastic structure is found in the entire chapter of Alma 36, with eighteen ideas presented, then repeated in eighteen mirror images, with the focal point being the atonement of Jesus Christ.

of soberness, that the said Smith has shown unto us, for we have seen and hefted, and know of a surety that the said Smith has got the plates of which we have spoken. And we give our names unto the world, to witness unto the world that which we have seen. And we lie not, God bearing witness of it" (Book of Mormon, the Testimony of Eight Witnesses).

But, some might say, these witnesses were all Joseph's friends . . . they were just in on the hoax, right?

Wrong. Most of these eleven men quit the LDS Church and severed their association with Joseph Smith at one point or another. Yet none of them ever denied what they witnessed nor recanted their testimonies. David Whitmer, one of the witnesses, made this statement at the end of his life as a non-practicing Mormon:

"'That the world may know the truth, I wish now, standing as it were, in the very sunset of life, and in the fear of God, once for all to make this public statement:

"'That I have never at any time, denied that testimony or any part thereof, which has so long since been published with that book, as one of the three witnesses.

"'Those who know me best, will know that I have always adhered to that testimony— And that no man may be misled or doubt my present views in regard to the same, I do now again affirm the truth of all my statements as then made and published.

"'He that hath an ear to hear, let him hear: It was no delusion.'"[19]

Oliver Cowdery, an excommunicated member of the LDS Church, nevertheless testified in a court proceeding:

"'"May it please your honor and gentlemen of the jury, this I say, I saw the angel and heard his voice—how can I deny it? It happened in the daytime when the sun was shining bright in the firmament; not in the night when I was asleep. That glorious messenger from heaven, dressed in white, standing above the ground . . . told us if we denied that testimony there is no forgiveness in this life nor in the world to come. Now, how can I deny it—I dare not; I will not!'"'[20]

There were others who also handled the golden plates, aside from the eleven witnesses whose testimonies are published in the Book of Mormon preface. Josiah Stowell, Lucy Mack Smith, Willam Smith, Katharine Smith, and Emma Smith all described having "'hefted and handled'" the golden plates at various times while they lay covered by a cloth.[21]

Joseph Smith's wife, Emma, said: "The plates often lay on the table without any attempt at concealment, wrapped in a small linen table cloth, which I had given him to fold them in. I felt of the plates, as they lay on the table, tracing their outline and shape. They seemed to be pliable like thick paper, and would rustle with a metalic sound when the edges were moved by the thumb, as one does sometimes thumb the edges of a book."[22]

As one Book of Mormon scholar has written, these testimonies, at a minimum, support the truth that "what emerges as alone indisputable is the fact that Joseph Smith does possess a set of metal plates."[23]

Wordprints

All of us have not only our own unique fingerprints, but also unique "wordprints"—how we write and string words and thoughts together. Wordprint statistical analysis is often used to determine authorship of documents. After subjecting portions of the Book of Mormon to wordprint analysis against Joseph Smith's personal writings, a Berkeley group concluded "that it is statistically indefensible to propose Joseph Smith . . . as the author. . . . The Book of Mormon measures multiauthored."[24] Another wordprint analysis found at least twenty-four unique authors in the Book of Mormon, concluding that the evidence is "overwhelming" that the book was not written by Joseph Smith or his contemporaries.[25]

All of us have our own unique "wordprints"— how we write and string words and thoughts together.

Wordprint analysis has shown that the Book of Mormon was not written by Joseph Smith or his contemporaries, but is actually multiauthored.

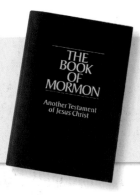

How Can I Get a Free Copy of the Book of Mormon?

If you would like a copy of the Book of Mormon to study for yourself, you can request one be sent to you at http://mormon.org/book-of-mormon/.

The complete Book of Mormon has been translated into 107 languages.

By the Numbers . . .

- 150 million copies of the Book of Mormon have been printed since 1830.
- Currently, 1 copy of the Book of Mormon is printed every 7 seconds.
- About 5 million copies of the Book of Mormon are distributed each year, or almost 14,000 copies per day.[26]
- The complete Book of Mormon has been translated into 107 languages.

Another Testament of Jesus Christ

Perhaps the greatest reason why Latter-day Saints love the Book of Mormon is that it testifies of the divinity of Jesus Christ. In fact, **the Book of Mormon testifies of Jesus Christ more than any other book.** The Book of Mormon mentions some form of Jesus' name **every 1.7 verses** (compared to 2.1 verses in the New Testament).[27] Jesus is referred to by **101 different titles** in the Book of Mormon. In the last thirteen pages alone, there are 215 references to Jesus.[28]

The pinnacle of the Book of Mormon is Jesus' ministry to His people on the American continent, shortly after His resurrection (see 3 Nephi 11–27). The closing message of the Book of Mormon is for all people to "come unto Christ, and be perfected in him" (Moroni 10:32). Truly it is "Another Testament of Jesus Christ" as its subtitle proclaims.

Great One-Liners from the Book of Mormon

The following are some memorable truths found in the Book of Mormon:

"FOR IT MUST NEEDS BE, THAT THERE IS AN OPPOSITION IN ALL THINGS" (2 NEPHI 2:11).

"MEN ARE, THAT THEY MIGHT HAVE JOY" (2 NEPHI 2:25).

"BY SMALL AND SIMPLE THINGS ARE GREAT THINGS BROUGHT TO PASS" (ALMA 37:6).

"WHEN YE ARE IN THE SERVICE OF YOUR FELLOW BEINGS YE ARE ONLY IN THE SERVICE OF YOUR GOD" (MOSIAH 2:17).

"IN THE STRENGTH OF THE LORD THOU CANST DO ALL THINGS" (ALMA 20:4).

"COME UNTO CHRIST, AND BE PERFECTED IN HIM" (MORONI 10:32).

"YE RECEIVE NO WITNESS UNTIL AFTER THE TRIAL OF YOUR FAITH" (ETHER 12:6).

"WICKEDNESS NEVER WAS HAPPINESS" (ALMA 41:10).

Chloroform in Print?

Mark Twain considered the Book of Mormon writing to be "chloroform in print." Well, many who have repeatedly studied the book would respectfully disagree with you, Mr. Samuel Langhorne Clemens. While there may be too many "Behold"s, "Wherefore"s, or "And it came to pass"es for some literary experts, the Book of Mormon is full of excellent writing, with extended metaphors and allegories, parallelisms and poetry, all organized into a deliberate, careful, and cohesively logical, integrated work. Some people have even argued that the Book of Mormon should be studied for its great literary qualities and structure, regardless of whether you believe in its divinity.[30]

Mark Twain considered the Book of Mormon writing to be "chloroform in print."

Here are a few examples of literary excellence found in the Book of Mormon.

- For an awesome allegory, read Jacob 5.

- For some great parallelisms, read 2 Nephi 9:52 and 1 Nephi 17:45.

- For a great logical syllogism, read 2 Nephi 2:13.

- For an amazing Hebrew chiasmus, read Alma 36.

- For a psalm that rivals one of David's, read 2 Nephi 4:15–35.

- For an extended metaphor, read Alma 32.

- For a symbolic dream, read 1 Nephi 8.

Can You Prove the Book of Mormon Is True?

Trying to use a scientific study to confirm or deny the truthfulness of the Book of Mormon is like using a heart-rate monitor to measure if you're in love.

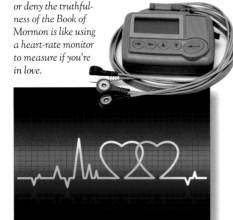

There are those who love to spout facts, studies, and evidence that supposedly prove the Book of Mormon is or isn't true. However, trying to use a scientific study to confirm or deny the truthfulness of the Book of Mormon is like using a heart-rate monitor to measure if you're in love: It's the wrong tool for the job. The chief evidence for the truthfulness of the Book of Mormon will not come from a scientific study, but from a personal study that includes reading its religious messages, feeling of its divine power, learning of its truths, living its teachings, and experiencing its spiritual fruits in your life.

The last prophet to write in the Book of Mormon, Moroni, closed the book with this promise to its future readers: "When ye shall receive these things [the Book of Mormon], I would exhort you that ye would ask God, the Eternal Father, in the name of Christ, if these things are not true; and if ye shall ask **with a sincere heart,** with **real intent, having faith in Christ,** he will manifest the truth of it unto you, by the **power of the Holy Ghost.** And by the power of the Holy Ghost ye may know the truth of all things" (Moroni 10:4–5).

Millions of Latter-day Saints the world over have put these words to the test, and we have found that they are true. We would invite all who want personal proof to sincerely read the Book of Mormon and to do the same.

In 2003, the Book of Mormon was ranked as one of the "20 Books That Changed America" by *Book* magazine.[31]

MEET a Mormon

Scan this QR code to meet **Chris** and read how his study of the Book of Mormon led him to join The Church of Jesus Christ of Latter-day Saints.

14 | Latter-day Prophets

On a summer evening in July 1838, the famous writer Ralph Waldo Emerson addressed the senior class of Harvard's Divinity School, speaking to the "causes of a decaying church and a wasting unbelief." Emerson said that "the assumption that the age of inspiration is past, that the Bible is closed . . . indicate[s] with sufficient clearness the falsehood of our theology. **It is the office of a true teacher to show us that God is, not was; that He speaketh, not spake."** [1]

God speaks to man through His authorized prophets on earth.

Little did Emerson know that a few states over in Missouri, a thirty-two-year-old frontier prophet named Joseph Smith was declaring that very doctrine: that God is still speaking to man, that the heavens aren't closed, that the scriptural canon is open, and that once again there were authorized prophets on the earth.

Latter-day Saints believe that not only did God speak to and call Joseph Smith to be a prophet, but we also believe that **God continues to speak to prophets today,** revealing His will and word to them just as He did to Abraham, Moses, and Isaiah. That's right: Mormons believe there is a modern-day prophet who acts and speaks as God's mouthpiece just as Moses did.

Mormons believe there is a modern-day prophet who acts and speaks as God's mouthpiece just as Moses did.

In this age of progress—when humankind is gaining seemingly exponential knowledge, and advancements are being made in almost every field of study—Latter-day Saints believe that God's final word wasn't spoken 2,000 years ago. We believe that God has more knowledge to give to the human family on the subject of salvation. In the words of Joseph Smith, Mormons "believe all that God has revealed, all that He does now reveal, and we believe that He will yet reveal many great and important things pertaining to the Kingdom of God" (Articles of Faith 1:9). Those revelations from God come to His authorized servants—the prophets.

God Calls Prophets

If there is one oft-repeated pattern in the Bible (other than some people being really, really good and other people being really, really bad), it is that God calls prophets to be His witnesses and mouthpieces. From the beginning, God has spoken to His chosen servants—prophets such as Adam, Enoch, Noah, Abraham, Isaac, Jacob (Israel), Moses, Isaiah, Jeremiah, Daniel, Peter, and Paul—and authorized them to make known to the people God's will and to act as His representatives.

Mormons believe that this same pattern of calling an authorized servant to lead God's people has existed in all ages and among all people to whom God's ordinances of salvation have been offered. This prophetic pattern was also followed in the Book of Mormon, where some of the Lord's people in ancient America were led by prophets named Lehi, Nephi, Alma, Mormon, and Moroni, among others. **And as God is "the same yesterday, and to day, and for ever"** (Hebrews 13:8; see also 1 Nephi 10:18), **we believe that**

Mormons don't think God is currently napping, but is actively working to bring about the salvation of His children.

God's pattern of calling prophets continues today. The prophet Amos said, "Surely the Lord God will do nothing, but he revealeth his secret unto his servants the prophets" (Amos 3:7). Mormons don't think God is currently napping, but is actively working to bring about the salvation of His children.

Therefore, **we believe that God calls living prophets today who receive divine revelation and communications from God to lead His people.** We believe that in these latter days God called a prophet named Joseph Smith to reestablish His authorized Church (see chapter 2 and chapter 12), and, just as the prophetic authority was passed from Moses to Joshua or from Elijah to Elisha, the prophetic mantle given to Joseph Smith has been passed on in an unbroken line to subsequent LDS prophets today.

We believe that just as the prophetic authority was passed from Elijah to Elisha, the prophetic mantle given to Joseph Smith has been passed on to subsequent LDS prophets today.

Who Are the LDS Prophets?

As of this book's printing, Thomas S. Monson is the prophet and President of The Church of Jesus Christ of Latter-day Saints. However, his two counselors in the First Presidency as well as the members of the Quorum of the Twelve Apostles are also considered to be prophets by faithful LDS Church members. Therefore, although the LDS Church President is called

At any given time, there are actually fifteen prophets for Latter-day Saints: three in the First Presidency and twelve in the Quorum of the Twelve Apostles.

"*the* prophet"—because we believe he is the authorized spokesperson for God—that simply denotes that he is the chief prophet of the prophets—the highest authority in the LDS Church (see Doctrine and Covenants 107:22). **At any given time, there are actually fifteen prophets for Latter-day Saints: three in the First Presidency and twelve in the Quorum of the Twelve Apostles.**

Like the Old and New Testament prophets and apostles, the modern prophets are common men with regular vocational backgrounds. However, like Peter and Andrew, when they were called by Jesus, "they straightway left their [occupational] nets" (Matthew 4:20) to dedicate the remainder of their lives in service to God and man. Although many modern prophets have advanced degrees and financial means, there is nothing in their background—not wealth, scholarly degrees, worldly positions, or physical stature—that prequalify them for their position. They are common men who experience the same life challenges and face unexpected difficulties like all of us do, but they hold an uncommon office and calling to bear witness of the Savior and His restored gospel to the entire world.

Before being called to the full-time apostleship, current LDS Apostle Russell M. Nelson was a world-renowned heart surgeon, Elder Dallin H. Oaks was a Utah Supreme Court justice, Elder Richard G. Scott was a nuclear engineer, President Henry B. Eyring and Elder David A. Bednar were university professors, and Elder Quentin L. Cook and Elder D. Todd Christofferson were lawyers. Modern LDS prophets and apostles dedicate their entire lives to the Lord, leaving their professional occupations behind upon receiving their apostolic call and serving God until their death.

Why Do LDS Prophets Wear Business Suits and Not Prophetic Robes?

When some people think of how prophets dress, they often picture long beards, flowing robes, and maybe even a walking staff for good measure (thanks, Charlton Heston). Thus, some may be surprised to see modern LDS prophets dressing in regular business suits and not in some sort of special clerical, priestly, or prophetic robes. **In Mormonism, we believe that "the preacher [is] no better than the hearer, neither [is] the teacher any better than the learner; and thus [we are] all equal"** (Alma 1:26) **in the eyes of God.** Mormons don't have any particular clothing or dress within the Church that sets one person apart from another based upon their respective call to serve the Lord, even if that call is to be a prophet. Thus, LDS prophets and apostles wear regular professional attire during the week and appropriate Sunday dress—usually business suits and ties for men—for Church meetings and functions.

Mormons don't have any particular clothing or dress within the Church that sets one person apart from another based upon their respective call to serve the Lord, even if that call is to be a prophet.

When some people think of how prophets dress, they often picture long beards, flowing robes, and maybe even a walking staff for good measure.

What Do Modern Prophets and Apostles Do?

Well, they do *not* do this. ⟶

The primary job of modern prophets and apostles is to be "special witnesses of the name of Christ in all the world" (Doctrine and Covenants 107:23). Modern prophets oversee and "build up the church, and regulate all the affairs of the same in all nations" (Doctrine and Covenants 107:33). The LDS guidebook *True to the Faith* says: "Like the prophets of old, prophets today testify of Jesus Christ and teach His gospel. They make known God's will and true character. They speak boldly and clearly, denouncing sin and warning of its consequences. At times, they may be inspired to prophesy of future events for our benefit."[2]

Modern prophets and apostles do NOT do this.

As a unified body, the First Presidency and Quorum of the Twelve Apostles obtain the Lord's will through divine revelation and, by inspiration, make decisions regarding LDS Church policy and doctrine (see Doctrine and Covenants 107:27). The modern prophets speak to the worldwide Church twice a year during the LDS Church's general conference and also through published articles in the LDS Church's magazines (such as the *Ensign*) and other media. Although their prophetic responsibilities are broad and global, in the words of current LDS Apostle Elder David A. Bednar, "the ministry of an Apostle is to find the one . . . [and] to bless individuals and families."[3]

How Do Prophets Receive Revelation?

Modern LDS prophets receive revelation the same way that ancient prophets received it: through divine manifestations of the Holy Ghost. Sometimes prophets (both ancient and modern) have and report visions; sometimes they have inspired dreams; sometimes they audibly hear the Lord's voice; sometimes they are visited and ministered to by angels, and sometimes even by the Lord Jesus Christ Himself.

However, although these types of revelation from God are real and have been experienced by modern LDS prophets, they are not common or daily occurrences. **Most forms of revelation come to individuals "line upon line"** (Isaiah 28:10; 2 Nephi 28:30) **through divine feelings and impressions to the mind and the heart by the power of the Holy Ghost, and most revelation comes to prophets the same way.**[4]

When former LDS Church President Gordon B. Hinckley (1910–2008) was asked by 60

Minutes interviewer Mike Wallace: "'The Mormons, Mr. President, call you a "living Moses," a prophet who literally communicates with Jesus. How do you do that?'" President Hinckley responded, "'I think the best way I could describe the process is to liken it to the experience of Elijah as set forth in the book of First Kings [see 1 Kings 19:11–12]. Elijah spoke to the Lord, and there was a wind, a great wind, and the Lord was not in the wind. And there was an earthquake, and the Lord was not in the earthquake. And there was a fire, and the Lord was not in the fire. And after the fire a still, small voice, which I describe as the whisperings of the Spirit. Now . . . one must have and seek and cultivate that Spirit, and there comes understanding and it is real. I can give testimony of that.'"[5]

Who Are the Past LDS Prophets?

Joseph Smith was the founding prophet of The Church of Jesus Christ of Latter-day Saints.

Since the death of Joseph Smith in 1844, an unbroken line of prophets has led the LDS Church. To date, there have been sixteen men called to lead as its president and prophet. Here is a brief summary[6] of each of their tenures and major contributions as Presidents of The Church of Jesus Christ of Latter-day Saints:

Joseph Smith (1830–1844): The founding prophet of The Church of Jesus Christ of Latter-day Saints. He is considered by Mormons as the great prophet and head of Jesus' latter-day work before the return of Christ at His Second Coming. (See chapter 12 for more about Joseph Smith.)

Brigham Young (1844–1877): As President of the Quorum of the Twelve Apostles, Brigham Young assumed leadership of the LDS Church after Joseph Smith's martyrdom. Sometimes known as the "Modern Moses," Brigham Young led the LDS Church in their epic exodus west across the American wilderness to the Salt Lake Valley. The longest tenured LDS Church President, he oversaw the building of the Salt Lake Temple, served as Utah's first territorial governor, and pioneered the establishment of more than five hundred settlements in the American West. A statue memorializing his greatness and contributions to America sits in the United States Capitol rotunda. The LDS Church's Brigham Young University is named in his honor.

Brigham Young led the LDS Church in their epic exodus west across the American wilderness to the Salt Lake Valley.

John Taylor is the LDS Church's only non-American President to date. He was born in England and immigrated to America from Canada.

John Taylor (1877–1887): The LDS Church's only non-American President to date—he was born in England and immigrated to America from Canada—John Taylor was in the room with Joseph Smith when Joseph was killed; he himself was severely wounded, being shot four times. John Taylor led the LDS Church during the tumultuous years of the American anti-polygamy campaign.

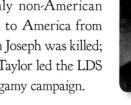

Wilford Woodruff (1887–1898): He received the revelation for Latter-day Saints to end plural marriage and oversaw the completion of the LDS Church's most historic landmark—the Salt Lake Temple. Wilford Woodruff was a prolific journal writer, and many of the teachings of early LDS Church leaders and accounts of other historic events have been preserved because of his detailed and daily efforts in chronicling the history of the LDS Church as it occurred.

Wilford Woodruff received the revelation for Latter-day Saints to end plural marriage.

Lorenzo Snow (1898–1901): Although brief, Lorenzo Snow's presidency was pivotal, as he assumed leadership of the Church when it was in dire financial circumstances. He was instrumental in reestablishing tithing (a voluntary payment of 10 percent of a person's income to the Church) as a divine commandment to be followed by faithful Latter-day Saints. The Saints' obedience to the commandment of tithing has provided the LDS Church with the financial means to grow and prosper as a worldwide faith.

Lorenzo Snow was instrumental in reestablishing tithing as a divine commandment to be followed by faithful Latter-day Saints.

Joseph F. Smith (1901–1918): A nephew of Joseph Smith, Joseph F. Smith was influential in starting some foundational LDS programs, such as adopting the Boy Scouts as an official program for American LDS young men and approving the LDS seminary system of religious instruction for high-school aged youth. He also called upon LDS members to hold family home evening one night per week (see chapter 7 for more about Mormons and families). Additionally, he made major doctrinal declarations for the Church, such as *The Origin of Man* (the LDS position on human evolution), and his vision of the redemption of the dead can be found in Doctrine and Covenants 138.

Joseph F. Smith was influential in starting some foundational LDS programs, such as family home evening.

Heber J. Grant (1918–1945): President of the LDS Church for nearly twenty-seven years, his tenure as its leader is second only to Brigham Young in longevity. He successfully led the Latter-day Saints through two world wars and the Great Depression. Under his direction, the LDS Church established the remarkable Church welfare program.

George Albert Smith (1945–1951): In conjunction with United States President Harry Truman, George Albert Smith oversaw the LDS Church's substantial welfare and relief efforts to address the suffering in Europe caused by World War II. *Time* magazine honored President Smith on its cover in July 1947. He also began to focus more concerted LDS missionary efforts in areas of the world such as South America, Africa, and Japan.

Heber J. Grant successfully led the Latter-day Saints through two World Wars and the Great Depression.

George Albert Smith oversaw substantial relief efforts in Europe after World War II.

David O. McKay (1951–1970): Beloved by President Lyndon B. Johnson[7] and honored by one US Secretary of State as "the best goodwill ambassador the United States had,"[8] David O. McKay looked like a prophet.[9] A masterful teacher, David O. McKay helped ground the LDS Church as a family-centered Church when he famously quoted J. E. McCulloch, who said, "'No other success can compensate for failure in the home.'"[10]

David O. McKay was honored by one Secretary of State as "the best goodwill ambassador the United States had."

Joseph Fielding Smith (1970–1972): The son of President Joseph F. Smith and great-nephew of Joseph Smith, Joseph Fielding Smith was a prolific gospel scholar and writer, and many of his doctrinal books and teachings are still referenced today by Latter-day Saints. Although he served as President of the Church for only a few years, he is the longest serving apostle in the Church to date, having served from 1910 to 1972.

Joseph Fielding Smith was a prolific gospel scholar and writer.

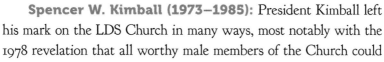

Harold B. Lee (1972–1973): As a local congregational leader, Harold B. Lee developed the pattern for the LDS welfare system and was called upon by Church leaders to expand it into a worldwide system. He was chairman of the Church's efforts to correlate all Church departments and auxiliaries under priesthood direction.

Harold B. Lee developed the pattern for the LDS welfare system.

Spencer W. Kimball (1973–1985): President Kimball left his mark on the LDS Church in many ways, most notably with the 1978 revelation that all worthy male members of the Church could be ordained to the LDS priesthood regardless of race. (See chapter 5 for more on the pre-1978 priesthood restriction.) He also oversaw the production and printing of the revised, cross-referenced LDS scriptures and Bible Dictionary, which have aided countless Latter-day Saints in their scripture study.

Spencer W. Kimball received the 1978 revelation that all worthy male members of the Church could be ordained to the LDS priesthood regardless of race.

Ezra Taft Benson (1985–1994): Perhaps no one other than Joseph Smith has done more than Ezra Taft Benson to establish the Book of Mormon as a global scripture. His call to "flood the earth with the Book of Mormon"[11] resulted in increased study and use of the Book of Mormon in LDS families, Church curriculum, and missionary efforts. He was also a former member of US President Dwight D. Eisenhower's Cabinet.

Howard W. Hunter invited Mormons "to look to the temple of the Lord as the great symbol of your membership."

Perhaps no one other than Joseph Smith has done more than Ezra Taft Benson to establish the Book of Mormon as a global scripture.

Howard W. Hunter (1994–1995): Although President of the Church for only nine months, President Hunter's invitation for Mormons "to look to the temple of the Lord as the great symbol of your membership"[12] continues to guide the Saints today in their desires to center their worship of Jesus Christ through the temple. (See chapter 8 for more about temples.)

Gordon B. Hinckley (1995–2008): Gordon B. Hinckley was instrumental in the Church's worldwide expansion, especially with its construction of temples across the world. During his twelve-year presidency, the Church announced seventy-nine new temples, nearly tripling the existing number of LDS temples worldwide.[13] Under his prophetic leadership, the Church released the doctrinal documents "The Family: A Proclamation to the World" and "The Living Christ: The Testimony of the Apostles." He established the LDS Church's Perpetual Education Fund, which provides money for schooling to poverty-stricken Latter-day Saints across the world. For his humanitarian and educational efforts, US President George W. Bush awarded President Hinckley the Presidential Medal of Freedom, the highest award given to a US civilian.

Gordon B. Hinckley was instrumental in the Church's worldwide expansion.

Thomas S. Monson (2008–present): Through his example and teachings, Thomas S. Monson has influenced and encouraged members of the Church to be more compassionate, loving, kind, and concerned for the poor and the needy—in short, to be more like the Savior Jesus Christ. One of his first major acts as President of the LDS Church was to add "caring for the poor and needy"[14] as one of the Church's stated purposes. Latter-day Saints look to Thomas S. Monson as the living prophet of God on the earth today, and will continue to do so until his death, when a new President and prophet will take his place.

Thomas S. Monson has influenced and encouraged members of the Church to be more compassionate.

#1 Over 80

In 2010, LDS Church President Thomas S. Monson was named by *Slate* magazine as the most influential person above eighty years old in America—for the second year in a row. He was ranked above such notable people as Warren Buffett, Barbara Walters, and President Jimmy Carter.[15] And in 2011, President Monson was named by Americans as one of the top ten "Most Admired Men,"[16] the first time an LDS Church president was so honored.

How Is a New President and Prophet of the LDS Church Chosen?

It's actually quite simple. Upon the death of an LDS Church President, the next most senior apostle (which is determined by length of service as an apostle, not by age) becomes the next President of the LDS Church.

Here is a little more detail about how that process happens.[17] When the current President of the LDS Church dies, the LDS First Presidency—the highest governing body of the Church—is dissolved and the two counselors revert back to their positions of seniority in the Quorum of the Twelve Apostles, which now numbers fourteen members.

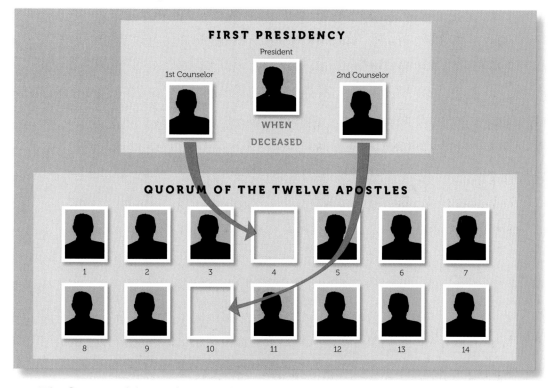

The Quorum of the Twelve Apostles assumes leadership of the LDS Church, and a motion is made to have the now-presiding, senior-most apostle ordained as President of the Church. Once the motion is discussed and accepted by the Quorum of the Twelve Apostles, the apostles lay their hands on the head of the senior-most apostle and set him apart as President of The Church of Jesus Christ of Latter-day Saints. The new president then selects two counselors from among the Quorum of the Twelve, regardless of seniority, and the three of them become the new First Presidency and highest governing body of the LDS Church.

Selecting and ordaining a new LDS President is a beautiful and simple system, which we feel is inspired by the Lord. There is no balloting. There is no campaigning or electioneering. There is no jockeying for power or position. The decision of who becomes the next Church President is, in essence, determined by longevity of life, and thus the selection of a new LDS Church President is left completely in the hands of God.

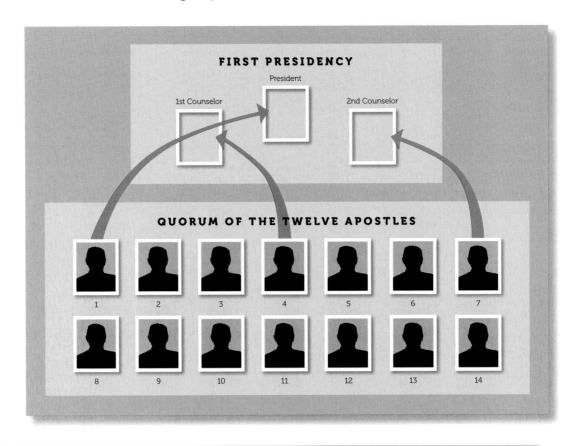

Scan this QR code or go to www.mormon .org/videos to meet a modern-day LDS apostle, **Elder Jeffrey R. Holland**, and hear him express his testimony and witness of the divinity of Jesus Christ.

MORMYTH: Mormons believe that their prophets will never lead them astray.

Answer: True.

Although none of the individual prophets or apostles claims to be perfect or infallible,[18] Latter-day Saints believe that the collective bodies of the First Presidency and the Quorum of the Twelve Apostles will not lead them astray in matters pertaining to salvation.

After receiving the revelation to end the practice of plural marriage, President Wilford Woodruff promised: "The Lord will never permit me or any other man who stands as President of this Church to lead you astray. It is not in the programme. It is not in the mind of God. If I were to attempt that, the Lord would remove me out of my place, and so He will any other man who attempts to lead the children of men astray" (Doctrine and Covenants, Official Declaration 1).

Elder James E. Faust (1920–2007) of the Quorum of the Twelve Apostles asked: "How can we be so sure that, as promised, the prophets, seers, and revelators will never lead this people astray? . . . One answer is contained in the grand principle found in the 107th section of the Doctrine and Covenants: 'And every decision made by either of these quorums must be by the unanimous voice of the same.' [D&C 107:27.] This requirement of unanimity provides a check on bias and personal idiosyncrasies. It ensures that God rules through the Spirit, not man through majority or compromise. It ensures that the best wisdom and experience is focused on an issue before the deep, unassailable impressions of revealed direction are received. It guards against the foibles of man."[19]

President Wilford Woodruff promised: "The Lord will never permit me or any other man who stands as President of this Church to lead you astray."

Although Mormons do not believe that the Lord will allow their collective leaders to lead them astray, Church members are counseled to gain their own, independent witness of the truthfulness of the teachings of latter-day prophets. Brigham Young taught: "I am more afraid that this people have so much confidence in their leaders that they will not inquire for themselves of God whether they are led by Him. . . . Let every man and woman know, by the whispering of the Spirit of God to themselves, whether their leaders are walking in the path the Lord dictates, or not."[20]

15 Temple Square

Welcome to Temple Square! Each year, more than five million people visit Temple Square in Salt Lake City, Utah, making it one of the top twenty-five most visited sites in the United States.[1] We hope you already have been or soon will be one of those five million people to visit this beautiful area. But if not, here's a quick tour.[2]

Church History Library

Completed in 2009, this building is home to many LDS Church history documents and is opened to all those interested in researching LDS history.

Conference Center

Built in 2000, the Conference Center seats 21,000 people. The LDS general conference is held there twice a year. Numerous concerts and performances are also held at the Conference Center each year. At 1.5 million square feet, the building is massive.

North Visitors' Center

The North Visitors' Center has an eleven-foot replica of Bertel Thorvaldsen's *Christus* statue, two art galleries, a replica of Jerusalem, and other exhibits.

Church History Museum

The Church History Museum is free to the public and tells the history of the LDS Church through exhibits and displays of artifacts and art.

Family History Library

This building houses the largest genealogical library in the world. It contains the names of more than three billion people from more than one hundred countries.

Salt Lake Tabernacle

This historic building was completed in 1867. Its eggshell design was envisioned by Brigham Young. It seats 2,900 people, and the Mormon Tabernacle Choir performs in the Tabernacle each Sunday. The Tabernacle is so acoustically sensitive that if you stand at the pulpit and drop a pin, the sound can be clearly heard at the back of the hall—about 170 feet away.[3]

Mormon Tabernacle Choir

Touted as "America's Choir" by President Ronald Reagan, the Mormon Tabernacle Choir is world renowned. Here are some interesting facts about the Choir:[4]

- **360:** Members of the choir, aged 25 through 60.
- **3.5 billion:** TV viewers who watched the Choir perform at the opening ceremonies of the Salt Lake City 2002 Olympic Winter Games.
- **13:** Performances at world's fairs and expositions.

Salt Lake Temple

The heart of Temple Square is the Salt Lake Temple—an iconic symbol of Mormonism throughout the world. It took the pioneers forty years to build the granite structure (1853–1893). The temple's exterior is rich in symbolism; symbols which are meant to teach spiritual truths.

Church Office Building

Built in 1972, the Church Office Building is one of the tallest buildings in Salt Lake City. From here, Church leaders and employees oversee various departments of the Church, from temple and chapel construction to Church education to Church media efforts to the worldwide missionary program, and much, much more.

Relief Society Building

This building is the headquarters for the three auxiliaries of the LDS Church that are headed by female presidencies: the Relief Society, Young Women, and the Primary.

Administration Building

The administration building houses the offices of many LDS Church leaders, including the First Presidency and the Quorum of the Twelve Apostles.

Lion House and Beehive House

These nineteenth-century homes are the former residences and office of President Brigham Young.

Joseph Smith Memorial Building

Built in 1911, the former Hotel Utah was renovated in 1993 and renamed in honor of LDS founder Joseph Smith. The building has a FamilySearch center (for family history beginners); the 500-seat Legacy Theater, where LDS films are shown for free; and three public restaurants.

South Visitors' Center

The South Visitors' Center features an exhibit on the family and an exhibit on the history of building the Salt Lake Temple. It also has a scale model and minutely detailed replica of the Salt Lake Temple, allowing visitors to see the inside of the house of the Lord.

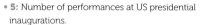

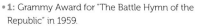

- **5:** Number of performances at US presidential inaugurations.
- **2 and 5:** Number of platinum and gold records, respectively.
- **1:** Grammy Award for "The Battle Hymn of the Republic" in 1959.
- **80:** Number of years *Music and the Spoken Word* has been broadcast (4,100 episodes). It is the oldest continuous nationwide network broadcast in America.

Assembly Hall

This amazing gothic-style building with stained-glass windows—constructed between 1877 and 1882—was built from cast-off stones used in the construction of the adjacent Salt Lake Temple. This building is primarily used for concerts.

Part 3: The Mormon Way of Life

16 Mo-cabulary
Understanding Mormon Vernacular

Imagine if you overheard a Mormon say this in conversation:

"At the stake center some elders who were heading to the MTC next Wednesday came and spoke to the Beehives at Mutual. Gosh, they were awesome! One elder taught us a message from the standard works (but I forgot my triple combination, or my quad!) and the other read an article from the *Ensign* about sealings and the priesthood keys that were lost during the Great Apostasy but that have been restored in our dispensation. I really felt a burning in my bosom when they spoke. It was like we were on Kolob, or in Zion. I think I'll bear my testimony about it next Fast Sunday."

No, that wasn't in Hebrew, but it might as well have been for some people. Like most organizations, Mormons have a unique vocabulary that is distinct to our doctrine and based on our beliefs. So, to help out in your conversations with Mormons or in the study of our religion, here is a list of some of the more prominent doctrinal words, acronyms, and Mormon jargon that often make up our "Mo-cabulary."[1]

Aaronic Priesthood: The lesser of the two priesthoods within the LDS Church, named after Moses' brother Aaron. The Aaronic Priesthood includes the offices of deacon, teacher, priest, and bishop (see Doctrine and Covenants 107:13–14; Hebrews 7:11).

Like most organizations, Mormons have a unique vocabulary that is distinct to our doctrine and based on our beliefs.

Agency: The God-given ability for all people to choose and act for themselves.

Apostasy: When a person, group, or nation turns away from or forsakes the truth.

Atonement: The suffering, death, and resurrection of Jesus Christ for the sins of the world in the Garden of Gethsemane and on the cross, thus overcoming the effects of sin and death for all mankind and making salvation possible.

Baptisms for the dead: The performing of proxy baptisms in LDS temples for and in behalf of deceased persons who died without the opportunity to be baptized by proper authority.

Bear testimony: To publicly express one's personal beliefs and convictions of gospel truths.

Beehive: A symbol for "Deseret," implying cooperation and industry. Also, the name for the LDS young women's group for girls ages twelve and thirteen.

Blessing: When a Melchizedek Priesthood holder(s) lays his hands on a person's head and pronounces a blessing of healing or comfort by inspiration.

This is NOT what we mean by "block."

Block: The three-hour Sunday meeting schedule for Latter-day Saints (i.e., sacrament meeting, priesthood or Relief Society meeting, and Sunday School).

BMW (Big Mormon Wagon): This is a humorous reference to a vehicle that transports a lot of people or a large LDS family (i.e., a big ol' Suburban or a twelve-passenger van that gets about as many miles per gallon as it holds passengers).

Born in the covenant: A term for when a baby is born to Latter-day Saints parents who have been sealed together for eternity in an LDS temple.

Burning in the bosom: A phrase that comes from Doctrine and Covenants 9:8, describing a manifestation of the Holy Ghost on a person's feelings.

Calling: A Church assignment given to and voluntarily accepted by a Latter-day Saint. Most callings are given and performed in the local LDS ward or stake congregation.

Celestial kingdom: The highest of the three heavens of eternal glory, where the faithful and righteous live for eternity.

Celestial marriage: See "Eternal marriage."

Confirmation: After baptism by water, a person is confirmed a member of The Church of Jesus Christ of Latter-day Saints and the gift of the Holy Ghost is conferred upon them through the laying on of hands by those who hold the Melchizedek Priesthood.

Consecration: The LDS communal law, designed to eliminate poverty and to unite a society, where all properties are given to the Church, and then each person is given a "stewardship"

"CTR" stands for "Choose the Right."

to live on "according to his family, according to his circumstances and his wants and needs" (Doctrine and Covenants 51:3; see also Acts 4:32; 4 Nephi 1:3). Also, to dedicate your time, talents, resources, and energies toward building up God's kingdom.

Covenant: A two-way agreement between God and His children where God sets the terms and we agree to abide by them. In return, God promises us blessings.

CTR: An acronym for "Choose the Right." The letters often appear on green, shield-shaped rings that are given to LDS Primary children.

Cumorah: The hill where the last battle of the Nephite civilization took place and where the ancient American prophet Mormon concealed many of the Nephite records in the ground. Also, the hill where Joseph Smith unearthed the golden plates.

Deseret: The word Brigham Young originally proposed as the name for the territory, and then the state, of Utah. The origin of the word is from the Book of Mormon, which states that the interpretation of *deseret* "is a honey bee" (Ether 2:3).

Dispensation: When the Lord reestablishes or "dispenses" His priesthood, doctrines, and ordinances among mankind. For example, Adam was the head of the first dispensation, and Joseph Smith is the head of this last dispensation.

Doctrine and Covenants: A collection of many of the revelations received by LDS founder, the Prophet Joseph Smith, as he was reestablishing Jesus Christ's Church on the earth. It also contains the revelations of a few other LDS Presidents, such as Brigham Young and Joseph F. Smith. It is considered to be holy scripture by Latter-day Saints.

Elder: A priesthood office in the Melchizedek Priesthood. Also, the title of male LDS missionaries. It is also the title given to members of the Quorums of the Seventy and the Twelve Apostles.

Endure to the end: This phrase, used in LDS scripture (see 2 Nephi 31:20), implies continued faithfulness to God and emphasizes our need to remain true throughout life despite temptations or trials.

The Ensign is the official monthly magazine of the LDS Church.

The Ensign: The name of the official monthly magazine of the LDS Church. The word "ensign" is used repeatedly in the writings of Isaiah (Isaiah 11:10, 12) and in Latter-day Saint scriptures. An ensign means a "sign," "signal," "standard," or "banner."

Eternal life: To live forever as families in God's presence (see Doctrine and Covenants 132:19–20).

Eternal marriage: This is synonymous with "celestial marriage" or being "sealed" in the temple as a husband and wife. It means just what it implies: that a marriage can last for eternity and can be sustained both in this life and the next.

Eternal progression: The promise of an endless increase in glory and dominion for those who are exalted in the celestial kingdom.

Exaltation: To become like God the Father and live in His presence in the celestial kingdom.

Fall (of Adam and Eve): The act of partaking of the forbidden fruit by Adam and Eve, thus introducing sin and physical death to humankind.

The act of partaking of the forbidden fruit by Adam and Eve is known as the Fall.

Family home evening: Monday evening has been designated by LDS Church leaders as the time for families to gather together to teach one another the gospel, strengthen relationships, and have fun together.

Fast offering: A monetary donation of the value of meals not eaten during a "fast" (two meals or twenty-four hours) given to the LDS Church for use in caring for the poor and needy.

Fast Sunday: The first Sunday of the month is designated for Latter-day Saints to fast, which means to refrain from any eating and drinking for two consecutive meals (or twenty-four hours).

A fast offering is a donation of the value of meals not eaten during a "fast."

First Presidency: The highest governing body in the LDS Church, consisting of the President of the LDS Church and his two counselors.

First Vision: When God the Father and Jesus Christ appeared in a vision to the fourteen-year-old boy Joseph Smith in Palmyra, New York, in 1820.

Garments: Sacred underclothing given to Latter-day Saints who have received their endowment in an LDS temple. The clothes remind the wearer of his or her covenants of faithfulness to God.

Home teaching: A Church program where each family in an LDS congregation is assigned two priesthood holders who briefly visit the family regularly to "watch over . . . and be with and strengthen them" (Doctrine and Covenants 20:53) in their spiritual and temporal needs.

Institutes of Religion: Weekday LDS religious instruction for young adults ages eighteen through thirty. Classes are usually held in buildings adjacent to college and university campuses.

Iron rod: A central feature of the visionary dream had by the Book of Mormon prophet Lehi (see 1 Nephi 8). The iron rod leads followers of Christ to the tree of life (representing Jesus). The iron rod is interpreted as the "word of God" (1 Nephi 11:25).

JST: The Joseph Smith Translation of the Bible where, through divine inspiration, Joseph Smith restored the original meaning or intent of certain Biblical verses.

Kingdom of God: The Church of Jesus Christ of Latter-day Saints. Also the theocratic government of God that will be implemented during the millennial reign of Jesus Christ after His return to earth.

According to Abraham, one day on Kolob is equal to a thousand years on earth.

Kolob: The planet residing "nigh unto the throne of God" (Abraham 3:9), where one day is equal to one thousand of our years (see Abraham 3:4).

Lamanites: One of the principal groups in the Book of Mormon, who were primarily the descendants of Laman, Lemuel, and Ishmael.

Law of chastity: The commandment to live a sexually pure life, defined as not having any sexual relationship outside the bonds of a legal marriage between a man and a woman.

Laying on of hands: Those who have been ordained to priesthood offices may lay their hands on a person's head to give a blessing, ordain to a priesthood office, or set someone apart in an official capacity in a Church calling.

Melchizedek Priesthood: The higher of the two priesthoods within the LDS Church, named after the great high priest and king of Jerusalem, "Melchisedec" (see Hebrews 7:1–3). The Melchizedek Priesthood includes the offices of apostle, seventy, patriarch, high priest, and elder (see Doctrine and Covenants 107:1–12; Hebrews 5:6; 6:20; 7:11, 7:17).

Millennium: The period of a thousand years of peace that will begin with the return of Jesus Christ to earth.

The Millennium is the period of a thousand years of peace that will begin with the return of Jesus Christ to earth.

Moroni: The ancient American prophet who, as a resurrected being, in 1823 revealed to Joseph Smith where the Book of Mormon record was concealed. Moroni is represented by the iconic golden statue on top of most LDS temples.

MoTab: The abbreviated slang name used to refer to the Mormon Tabernacle Choir.

MTC: The Missionary Training Center, where LDS missionaries go to receive training and instruction at the beginning of their full-time missionary service.

Mutual: The name of the weeknight activities which take place at local LDS meetinghouses for LDS young men's and young women's groups.

Nephites: One of the principal groups in the Book of Mormon, the Nephites were primarily the descendants of Nephi, Jacob, Joseph, Sam, and Zoram.

Nauvoo: The name of the city formerly known as Commerce, Illinois, that was built along the banks of the Mississippi River by Joseph Smith and his followers after they were expelled from the state of Missouri. Today, the city of Nauvoo is a national historical site.

Ordinance: A sacred, formal act performed by the authority of the priesthood that has religious meaning and is designed to teach spiritual truths. Latter-day Saint ordinances include baptism, confirmation, the sacrament, and the temple endowment. Saving ordinances (such as baptism) are always entered into by covenant.

Outer darkness: The eternal place of hell designated for Satan and his followers who rebelled against God (see Doctrine and Covenants 76:25–49).

Nauvoo Temple.

Patriarchal blessing: A blessing given to worthy Latter-day Saints by an ordained patriarch, containing a declaration of the person's lineage within the house of Israel as well as lifelong personal counsel and promised blessings from God.

Pearl of Great Price: A small selection from the revelations and translations of Joseph Smith. It includes five sections: selections from the Book of Moses, the Book of Abraham, Joseph Smith—Matthew, Joseph Smith—History, and the Articles of Faith. (See chapter 9 for more about these books.)

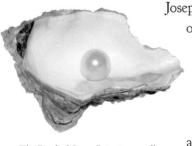

Pioneer: In the LDS context, the word "pioneer" has dual meanings. It can refer to a mid-1800s Latter-day Saint who traveled great distances to gather to Utah and its surrounding territories. It can also refer to a modern Latter-day Saint who is among the first converts in a city or country to accept the gospel and become a Mormon.

The Pearl of Great Price is actually a book of scripture, not a pearl.

Plan of salvation: God the Father's plan to enable His children to become more like Him and receive a fullness of joy.

Plural marriage: The practice of a man being authorized by God to marry more than one woman at a time.

Premortal life: Also called "premortality," this refers to the time we spent living in the presence of God as His spirit children (without mortal bodies) before we were born on the earth.

Priesthood: God's eternal power and authority. God gives priesthood authority to all worthy male Latter-day Saints to act in His name, preach the gospel, provide the ordinances of salvation, and govern the Church.

Priesthood keys: The authority God has given to priesthood leaders to direct, control, and govern the use of His priesthood on earth.

Primary: The organization in the LDS Church for children aged eighteen months to twelve years old.

"Priesthood keys" refers to the authority God has given to priesthood leaders to direct the priesthood.

Quad: Shorthand reference for the four books of LDS scripture (the Bible, the Book of Mormon, the Doctrine and Covenants, and the Pearl of Great Price) that have been bound together in one volume.

Quorum: A group of LDS priesthood holders delineated by priesthood office.

Relief Society: The women's organization in the LDS Church for females aged eighteen and older. The Relief Society is designed to help those in need, increase the gospel knowledge and faith of LDS women, and strengthen their homes and families.

Restoration: In the LDS context, this means the reestablishment of Jesus Christ's authorized Church on earth through the Prophet Joseph Smith.

"Quad" is shorthand for the four books of LDS scripture that have been bound together in one volume.

Revelation: Any form of communication between God and His children, most often occurring through personal impressions made on an individual's mind and heart by the Holy Ghost (see Doctrine and Covenants 8:2–3).

RM: A "returned missionary," or an LDS member who has completed serving an LDS mission.

Sacrament: In Mormonism, the sacrament is the partaking of blessed bread and water in remembrance of the body and blood of Jesus Christ.

Saint: As implied by scripture, a saint is anyone who strives to follow the teachings of Jesus Christ and believes in His divinity (see 2 Nephi 9:18; Romans 1:7; 1 Corinthians 1:2). Thus, Mormons consider themselves to be latter-day (last days) saints.

The sacrament is the partaking of blessed bread and water in remembrance of the body and blood of Jesus Christ.

Sacred Grove: The grove of trees behind the boyhood home of Joseph Smith where he saw God the Father and Jesus Christ in a vision in 1820.

Sealing: An ordinance that takes place by priesthood authority in an LDS temple where a man and a woman are joined together as husband and wife for eternity. Also, when parents are joined together with their child (or children) for eternity.

Seminary: Weekday LDS religious instruction for Mormon youth ages fourteen to eighteen. Most youth attend seminary classes either in the morning before school starts or during a class period when they are released from public school.

Set apart: When a person accepts a volunteer assignment (a "calling"), he or she is officially authorized to act in that position through the laying on of hands by those who have the priesthood authority to call them to that position.

Singles ward: An LDS congregation of young adults ages eighteen to thirty who are not married.

Spirit world: The place where the spirits of mankind dwell after they die as they await the resurrection.

Stake: An LDS congregation consisting of five to twelve LDS wards in a geographical area.

Stake center: The LDS meetinghouse for stake events.

Standard works: The accepted Latter-day Saint scriptures: the Bible, the Book of Mormon, the Doctrine and Covenants, and the Pearl of Great Price.

The LDS meetinghouse for stake events is called the stake center.

Telestial kingdom: The lowest of the three heavens of eternal glory.

Temple: The house of the Lord and the most sacred building in Mormonism, where the holiest Latter-day Saint ordinances (such as the endowment and eternal marriage) are performed. It is also where gospel ordinances are performed vicariously for and in behalf of those who died without receiving the saving ordinances of the gospel.

Temple recommend: A recommend given by LDS ecclesiastical leaders for a worthy Latter-day Saint to enter the temple and perform or receive its ordinances.

Terrestrial kingdom: The middle of the three heavens of eternal glory.

Tithing: The payment of one-tenth of an individual's income to the Lord through His Church.

Triple Combination: The shorthand name for the three-in-one book of LDS scripture containing the Book of Mormon, the Doctrine and Covenants, and the Pearl of Great Price.

Tithing is one-tenth of an individual's income.

True to the Faith: A book of alphabetical listings of religious topics designed to aid members in their study of the scriptures and words of the prophets. It is endorsed by the First Presidency of the LDS Church.

Urim and Thummim: The name of the translation tool given to Joseph Smith to aid him in the translation of the golden plates of the Book of Mormon. It consisted of two stones fastened to a breastplate (see Joseph Smith—History 1:35).

Ward: The name of the basic Latter-day Saint local congregation.

War in heaven: The name given to the conflict in the premortal life between those who followed God and His plan of salvation and those who rebelled against God. The rebellion was led by Lucifer, later known as Satan (see Revelation 12:7–11; Moses 4:1–4).

Word of Wisdom: The health code followed by Latter-day Saints that stipulates the avoidance of coffee, tea, alcohol, and tobacco; it also advocates the eating of grains, vegetables, and fruits (see Doctrine and Covenants 89).

The "Y" is short for Brigham Young University, the LDS Church's university in Provo, Utah.

The "Y": Short for BYU, or Brigham Young University, the LDS Church's university in Provo, Utah.

Zion: Zion can mean a place or a group of people or a state of being. As a place, it refers to the holy city that will be built on the American continent in Independence, Missouri (see Doctrine and Covenants 57:1–3). As a group it can refer to the Church and the people of God (see Moses 7:18; 1 Nephi 22:14, 19).

17 What Does It Take to Be a Mormon?

LDS Standards

believe in the Ten Commandments, not the Suggestions.

Although many Americans might be unaware of the specifics of LDS doctrines and beliefs, our moral standards are no secret. A 2008 study indicated that **nearly three-fourths of Americans associate Latter-day Saints with high moral standards.**[1] Whether it's being honest, or not drinking alcohol, or maintaining moral purity, or embracing family values, the bar is set high for a faithful Mormon, which is a good thing. The Lord has set high standards so that He can bless us, as living these principles helps us be in harmony with God and our fellow man.

This chapter outlines some of what is required to be a Mormon and details some of the more common standards and commandments that faithful members of The Church of Jesus Christ of Latter-day Saints strive to live.

High Commitment = High Faith

Joseph Smith taught that a religion that requires sacrifice produces commitment and faith.[2] President Gordon B. Hinckley also linked the appeal of the LDS Church for its members to the Church's high standards: "We expect things of our people. We expect them to do things. We expect them to measure up to certain standards. It isn't always easy to be a member of this church. It's demanding. But it's wonderfully fruitful and has a tremendous affect upon people."[3]

Sociologist Rodney Stark, who describes Mormonism as a demanding faith,[4] has concluded the same: **a higher-demanding faith produces higher commitment to that faith.**

To illustrate, he found that the higher the percentage of those who give at least $2,000 per year to their church in donations, the higher satisfaction rating (on a scale from zero to four) that its members gave the church.[5]

The Contributions and Satisfaction of Church Membership	Percentage who contributed $2,000 or more to their church in the past year	GPA* of the religious group graded by members
Roman Catholics (n=386)	2	2.3
Liberal Protestants (n=372)	3	2.3
Conservative Protestants (n=338)	1.4	3.1
Latter-day Saints (n=30)	48	3.8

Source: Calculated from General Social Survey, 1989. *Grade point average: 4.0 is the highest possible grade; 0 is the lowest.

The Building Blocks of the Gospel: The First Principles and Ordinances

The first principles and ordinances are the building blocks of the gospel.

To become an official Latter-day Saint, a person must believe in and be willing to follow the gospel of Jesus Christ. What is "the gospel" according to Mormons? Well, here it is in a nutshell: "We believe that the first principles and ordinances of the Gospel are: first, Faith in the Lord Jesus Christ; second, Repentance; third, Baptism by immersion for the remission of sins; fourth, Laying on of hands for the gift of the Holy Ghost" (Articles of Faith 1:4).

Here is a little more about each of those requirements.

Faith: The first requirement of being a Latter-day Saint is to have faith in the Lord Jesus Christ. **Faith in the Lord Jesus Christ means to trust in His divinity and His power as the Savior of mankind,** recognizing that "no flesh . . . can dwell in the presence of God, save it be through the merits, and mercy, and grace of the Holy Messiah" (2 Nephi 2:8). Faith in Christ also means to rely on His infinite power, goodness, and love, and to believe in His teachings and strive to live them.[6]

The first requirement of being a Latter-day Saint is to have faith in the Lord Jesus Christ.

Repentance: A natural result of faith in Jesus Christ is an increased desire to show our love for and belief in Him by striving to learn more about and follow His commandments (see John 14:15). Thus, our faith in Jesus Christ leads us to repent, or **to change our thoughts, beliefs, and behaviors** to align with His teachings. Although all of us will fall short of Jesus' standard of perfection (see Matthew 5:48; Romans 3:23), we nevertheless strive to do His will as His disciples and to correct our behavior through repentance as we fall short. Sufficient evidence of repentance is a necessary precursor to being baptized and becoming an official member of the LDS Church (see Doctrine and Covenants 20:37).

We strive to do Christ's will and to correct our behavior through repentance as we fall short.

Baptism: To become a member of The Church of Jesus Christ of Latter-day Saints, a person must be baptized by the proper priesthood authority and receive the gift of the Holy Ghost. **When someone is baptized into the LDS Church, he or she makes a covenant (or a sacred agreement) with God** that they "are willing to take upon them the name of Jesus Christ, [and] to serve him to the end" (Doctrine and Covenants 20:37; see also Mosiah 5:5, 18:10). As part of our baptismal covenant, we promise that we are willing to always remember Christ and keep His commandments (see Doctrine and Covenants 20:77).

Mormons believe that baptism by immersion is "symbolic of the death of a person's sinful life and the rebirth into a spiritual life, dedicated to the service of God and His children."[7] We believe that baptism is necessary for salvation (see Mark 16:16; John 3:5) for all those capable of sin. Therefore, we do not believe in baptizing little children (see Moroni 8:4–24), as our doctrine states children are not accountable for sin until they are eight years old (see Doctrine and Covenants 68:27).

We believe that baptism is necessary for salvation for all those capable of sin.

Confirmation and Receiving the Holy Ghost: After a person has been baptized by immersion by the proper priesthood authority, two men who hold the Melchizedek Priesthood lay their hands on the newly baptized person's head and confirm him or her a member of The Church of Jesus Christ of Latter-day Saints and confer the gift of the Holy Ghost with the injunction to "receive the Holy Ghost."[8]

We believe that **receiving the gift of the Holy Ghost,** or the baptism "of the Spirit" (John 3:5) **is also necessary for salvation,** as the reception of the Holy Ghost cleanses us from sin and helps to change our natures so we can become better people (see 2 Nephi 31:17; 3 Nephi 27:20).

The reception of the Holy Ghost cleanses us from sin and helps to change our natures so we can become better people.

After a person is baptized and is confirmed a member of the LDS Church, they are expected to continue in the faith until the end of their lives, or to "endure to the end" as it is commonly referred to in Mormonism (2 Nephi 31:20). This simply means we try to live the teachings of Christ and be faithful to our covenant with God, and that when we fail, we will repent of our mistakes and continue to love Jesus and follow Him. **Enduring to the end doesn't imply perfection like Christ** (as that is impossible), **but dedication to Christ.**

Just Like Mom and Dad

So, can someone be considered a Mormon just because of their family lineage or their lifestyle, even if they don't belong to the Church?

Just because a man's parents were Mormon doesn't mean he is a Mormon. It isn't like Judaism, where because of a person's ancestry and bloodlines, he or she can still be considered Jewish, regardless of his or her personal belief system. Similarly, there are some who accept some LDS doctrines and follow LDS lifestyles or cultural practices, but who are not official members of the Church. To truly be a Mormon, a person must be a baptized member of The Church of Jesus Christ of Latter-day Saints.

Latter-day Saint Standards

The following are some of the more common standards that faithful Latter-day Saints strive to live. To be clear, we make no pretensions of perfection or claim that we always fully live these standards. Obviously, we all do not. Elder Neal A. Maxwell (1926–2004) said the LDS Church "is not a well-provisioned rest home for the already perfected."[9] Or in the words of Jesus: "They that be whole need not a physician, but they that are sick" (Matthew 9:12).

Mormons are still and ever will be involved in the ongoing process of "perfecting of the saints" (Ephesians 4:12). However, we believe these standards are right and good and that striving to live by them is part of the baptismal covenant we make to be willing to keep Christ's commandments. Living these gospel teachings helps a person be worthy of the influence of the Holy Ghost and enjoy its fruits, which include personal joy and peace.

Sabbath Day Observance

Mormons worship on Sunday as their Sabbath day, and we believe in keeping it holy.

Mormons worship on Sunday as their Sabbath day, and we believe in keeping it holy as commanded in the scriptures (see Exodus 20:8; Mosiah 13:16; Doctrine and Covenants 68:29). As part of keeping the Sabbath day holy, Latter-day Saints are expected to attend church meetings and partake of the sacrament (see Doctrine and Covenants 59:9–10). We are advised not to work on Sunday so that we can attend our church meetings and use our time to do things that will "bring [us] closer to the Lord" and enjoy "needed rest and rejuvenation."[10]

Some appropriate Sabbath day activities include "spending quiet time with your family, studying the gospel, fulfulling your Church callings and responsibilities, serving others, writing letters, writing in your journal, and doing family history work."[11] However, the specific and individual interpretation and application of those principles is primarily left up to members of the Church and their families. For example, some Mormons choose not to watch football on TV on Sundays as a way to help keep the day holy, whereas other faithful Mormons choose to cheer away. ("Hey, I'm with my family, and I'm resting from my labors. Plus, Steve Young is doing color commentary, and Austin Collie is playing. First down!")

Tithing

Faithful Mormons pay one-tenth of their income to the Church.

Faithful Mormons voluntarily pay one-tenth of their annual income to the Church. Paying tithing is a way of showing God that we place no other god—even the god of money and possessions—before Him (see Exodus 20:3). **We believe that great temporal and spiritual blessings come from paying tithing** and that God opens up "the windows of heaven [to] pour you out a blessing" (Malachi 3:10) for the sacrifice of paying tithing.

Tithing money is used to build and maintain LDS temples and meetinghouses, print materials (such as the Book of Mormon), fund the Church Educational System, and support other Church programs (such as family history centers) that help the Church fulfill its mission and purpose (see chapter 24 for more on tithing). It is a requirement for a person to commit to being a full tithe payer before being baptized[12] and to be an actual full tithe payer before entering an LDS temple.

> A 2002 study of American generosity found the average American gave 2.3 percent of their income to charitable organizations. Utah (which was 60 percent Mormon) led the nation in charitable donations with an average of 5.1 percent per person—more than double the national average.[13]

Sexual Purity

This is commonly called the "law of chastity" in Mormonism, and it means that we do not have "any sexual relationship outside the bonds of a legal marriage between a man and a woman."[14] Latter-day Saints believe that sex within marriage is "beautiful and sacred,"[15] but that—like rinsing with mouthwash before drinking a glass of orange juice—sex before or outside of marriage turns something that is sweet into something that is sour. (Consider the uncountable broken hearts and homes, affairs and divorces, abortions and diseases, single mothers and welfare needs that result from sexual immorality, and you might agree that chastity is a smart standard to have.)

We believe that living a standard of sexual purity helps foster success in our personal, family, societal, and spiritual lives. Additional LDS standards related to sexual purity are the expectation of dressing modestly (wearing clothing that is neat and clean and not overly revealing) and avoiding and resisting pornography in all its forms. (See chapter 18 for more about these principles of moral cleanliness.)

A 2009 Pew Study on religion and public life reported that "On a host of religious measures, Mormons stand out for having exceptionally high levels of religious commitment."[16]

Attend Church Services at Least Once Per Week

76% OF LATTER-DAY SAINTS

39% OF GENERAL POPULATION

Read the Scriptures on Their Own at Least Once Per Week

76% OF LATTER-DAY SAINTS

35% OF GENERAL POPULATION

Pray at Least Once Per Week

90% OF LATTER-DAY SAINTS

75% OF GENERAL POPULATION

Pray Daily

82% OF LATTER-DAY SAINTS

58% OF GENERAL POPULATION

Pray or Read Scriptures with Their Children Aged 18 and Under

91% OF LATTER-DAY SAINTS

63% OF GENERAL POPULATION

Honesty

Mormons "believe in being honest" (Articles of Faith 1:13) with ourselves, with each other, and with God. Honesty is more than truth telling, it is truth living, as dishonesty is at the heart of many other sins, such as adultery, fraud, hypocrisy, cheating in school, and shoplifting (to name only a few). Latter-day Saints strive to be honest in all their dealings with other people. We believe that living a life of honesty helps us have peace of mind and helps to maintain our self-respect and integrity. It helps others to trust us and fosters healthy relationships. Honesty really is the best policy—both for individuals and for society.

In a survey study with non-Mormons who were asked to select words they thought described Latter-day Saints, 78 percent selected "honest."[17]

Media

Latter-day Saints try to be selective with our entertainment by consuming media that "inviteth and enticeth to do good" (Moroni 7:13) and by avoiding media "that is vulgar, immoral, violent, or pornographic in any way" or that "presents immorality or violence as acceptable."[18] That is because what we see, hear, and read influences what we desire and, therefore, how we act. Guided by latter-day prophets' counsel to youth, many Latter-day Saint adults and families have adopted a policy of not watching any movies rated "R."[19]

Latter-day Saints try to choose media that "inviteth and enticeth to do good."

Education

We believe that "the glory of God is intelligence" (Doctrine and Covenants 93:36). Thus, Latter-day Saints place a heavy emphasis on education, both formal schooling and our continued life education as we gain and improve our skills and abilities. Part of our doctrinal desire for education is to help us become more like God, but there is a practical side as well: Latter-day Saints believe in being self-reliant, and having a good education helps us in that goal.

The greatest education that a Latter-day Saint is expected to obtain is a spiritual education through a study of the scriptures and living the gospel. Mormons are regularly directed by prophets and other Church leaders "to study the scriptures every day, both individually and with our families."[20] (See chapter 9 for more on the scriptures.)

A 2009 Pew Study found that **the more education Latter-day Saints had, the greater their religious dedication.** They found that "A similar pattern emerges on belief in God, frequency of prayer and religious exclusivity. On each of these questions, Mormons with more formal education are more religiously committed, whereas in the general population the opposite is true."[21]

Additionally, we believe that the more educated we are, the more good we can do in the world in service to mankind.

Language

Joseph Smith once said, "I love that man better who swears a stream as long as my arm yet deals justice to his neighbors and mercifully deals his substance to the poor, than the long, smooth-faced hypocrite."[22] That may be, but Mormons still try to use clean and appropriate language and to follow the scriptural injunction to "let no corrupt communication proceed out of your mouth, but that which is good" (Ephesians 4:29). Mormons are taught to avoid taking the name of God or Jesus Christ in vain, as well as to avoid any language that is harsh or degrading. Not only do we try not to swear, but we strive to avoid any language that is dishonest, profane, or crude. Dirty or racist jokes, gossip, and putting other people down (even as a joke) are all against our verbal standards as well. We believe that speaking cleanly, kindly, and intelligently helps us remain in harmony with God's Spirit.

"Failure to express yourself in language that is clean marks you as one whose vocabulary is extremely limited."—LDS Church President Gordon B. Hinckley (1910–2008)[23]

When we say things that are degrading, our words usually say more about us than anything else.

The Word of Wisdom

Latter-day Saints follow a health code known as the Word of Wisdom, which stipulates the avoidance of tea, coffee, tobacco, alcohol, and harmful drugs, as well as advocating the eating of nutritious foods such as grains, vegetables, and fruits. The Word of Wisdom was given by revelation to the Prophet Joseph Smith in 1833 (see Doctrine and Covenants 89), long before medical science and society commonly supported its health practices. The governing principles of the Word of Wisdom are for us to take good care of our physical bodies, to remain active, alert, and in control, and to avoid anything that can be addictive, harmful, damage our bodies, shorten our life, or weaken our judgment.[24] We believe that living the principles of the Word of Wisdom helps us to be more in tune with the subtle impressions from God's Spirit on our minds and hearts (see Doctrine and Covenants 8:2) and that living by its principles will bless us physically, intellectually, and spiritually.

"Health in Their Navel" . . .
for Eight to Eleven Years Longer

The final promise of the Word of Wisdom to those who follow it is that they "shall receive health in their navel and marrow to their bones" (Doctrine and Covenants 89:18). That's quite a promise. But consider this: A fourteen-year selective study conducted by UCLA epidemiologist James E. Enstrom tracked the health of 10,000 moderately physically active LDS people in California. Of these nonsmoking, monogamous nondrinkers, Enstrom concluded from the study "that LDS Church members who follow religious mandates barring smoking and drinking have one of the lowest death rates from cancer and cardiovascular diseases—about half that of the general population. . . . Moreover, the healthiest LDS Church members enjoy a life expectancy eight to eleven years longer than that of the general white population in the United States."[25]

Can You Tell Which One Is LDS? Study Says You Can

A 2010 research study stated that "subtle markers of group membership can influence how others are perceived and categorized. Perceptions of health from non-obvious and minimal cues distinguished individuals according to their religious group membership."

Translation: You can pick a Mormon out of a crowd because of how their beliefs and standards affect their facial appearance.

The researchers tested this premise specifically by showing participants 160 randomly selected facial photos—eighty of Mormons and eighty of non-Mormons. The researchers trimmed the photos from the hairline to the bottom of the chin, to eliminate any other visible cues, and then asked each participant to identify, based on facial features alone, which ones were Mormon and which ones were not.

Surprisingly, the researchers found that "participants' accuracy . . . in categorizing the faces was significantly better than the chance guessing rate [(r = .58, p = .003)]." The researchers concluded that "information about health from the faces seemed to form the basis for perceivers' categorizations of Mormon/non-Mormon group membership, with facial skin quality serving as the primary cue."[26]

Service to Others

We believe that "service to others is an important characteristic of a disciple of Jesus Christ."[27] The Book of Mormon states that part of the covenant we make at baptism is to be "willing to bear one another's burdens, that they may be light; yea, and [be] willing to mourn with those that mourn; yea, and comfort those that stand in need of comfort" (Mosiah 18:8–9).

As a person increasingly develops Christlike attributes, his or her thoughts and concerns turn outward toward others.

As people increasingly develop Christlike attributes, they will continue to turn their thoughts and concerns outward toward others—engaging in simple everyday acts of kindness and selflessness toward family and friends—from missionary work, to serving in Church callings, to participating in and making donations toward the LDS Church's vast welfare system and programs. A classic LDS scripture teaches that "when ye are in the service of your fellow beings ye are only in the service of your God" (Mosiah 2:17).

A 2010 study called *American Grace: How Religion Divides and Unites Us* found that "collectively Mormons are among the most charitable of Americans with their means and time, both in religious and nonreligious causes."[28]

The BYU Honor Code Test

The nation caught a glimpse of just how serious Latter-day Saints are about living gospel standards in March 2011. With the LDS-Church-owned Brigham Young University men's basketball team ranked #3 in the nation, and the

team poised to make a run at the Final Four, BYU suddenly suspended a star player after they learned he had violated the school's honor code. (All students at BYU agree to live by an honor code that is consistent with many LDS Church standards, including not engaging in pre-marital sex and abstaining from alcohol.)

The school could have easily turned a blind eye to the honor code violation until after the basketball season was over and allowed the player to continue to play. But honor, integrity, responsibility, and faithfulness—coupled with forgiveness—were more important to BYU than pursuing fame and glory. *Time* magazine said of the decision: "You have to admire an institution that sticks by its principles. . . . Would any other school pay that price? More than likely, too few would pass the [BYU] test."[29]

18 Mormons and Sex

So what do Mormons say about sex? (Can Mormons even say the word "sex" or do they have to say "physical intimacy"?) Is sex good and right, or is it evil and wrong? Well, Utah does have the highest birthrate in America,[1] so apparently a lot of Mormons do actually think sex is good—under the right circumstances.

Practically everything that relates to Mormons' views on sexuality comes back to three beliefs: (1) The human body is sacred and divine, including its power to procreate, (2) marriage between a man and a woman is central to God's plan of happiness for His children, and (3) the family is the fundamental unit of society.[2] Therefore, sex between a married man and woman? Good—it brings children into married families, and it is a way to express love and total commitment between husband and wife. Sex between unmarried people? Not good—it can lead to pre-marriage pregnancy, single parenthood, abortion, adultery, divorce, mistrust, guilt, and sexually transmitted diseases.

Utah has the highest birthrate in America, so apparently Mormons do actually think sex is good.

Here's a little bit more about how Mormons view sex and other issues related to "physical intimacy."

The Human Soul

"The spirit and the body are the soul of man" (Doctrine and Covenants 88:15). In other words, we believe that our physical body affects our spirit. Treat the body well, and the spirit feels well. Treat the body wrong, and the spirit—and therefore the soul—is affected negatively.

Physical Intimacy Is Beautiful and Sacred

The LDS First Presidency has proclaimed: "Physical intimacy between husband and wife is beautiful and sacred. It is ordained of God for the creation of children and for the expression of love between husband and wife. God has commanded that sexual intimacy be reserved for marriage."[3]

"Physical intimacy between husband and wife . . . is ordained of God."
—The First Presidency

SEXUAL ABSTINENCE BEFORE MARRIAGE AND COMPLETE FIDELITY WITHIN MARRIAGE

This is the basic rule for Mormons regarding sex.

The Law

The basic rule for Mormons regarding sex is this: **abstinence before marriage; complete fidelity to one's spouse after marriage.**[4] You may think it old-fashioned, but when you consider the millions of abortions, the high incidence of sexually transmitted diseases, the fact that 40 percent of all US births are to single women,[5] and the countless broken hearts and homes that result from sexual immorality, adhering to the Mormon standard of sexual morality appears to be not only a spiritual blessing but a societal blessing as well. No society, and therefore no country, can be stronger than the collective moral fiber of its people. We believe this moral standard of chastity helps foster the most potential success in our personal, family, societal, and spiritual lives.

The Consequences of Sexual Immorality

- From 1973 to 2008, nearly 50 million abortions were legally performed in the United States, and four of every ten unintended pregnancies ended in abortion.[6]
- There are 19 million new cases of sexually transmitted diseases reported each year in the United States, and one in four sexually active teenage girls in the United States has a sexually transmitted disease.[7]
- The US Census Bureau data shows that the birthrate for unmarried women has risen in each reported year, from 43.8 percent in 1990 to 52.5 percent in 2008.[8]

Why Wait?

But isn't it better for people to have sex before they get married to make sure the relationship is compatible?

In a 2010 study of 2,035 married couples across the United States, researchers found that the couples who waited to have sex until they were married rated their current married relationship stability 22 percent higher, their marital satisfaction 20 percent higher, the sexual quality of their relationship 15 percent better, and the communication between them and their spouses 12 percent higher than those married couples who had sex before they were married.[9]

Sex after marriage   Sex before marriage

One holds up a relationship much better than the other.

We believe that one of the benefits of waiting to have sex until we are married is that the marriage relationship is then built on a foundation of communication, trust, respect, shared goals, and social enjoyment. When those things are in place, the addition of sexual intercourse after marriage only helps solidify an already healthy relationship. The researcher of the study concluded, "The longer a couple waits, the better."[10] We agree.

Abortion

The LDS position on abortion is clear: "Members of The Church of Jesus Christ of Latter-day Saints must not submit to, perform, encourage, pay for, or arrange for an abortion."[12] This position stems from our belief in the sanctity of life and from our belief that God is the Father of our spirits and that He has spirit children who desire to come to earth to inherit a physical body, be born, and progress through life on earth. (See chapter 4.)

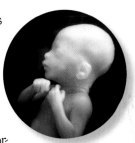

The LDS position is clearly against abortion, with possible exceptions in certain situations.

There are, however, some exceptional circumstances that *may* justify an abortion from an LDS view, including "when pregnancy is the result of incest or rape, when the life or health of the mother is judged by competent medical authority to be in serious jeopardy, or when the fetus is known by competent medical authority to have severe defects that will not allow the baby to survive beyond birth."[13]

So what is the Church's policy for what to do when a woman becomes pregnant outside of marriage? "When a child is conceived out of wedlock, the best option is for the mother and father of the child to marry and work toward establishing an eternal family relationship. If a successful marriage is unlikely, they should place the child for adoption."[14]

The Human Element

Our bodies have the power to create another human life. A unique person—someone never before seen or duplicated—with eyes and ears and fingers and toes—and with a divine potential and infinite worth.[15] For Mormons, perhaps nothing is more divine than to share with God the titles of "creator" and "parent." That is why married Mormons have and enjoy sex as something sacred, but at the same time aren't flippant or careless about it either.

If the human element is the most powerful element on earth, then perhaps the ability to create a human life is the greatest power given to man. Societies enforce strict laws to control who can access the power of guns or cars or chemicals as well as establish severe and somber laws to regulate the power over who can and can't take away life. For Mormons, the greatest power of all—the power to create life—has similar restraints and approvals for who can use it.

MORMYTH: The reason Mormons have such big families is that the Church tells them not to use birth control.

Answer: False.

The reason Mormons have larger families than the average American family has nothing to do with birth control being prohibited (it's not), but has everything to do with our belief that children are a blessing and that married couples have a divine responsibility to assist in God's work by providing physical bodies for God's spirit children. (See chapter 7.)

The Church's official position regarding birth control is stated in the book *True to the Faith*. Married LDS couples should "prayerfully decide how many children to have and when to have them. Such decisions are between the two of you and the Lord."[16] Church members are counseled to consider such things as the physical and mental health of the mother and father, as well as their ability to provide the necessities of life, when making personal decisions about when and how many children to have.[17]

Sex—A Sacred Symbol

We see sex in marriage as a physical symbol of total union.

For Mormons, sex in marriage is a *symbol* of the total union of a marriage. When a man and woman have given their whole lives to each other—all that they are or ever hope to be, all their hopes, dreams, and desires—and have joined their lives together in a covenant of marriage, then sex becomes a physical symbol of that union. It is a reminder that in every way—spiritually, mentally, emotionally, and physically—a married man and woman can and should "cleave unto" each other and be "one flesh" (Genesis 2:24).

"But We Didn't 'Go All the Way'"

Some people who strive for sexual abstinence before marriage think that as long as they remain virgins, anything else goes regarding sex. For faithful Mormons however, any use of the procreative powers outside of marriage—whether it be on first, second, or third base—is considered a sin. This goes back to our beliefs about the purposes of sex, which is to create children within the covenant of marriage and to express affection and commitment between husband and wife, and our belief in the sanctity of the power to procreate.[18]

Whether it be on 1st, 2nd, or 3rd base, any use of the procreative powers outside of marriage is considered a sin for faithful Mormons.

Adultery

The command from Sinai rings just as loud and clear today as it did in Moses' day: "Thou shalt not commit adultery" (Exodus 20:14). In fact, LDS scriptures (including the Book of Mormon and the Doctrine and Covenants) reemphasize at least twenty times the commandment not to commit adultery.[19]

Pornography

Pornography is considered an influence as destructive to the soul as the black plague was to the body, and faithful Mormons shun anything associated with it. It is degrading to the human body and undermines the purposes of physical intimacy. It is also most often degrading to women by objectifying them and demeaning their divine character.

Mormon leadership has spoken out on pornography in its worldwide general conference more than 140 times since 1986.[20] Why do Mormons take the issue of pornography so seriously? Well, we take Jesus at His word when He said, "Whosoever looketh on a woman to lust after her hath committed adultery with her already in his heart" (Matthew 5:28). If someone views immoral images, it can create immoral thoughts, which leads to immoral desires, actions, and character.

Additionally, pornography can be addicting and can take control of a person's life. Mormons believe in avoiding all aspects of behavior that can lead to addiction and diminish a person's ability to control their desires and behavior—including sexual addictions such as pornography. LDS scripture is clear on the point, giving a commandment to men: "Thou shalt love thy wife with all thy heart, and shalt cleave unto her and none else" (Doctrine and Covenants 42:22).

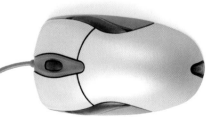

Pornography can be addicting and take control of one's life. Addiction diminishes a person's ability to control desires and behavior.

Elder Dallin H. Oaks (1932–) taught: "Pornography is also addictive. It impairs decision-making capacities and it 'hooks' its users, drawing them back obsessively for more and more. A man who had been addicted to pornography and to hard drugs wrote me this comparison: 'In my eyes cocaine doesn't hold a candle to this. I have done both. . . . Quitting even the hardest drugs was nothing compared to [trying to quit pornography].'"[21]

Mormon Modesty

Mormon women do *not* look and dress like this. (Unless it's for a stage play about pioneers.)

They look and dress more like this. ⟶

While we don't walk around wearing pioneer dresses or clothing from the 1800s, Mormons still believe in maintaining modesty in our dress and appearance. Because the human body is sacred, we treat it with respect in our dress and appearance. That doesn't mean that Mormons can't still be stylish and beautiful; it just means that faithful Mormon girls avoid wearing anything that is too tight, too low, too high, or too revealing. Similarly, Mormon guys try to dress cleanly and keep their bodies appropriately covered.

Miracle of miracles, by following this standard of modesty, Mormons still manage to attract, meet, and marry people of the opposite gender—sometimes more quickly than the rest of the nation.[22] We think that **the Mormon standard of modesty makes it easier for people to see and be attracted to us for who we are—not just for what our bodies look like.**

Do Mormon Leaders Practice Celibacy?

While Latter-day Saints believe in controlling our appetites and passions, a celibate life is inconsistent with our beliefs that God's plan for His children, and the purpose of life itself, centers on marriage and family. Therefore, not only do regular Mormons get married, but our elders and bishops and apostles and prophets can, do, and are encouraged to marry and have children. In fact, they should. Mormon scripture says: "For marriage is ordained of God unto man . . . that the earth might answer the end of its creation" (Doctrine and Covenants 49:15–16).

Mormons believe that marriage is an essential part of the Lord's purposes in creating the earth.

What's the Mormon View on Homosexuality?

We believe that people with same-gender orientation are children of God, beloved by Him, and are of infinite worth and potential, just like all of God's children. However, Mormons believe homosexuality is contrary to the physical and spiritual purposes of human sexuality, which purposes are closely tied to the creation of children by a man and woman within a marriage. As is self-evident, a same-gender relationship is inconsistent with the natural process of creating children.

The expectation of sexual abstinence outside of marriage is the same for all Mormons, regardless of whether they face heterosexual or same-gender attraction. Although the LDS Church has no official position on the causes of same-gender attraction,[23] LDS theology teaches that each person has the power to control their own behavior.

Mormons believe homosexuality is contrary to the physical and spiritual purposes of human sexuality.

In the LDS view, there is a difference between same-gender *actions* and same-gender *attractions*. As long as a Mormon with same-gender feelings lives the moral standards of the LDS Church, they are welcome to—and do—worship, serve, attend, and participate fully in the Church. (See chapter 6 for more about the LDS position on homosexuality and same-sex marriage.)

Attraction versus Action

In the official LDS Church pamphlet on homosexuality, *God Loveth His Children,* Church leaders have said, "Attractions alone do not make you unworthy. If you avoid immoral thoughts and actions, you have not transgressed even if you feel such an attraction. The First Presidency stated, 'There is a distinction between immoral thoughts and feelings and participating in either immoral heterosexual or any homosexual behavior.'"[24]

And in the LDS Church's official handbook, Church leaders have said, "If members feel same-gender attraction but do not engage in any homosexual behavior . . . [they] may hold temple recommends and receive temple ordinances."[25]

Are Mormons Who Have Sex outside of Marriage Doomed to Hell?

The moral standards of the LDS Church are high and often not easy to uphold. Mormons who have sex outside of marriage are subject to Church discipline, which—depending on the situation—can mean not being able to participate in Church ordinances like taking the sacrament, not being able to serve or teach in the Church, the suspension of membership, or most severe—removal of Church membership through excommunication.

Although we believe sexual sin to be very serious (see Alma 39:5), we also believe that God is merciful and that through the atonement of Jesus Christ someone who has been sexually immoral can repent, change his or her behavior, recommit to follow Christ, and be totally forgiven of sexual sin.

19 Mormon Women

Author and Pulitzer Prize–winner Wallace Stegner wrote a book in 1964 about the Mormon pioneers' westward migration. In it, he said, "I shall try to present [the Mormons] in their terms and judge them in mine. That I do not accept the faith that possessed them does not mean I doubt their frequent devotion and heroism in its service. Especially their women. **Their women were incredible.**"[1]

Although they don't don the pioneer dresses of the 1800s any more, modern Mormon women still lead remarkable lives and have a profound effect upon other people. Commenting on modern LDS women, a self-described "standard-issue late-20-something childless overeducated atheist feminist" recently confessed her infatuation with reading Mormon housewife blogs, calling them "uplift-ing" and saying that their lives send the message: "It is possible to be happy. . . . We love our homes. We love our husbands. . . . Family is wonderful, life is meant to be enjoyed."[2]

Women have a profound effect upon other people.

So who are LDS women, and what makes them so incredible? Where do they fit into the LDS Church, its society, and its theology? Here are some answers.

LDS Women and Motherhood

In an age when some people consider marriage and motherhood a stifling, feminine-fettered trap, Latter-day Saint theology celebrates it as something ennobling, enabling, and divine. Mormons believe the family is central to God's plan for the happiness of His children and the fundamental unit of society,[3] and thus no work can be nobler than that given to those who rear and raise, nurse and nurture those families: the mothers. Mormons believe that **"Motherhood is near to Divinity.** It is the highest, holiest service to be assumed by mankind. **It places her who honors its holy calling and service next to the angels.**"[5]

"Are We Not All Mothers?"

Latter-day Saints believe that all women, whether they have children or not, are moth-ers in the sense that the female gender has a divine, innate capacity to nurture and teach and care for others.[4]

Although motherhood can sometimes be monotonous (seriously, child, are you getting out of bed for the *four thousandth* time?), usually tedious, oftentimes thankless, and altogether paycheck-less, the eternal value of motherhood and mothering has almost no equal in Mormonism's teachings. Moms aren't just changing soiled diapers—through their divine work at home they are changing soiled societies. They aren't making meals and doing laundry—in a very real sense, they are doing

Mothers, in a very real sense, "clothe the naked and feed the hungry" (Jacob 2:19).

exactly what the Savior said the greatest among us should do: "clothe the naked, and . . . feed the hungry" (Jacob 2:19; see also Matthew 23:11). Within the daily work of mothers that some might see as drudgery, Latter-day Saints see something divine. We believe that the divine work of motherhood is ultimately focused on leading God's children to the source of salvation—Jesus Christ. In the words of LDS Relief Society general president Julie B. Beck (1954–), "There is eternal influence and power in motherhood."[6]

> A 2007 Pew Forum survey indicated that **American Mormons have the largest families of any faith**, with about 20 percent of LDS adults having three or more children at home.[7]

What about Women Who Don't Marry or Have Children but Would Like To?

There are many women who do not have the opportunity to marry and bear or raise children but very much want to. These women make up a large and significant portion of the LDS Church, and they contribute an equally large and significant portion to the Church and its programs. Latter-day Saint prophets have repeatedly taught that those "whose circumstances do not allow them to receive the blessings of eternal marriage and parenthood in this life will receive all promised blessings in the eternities."[9]

Who's More Influential— Mothers or Congress?

"When the real history of mankind is fully disclosed, will it feature the echoes of gunfire or the shaping sound of lullabies? The great armistices made by military men or the peacemaking of women in homes and in neighborhoods? Will what happened in cradles and kitchens prove to be more controlling than what happened in congresses? When the surf of the centuries has made the great pyramids so much sand, the everlasting family will still be standing, because it is a celestial institution, formed outside telestial time. The women of God know this."—LDS Apostle Neal A. Maxwell (1926–2004)[8]

The LDS Women's Relief Society

The Relief Society is the Latter-day Saint women's organization. Founded in 1842 by Joseph Smith in Nauvoo, Illinois, it is one of **the oldest and largest global women's organizations functioning today.**[10] As of 2011, there are 5.5 million women who belong to the Relief Society spread throughout 170 countries across the world.[11]

All LDS adult women belong to the Relief Society; women usually enter into the organization at the age of eighteen.[12] Women with and without children, married and not married, old and young, employed and unemployed meet together to learn from and strengthen each another in living the gospel. The purpose of the Relief Society "is to build faith and personal righteousness, strengthen families and homes, and help those in need."[13] Joseph Smith said it is for **the relief of the poor, the destitute, the widow and the orphan,** and **for the exercise of all benevolent purposes" and "not only to relieve the poor, but to save souls."**[14]

All LDS women belong to the Relief Society, both old and young.

The Relief Society meets together once a week in a class during Sunday congregational meetings where they teach each other the doctrines and principles of the gospel. They also sometimes have a Relief Society activity on a weeknight. The topics of these activities usually surround ways to help strengthen marriages and families; improve homemaking skills; learn self-reliance and provident living; engage in compassionate service, temple work, or family history work; as well as sharing the gospel.[15]

The Relief Society organization has a presidency on the ward, stake, and general Church level. The ward Relief Society president is part of the ward council and meets regularly with the bishop to discuss issues that may have risen within the congregation and to suggest ways to respond to them.[16]

Relief Society sisters watch over and care for one another.

Additionally, Relief Society sisters watch over and care for one another by regularly visiting each other's homes with assigned partners, providing uncounted varieties of service such as sharing spiritual messages, taking meals to those who are in need, watching children, or just offering a listening ear.

Preparing meals for those in need is one example of Relief Society service.

Women and Leadership within the LDS Church

It is true that the LDS Church is ultimately a male-led organization. The presiding authority in the ward, the stake, and the global Church is male, and women in the LDS Church are not ordained to priesthood office. (See chapter 5.)

However, **of all faiths, Mormon women are the most satisfied with their roles in Church leadership.**[17] Mormon women serve as leaders within the LDS Church in a variety of ways. There are female general Church officers—the Relief Society general presidency, Young Women's presidency, and Primary presidency—who speak in LDS general conference and sit on general LDS Church boards and committees. On local congregational levels, women serve as presidents of auxiliaries and organizations. They sit in ward councils and have equal voice with the men.[18]

Women vote side-by-side with men to sustain members and leaders in their Church callings. They regularly pray and give sermons in LDS worship meetings. Women teach adult gospel doctrine classes and other Sunday School classes. They are fully involved in all aspects of the work of the LDS Church, from full-time missionary work to member missionary work to temple and family history work to their work in the Relief Society in ministering to the needy.

Above all, LDS women lead as coequals with their husbands in the most important organization within the Church: the family.

About 40 percent of LDS women surveyed say that the role and influence of women in the LDS Church was the "right amount." The next closest faith measured was Evangelical Protestants, with only about 15 percent saying women had the "right amount" of leadership influence in their Church, followed by 10 percent of Anglo-Catholics and about 8 percent of Jews.[19]

40% — Latter-day Saints
15% — Evangelical Protestants
10% — Anglo-Catholics
8% — Jews

Now That's Leadership!

Linda K. Burton, Relief Society general president

Elaine S. Dalton, Young Women general president

Rosemary M. Wixom, Primary general president

As of 2011, the Relief Society general president of the LDS Church leads roughly 5.5 million adult Mormon women.[20] The LDS Young Women's general president guides more than 1 million teenage girls globally.[21] And the LDS Primary general president directs the teaching and learning of an estimated 1 million children worldwide.[22]

LDS Women and the Priesthood

Latter-day Saint women are not ordained to priesthood offices in the LDS Church, and we don't really know why.[23] President Gordon B. Hinckley (1910–2008) simply said, "'Women do not hold the priesthood because the Lord has put it that way. It is part of His program.'"[24]

Although Mormon women do not hold priesthood office, **all the blessings and saving ordinances available through the priesthood are made equally available to both men and women.** (See chapter 5.)

Mormons in Women's Suffrage and Feminism

Many people may not know that LDS women were involved in, and in some ways led, the US women's suffrage movement. In 1870, Utah was the second territory (behind Wyoming) to grant women the right to vote under law, and after gaining statehood, Utah became the third state in the Union to give women equal suffrage.[25]

In fact, because Utah held an election before Wyoming, the first political votes ever cast by women in America were from Utah. Soon thereafter, the first woman to become a state senator was a Mormon woman from Utah, Martha Hughes Cannon, who beat out her own husband, Angus, in the election for the office.[26]

The first woman in America to become a state senator was a Mormon woman from Utah, Martha Hughes Cannon.

Regarding feminism—if defined as the "social, political, and economic equality of the sexes"[27]—LDS beliefs support the foundational concept of equality. God said equally to *both* Adam and Eve, "let *them* have dominion . . . over all the earth" (Genesis 1:26; emphasis added), and "The Family: A Proclamation to the World" by the LDS First Presidency and Quorum of the Twelve Apostles states that men and women are "equal partners"[28] in a marriage and family relationship. Nowhere in LDS scripture or official doctrine is it indicated that God favors one gender above the other. In fact, the Book of Mormon specifically teaches that "male and female . . . are alike unto God" (2 Nephi 26:33). However, much of radical feminism—which can suggest a rejection of men, motherhood, and marriage—is at odds with LDS doctrine and thus not embraced by most Latter-day Saints.

Can LDS Women Work Outside the Home?

The idea that faithful Mormon women can't, shouldn't, or don't work and pursue careers is not accurate.

Latter-day Saint women across the world hold professional titles of CEO, vice president, doctor, professor, attorney, author, artist, teacher, athlete, and business owner—just to name a few. The idea that faithful Mormon women can't, shouldn't, or don't work and pursue careers is not accurate, nor is it what the LDS Church teaches.

That being said, Mormons place the family in highest regard, believing it to be the fundamental unit of society and central to our faith. Thus, we believe that all decisions regarding a wife's or mother's employment should be weighed carefully on how it will affect the family and the rearing of children.

"The Family: A Proclamation to the World" teaches that, although husband and wife "are obligated to help one another as equal partners," each gender does have principal assignments related to the family: "Mothers are primarily responsible for the nurture of their children" and fathers are "responsible to provide the necessities of life," but "disability, death, or other circumstances may necessitate individual adaptation."[29]

Therefore, the ideal is that mothers nurture children at home while fathers provide temporally for the family. However, **the matter of an LDS woman working outside the home or pursuing a career is left to her to decide and is entirely dependent upon her individual, marital, family, and social situation.** Latter-day Saints are counseled not to be judgmental of mothers who choose to work outside the home, regardless of the situation.

> "We should all be careful not to be judgmental or assume that sisters are less valiant if the decision is made to work outside the home. We rarely understand or fully appreciate people's circumstances. Husbands and wives should prayerfully counsel together, understanding they are accountable to God for their decisions."
> —LDS Apostle Quentin L. Cook (1940–)[30]

Women and Mormon Theology

Latter-day Saint theology holds women in high spiritual regard. Perhaps most significantly and unique to Mormonism is our belief that if we have a Father in Heaven, we logically and doctrinally have a Mother in Heaven as well. A famous LDS hymn asks:

> *In the heav'ns are parents single?*
> *No, the thought makes reason stare!*
> *Truth is reason; truth eternal*
> *Tells me I've a mother there.*[31]

We are all children of "heavenly parents,"[32] and although we don't know much about our Heavenly Mother, she is evident in Mormon thought and theology. LDS President Spencer W. Kimball (1895–1985) taught, "You [women] are daughters of God. You are precious. You are made in the image of our heavenly Mother."[33] And in 1909, the LDS First Presidency officially declared, "All men and women are in the similitude of the universal Father and Mother, and are literally the sons and daughters of Deity."[34]

We believe that Eve chose to move God's plan of salvation forward by partaking of the forbidden fruit, thus enabling mankind to experience birth and death.

Additionally, Latter-day Saint theology is not critical of the first woman on the earth, Eve, but rather praises her as the "glorious Mother" (Doctrine and Covenants 138:39) of humanity and celebrates her decision in the Garden of Eden (see Moses 5:11). We believe that Eve chose to move God's plan of salvation forward by partaking of the forbidden fruit, thus enabling mankind to experience birth and death. The *Encyclopedia of Mormonism* says, "The Church of Jesus Christ of Latter-day Saints strongly affirms that in partaking of the fruit of the tree of knowledge of good and evil, Eve along with Adam acted in a manner pleasing to God and in accord with his ordained plan."[35]

Mormons believe that not only can men prophesy, receive revelations, have visions, speak in tongues, and work miracles, but women can equally participate in and enjoy those gifts of the Spirit as well (see Doctrine and Covenants 46:11–26; Joel 2:28). The Book of Mormon specifically teaches that God "imparteth his word by angels unto men, yea, not only men but women also" (Alma 32:23). The book of Revelation also teaches that "the testimony of Jesus is the spirit of prophecy" (Revelation 19:10). Countless women are filled with the spiritual knowledge that Jesus is the Christ and enjoy personal access to prophecy and revelation.

Last, of all the beautiful creations on earth, we believe that women are God's crowning creation, His signature stroke in the masterpiece of the universe.

Scriptural "Prophetess"

Notable women in the scriptures who are identified as "prophetess" include:

Miriam (see Exodus 15:20).
Deborah (see Judges 4:4).
Huldah (see 2 Kings 22:14).
Anna (see Luke 2:36).

Deborah was identified as a prophetess.

LDS Women and Education

Latter-day Saint theology encourages women to gain an education and develop their minds and abilities. In 1830, a revelation given for Joseph Smith's wife, Emma, directed her to "be given to writing, and to learning much" (Doctrine and Covenants 25:8). Later, Brigham Young taught, "We have sisters here who, if they had the privilege of studying, would make just as good mathematicians or accountants as any man; and we think they ought to have the privilege to study these branches of knowledge that they may develop the powers with which they are endowed."[40] That emphasis on education for LDS women continues today. LDS Church President Spencer W. Kimball (1895–1985) said simply, "We want our women to be well educated."[41]

The LDS First Presidency has given the following counsel to both male and female LDS youth: "[God] wants you to educate your mind and to develop your skills and talents. . . . Education will prepare you for greater service in the world and in the Church. It will help you better provide for yourself, your family, and those in need. It will also help you be a wise counselor and companion to your future spouse and an informed and effective teacher of your future children."[42]

"Something Divine"

A 2010 study found that women of all faiths "believe more fervently in God" than men, and that "by virtually every measure they are more religious" than their male counterparts.[37]

This is consistent with what President James E. Faust (1920–2007) said: "Surely the secret citadel of women's inner strength is spirituality. In this you equal and even surpass men, as you do in faith, morality, and commitment when truly converted to the gospel."[38]

We believe that "God planted within women something divine."[39]

Latter-day Saint theology encourages women to gain an education and develop their minds and abilities.

MORMYTH: LDS women are more depressed than other women.

Answer: False.

A common myth has circulated that LDS women are more depressed than any other women in America due to the demands, expectations, and religious lifestyle of Mormonism. The rumor probably started when Express Scripts reported in 2001, and again in 2007, that Utah (with its population of 60 percent Latter-day Saints) led the nation in rates of antidepressant prescriptions, causing some people to jump to the faulty conclusion that the high rates of depression were directly related to Mormonism.[43]

Many studies have been conducted examining the relationship between religion and depression, and specifically Mormonism and depression. The vast majority of the research indicates that LDS women are no more likely to experience depression than any other women in any other religious group.[44] A 2010 study compared thousands of LDS men and women with thousands of non-LDS men and women on twelve indicators of depression and found that, on average, LDS men who served missions (indicating high religiosity

and activity in the LDS Church) reported less incidence of depression than the national sample.

And how did the LDS women fare? LDS women who served a mission (once again, indicating high activity in the LDS Church) had significantly less depression than the national sample, reporting an average score of 1.0 days per week where depression symptoms occurred, compared to 1.39 days per week by the women on the national sample. (LDS women who did not serve a mission also reported a lower number than the national sample—1.11 days.)

The researchers concluded that "this study found no evidence that members of The Church of Jesus Christ of Latter-day Saints experience depression more often than others across the nation. In fact, we discovered that, on the whole, LDS men and women with higher rates of religiosity had significantly lower levels of depression that the average American. Apparently, the religious LDS lifestyle acts as a buffer against depression rather than heightening it, as some have previously assumed."[45]

Scan this QR code to meet **Sarah Osmotherly**, a vibrant and outgoing LDS Australian woman who is taking a break from her public relations career to spend more time at home with her daughter. She says, "I love my career, but recently trading the stilettos for flip-flops and walking the red carpet for walking my little girl to school has been a life-changing decision. I have never been happier."[46]

20 LDS Teenagers

The standards of The Church of Jesus Christ of Latter-day Saints help our youth retain their moral alignment. A four-year study by the National Study of Youth and Religion examined the influence of religion among American teens and found that **Latter-day Saint youth, when compared to their peers of other religions, were the most engaged in their faith.** The longitudinal study found that LDS teens were **less likely** than any other group to

- "engage in sexual intercourse (12 percent);
- "have ever smoked pot (15 percent);
- "drink alcohol a few times a year (10 percent);
- "[have] watched an X-rated or pornographic program in the past year (15 percent)."

Additionally, LDS youth "were found **more likely** to:

- "hold religious beliefs similar to their parents' (73 percent).
- "attend religious services once a week (43 percent . . .).
- "rate the importance of religious faith in shaping their daily life as 'extremely important' (43 percent).
- "engage in fasting or some other form of self-denial (68 percent).
- "have no or few doubts about religious beliefs (91 percent)."[2]

"Too many of today's children have straight teeth and crooked morals."
—Unidentified high school principal[1]

Researcher John Bartowski concluded: "The story we tell about Mormon youth is not that all is well, but compared with other teens they're more knowledgeable about their faith, more committed to their faith, and have more positive social outcomes associated with their faith." Christian Smith, who led the National Study of Youth and Religion, said, "I'm not saying they're all perfect. . . . I'm not trying to idealize Mormon kids . . . [but] Mormon kids tend to be on top."[3]

Latter-day Saints have the same hopes for their youth that Paul had for Timothy: "Let no man despise thy youth; but be thou an example of the believers, in word, in conversation, in charity, in spirit, in faith, in purity" (1 Timothy 4:12).

Here's a brief summary of the standards and programs of the Church that help LDS youth strive to be faithful teens.

For the Strength of Youth

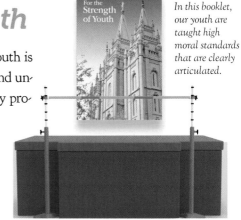

In this booklet, our youth are taught high moral standards that are clearly articulated.

We believe that one key to the spiritual success of our youth is to set high moral standards that are clearly articulated and understood. To this end, the LDS Church's First Presidency provides a booklet for each Latter-day Saint youth called *For the Strength of Youth*, in which various behavioral standards and expectations are laid out. In this booklet (which is studied regularly in LDS Church classes and other settings), youth are taught about the necessity of being grateful, the importance of education, the divine purpose of families, how to choose and be a good friend, and the need to serve other people. *For the Strength of Youth* also discusses essential moral standards such as dressing modestly, being sexually pure, using clean language, keeping the Sabbath day holy, listening to uplifting music, avoiding pornography, abstaining from alcohol and drugs, and being honest.

However, the "strength" in these standards is that they are more than mere moral or ethical values, which are often societal and situational; rather, they are placed in the context of the eternal truths and enduring principles found in the gospel of Jesus Christ.

Mormon youth are not only taught what to do (the standard), but more importantly, they are given the reasons why they should live the standard (the doctrine). Knowing the "why" helps provide powerful answers and practical reasons for LDS youth to live high standards. Here's an example, taken from the "Physical Health" section of the *For the Strength of Youth* booklet. (The *whats* are highlighted in green, and the *whys* are highlighted in red.)

"Your body is a temple, a gift from God. You will be blessed as you care for your body. Choose to obey the Word of Wisdom (see D&C 89). When you are obedient to this law, you remain free from harmful addictions and have control over your life. You gain the blessings of a healthy body, an alert mind, and the guidance of the Holy Ghost. . . .

"To care for your body, eat nutritious food, exercise regularly, and get enough sleep. Practice balance and moderation in all aspects of your physical health. Also, avoid extremes in diet that could lead to eating disorders. Do not intentionally harm your body. Avoid dangerous activities that put your body at risk of serious injury.

"Do not drink coffee or tea. Never use tobacco products or any form of alcohol; they are addictive and harmful to your body and spirit. Being under the influence of alcohol weakens your judgment and self-control. Drinking can also lead to alcoholism, which destroys individuals and families.

"Avoid any drink, drug, chemical, or dangerous practice that is used to produce a 'high' or other artificial effect that may harm your body or mind. . . . Use of these substances can lead to addiction and can destroy your mind and your body."[4]

Shield of Faith

A recent study in *Time* magazine reported that 65 percent of teens have participated in all four of the following illegal activities: drinking alcohol, smoking cigarettes, smoking marijuana, and abusing prescription drugs.[5]

In contrast, the effect of the LDS religion on youth in lessening substance abuse is convincingly evident: **LDS males are about three times less likely to abuse substances and LDS females are about four times less likely than their American high school counterparts.** The following report compares Latter-day Saint high school seniors with their national peers in these areas:[6]

The standards taught to LDS youth form a shield of protection.

While some LDS youth may struggle to live up to these high standards and sometimes they fall short ("standard deviation" is not just a statistical term after all), overall we feel that our youth do an excellent job. The book *Souls in Transition* reports that LDS youth have the highest rates of church attendance (60 percent), personal prayer (54 percent), Sabbath observance (71 percent), and daily scripture reading (23 percent) compared to teens from other religions.[7]

	BOYS		GIRLS	
	Nation	LDS	Nation	LDS
Smoked Cigarettes	64%	25%	60%	15%
Drank Alcohol	87%	25%	87%	22%
Used Marijuana	39%	13%	31%	8%
Got Drunk or High	76%	18%	69%	14%

And for those who think that expecting sexual abstinence from teenagers is unrealistic, recent findings report that **LDS high school seniors have significantly lower rates of premarital sex than the general population of high school seniors:** 11 percent for LDS boys compared to 58 percent for boys nationally, and 19 percent for LDS girls versus 59 percent nationally.[8]

We believe that the standards set in *For the Strength of Youth* do not limit or inhibit our youth, but in fact do the opposite: they provide freedom from many of the problems plaguing youth today and give them strength to live good, clean, honorable, productive, faithful, and virtuous lives.

What Happens When LDS Youth Break Their Standards?

But Mormon youth are not perfect; they have moral struggles just like other teenagers. For example, although LDS rates of premarital sex are significantly lower than the national average, 11 percent of LDS high school senior boys and 19 percent of senior girls still reported that they had been sexually active, and 25 percent of LDS boys and 22 percent of girls had consumed alcohol, both of which are activities contrary to our standards.

To repent, Mormon youth are taught that they must abandon and feel sorrow for the sin.

For the Strength of Youth teaches LDS teens who violate moral standards of the LDS Church that through Jesus Christ "you can receive forgiveness and be cleansed from your sins when you repent."[9] To repent, Mormon youth are taught that they must abandon and feel sorrow for the sin, exercise faith in Christ's ability to cleanse and forgive, confess the sin to God (and, if necessary, meet with their local bishop for guidance in overcoming more serious sin), make restitution for the mistake, and strive to live an overall righteous life in harmony with the teachings of Christ.[10]

We believe that God is merciful and that through Jesus Christ anyone who has violated God's standards can indeed repent, change their minds and hearts, recommit themselves to following Christ, and be totally forgiven of the sin (see Doctrine and Covenants 58:42).

Sweet Sixteen . . . Wanna Double?

Mormon youth are encouraged not to begin dating until they are sixteen years old, and even then to "avoid going on frequent dates with the same person"[11] and to go in groups or on double dates while in their teens. Additionally, they are advised to date only "those who have high moral standards and in whose company [they] can maintain [their] standards."[12]

While these dating standards are difficult for some LDS teens to uphold, most realize that early and serious dating during their teenage years only leads to problems. Research has shown that dating during early adolescence is highly correlated with other at-risk behaviors such as poor school performance, drug use, delinquency, and sexual activity.[13] Most parents agree: In a national study of 300 parents of teens, 87 percent reported that they thought a teenager should be sixteen before beginning one-on-one dating.[14]

Mormon youth are encouraged to avoid going on frequent dates with the same person and to go in groups or on double dates.

Responsibility... What's That? Well, for LDS Youth, It's a Lot

In a world that often accepts finger-pointing as a way of life, LDS youth are taught that they have agency, which is the power of independent action to choose for themselves.

As *For the Strength of Youth* explains, "You are responsible for the choices you make. God is mindful of you and will help you make good choices.... While you are free to choose your course of action, you are not free to choose the consequences. Whether for good or bad, consequences follow as a natural result of the choices you make."[15]

Not only do we strive to help our youth understand that they are accountable for their own actions, we teach them that they should also learn to be responsible at a young age. From the time they are twelve, LDS young men and young women are given leadership opportunities within their local congregations. They serve in youth presidencies, on committees, and in councils. They conduct meetings, make agendas, organize projects and activities, delegate assignments, and follow up with others. They teach one another, pray in our public meetings, and even address the entire congregation as speakers in our sacrament meetings (see chapter 22).

Mormon Youth and Temple Work

When an LDS youth turns twelve years old, he or she is able to enter a Latter-day Saint temple and participate in baptisms for the dead. (See chapter 8 for more on baptisms for the dead.)

On My Honor: Latter-day Saint Youth and Scouting

In 1913, the LDS Church adopted the Scouting program as a way to help LDS young men prepare to become better priesthood holders through embracing the moral, ethical, and leadership values espoused in Scouting. Today, the LDS Church is the single largest chartered religious organization supporting the Boy Scouts of America, with about 400,000 LDS young men involved in 2010.[16]

LDS Church President Thomas S. Monson (1927–) said, "'We are builders of boys and menders of men. In doing so, we remember that the greatest verb in the vocabulary is to love; the second is to help. It is the mission of the Boy Scouts of America to serve others by helping to instill values in young people and, in other ways, to prepare them to make ethical choices over their lifetime in achieving their full potential.'"[17]

LDS Young Men's Priesthood Quorums

Based on their age and priesthood office (see chapter 5), LDS boys are placed into different priesthood groups, or quorums. Usually, boys who are twelve and thirteen are part of the deacons quorum, boys who are fourteen and fifteen are part of the teachers quorum, and boys who are sixteen and seventeen are part of the priests quorum. Each of these quorums is headed by a president and his two counselors, who have been chosen from among the youth in the quorum. (That's right—a twelve- or thirteen-year-old deacons quorum president leads the way for his fellow quorum members. Although it sometimes results in the blind leading the blind, it still provides a great leadership experience for Mormon youth).

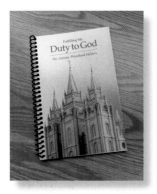

In these quorums, young men meet together with adult advisers on Sundays to better learn their priesthood duties, teach one another, and study the gospel of Jesus Christ together. These young men are taught to watch over and care for one another as a brotherhood. The Church has also implemented the Duty to God program for Aaronic Priesthood holders to help LDS young men better strengthen their testimony of and relationship with God, learn and fulfill their priesthood duties, and apply standards from *For the Strength of Youth*.[18] Through this program, LDS young men are guided to learn gospel principles, make plans in each of these areas to implement the principles in their lives, and then to act on those plans and share their experiences with others.

The Duty to God program helps LDS young men improve themselves.

LDS Young Women's Classes

LDS young women are grouped into one of three classes: Beehives (twelve- and thirteen-year-olds), Mia Maids (fourteen- and fifteen-year-olds), and Laurels (sixteen- and seventeen-year-olds). Weird class names? Perhaps. But do the classes have meaning and purpose? Definitely.

Each of these classes is also led by a president and two counselors, who are chosen from among the young women in the class (and who, as you might suspect, are usually just a wee bit more organized than the young men's quorum presidencies).

Young Women's classes meet each Sunday for about an hour, where they learn the gospel of Jesus Christ and where they strive to accomplish the objectives of the LDS Young Women's program, which are encapsulated in a theme they recite each week:

The Personal Progress program helps LDS girls learn and apply the Young Women Values.

We are daughters of our Heavenly Father, who loves us, and we love Him. We will "stand as witnesses of God at all times and in all things, and in all places" (Mosiah 18:9) as we strive to live the Young Women values, which are:

Faith
Divine Nature
Individual Worth
Knowledge
Choice and Accountability
Good Works
Integrity
and Virtue

The Young Women pledge to stand as witnesses of God at all times.

We believe as we come to accept and act upon these values, we will be prepared to strengthen home and family, make and keep sacred covenants, receive the ordinances of the temple, and enjoy the blessings of exaltation.[19]

To help LDS girls learn and apply the Young Women Values, the LDS Church has instituted the Personal Progress program, which is designed to allow the young women to learn about each of the eight Values in depth as well as complete a project related to each Value. When a young woman completes the Personal Progress program, she receives a Young Womanhood Recognition award, which is akin to a young man receiving his Duty to God or Eagle Scout award.

LDS "Mutual" (No, It's Not an Insurance Company)

Go to youth.lds.org to check out many of the LDS youth programs described in this chapter and to see videos and articles directed specifically to Latter-day Saint youth.

Mormon youth also participate in "Mutual," a one- to two-hour activity for young men and young women. Mutual is normally held once a week on a weeknight at a local LDS meeting-house. At Mutual, LDS youth usually divide into their specific quorums or classes and hold meaningful activities that help them to accomplish the requirements for Scouting merit badges, for their Duty to God award, or for their Personal Progress award. (We say "usually" because every now and then, we admit, plans fall through and, to the delight of many LDS boys, a game of basketball breaks out instead.) About once a month most LDS youth will hold a "combined" activity where all the young men and young women enjoy an activity together.

The LDS Seminary System

When most people hear of a "seminary," they think of a place to train monks, priests, or pastors. However, LDS seminary is not designed to prepare a professional clergy or to ordain persons to a religious ministry. **It is a four-year religious education program designed for all LDS youth ages fourteen to eighteen and is intended to teach them the basic doctrines of the LDS Church,** familiarize them with LDS scriptures, help them "under-

When most people hear of a "seminary," they think of a place to train monks, priests, or pastors. But the LDS seminary program is something different.

stand and rely on the teachings and atonement of Jesus Christ,"[20] and "deepen their faith, testimony, and conversion."[21] To date, there are approximately 350,000 LDS youth enrolled in seminary in 140 countries worldwide.[22]

One purpose of seminary is to familiarize Mormon youth with the scriptures.

The two most common types of LDS seminary are early-morning seminary and released-time seminary. Early-morning seminary classes meet for about an hour *before* public school starts each day. (Yes, that's right—Mormon youth voluntarily go to a religious meeting at about 6:00 A.M. every weekday for four years to learn the gospel. And people say miracles have ceased!) Early-morning LDS seminary students are taught by a volunteer teacher called from their local congregation, and they usually meet in a local Church-owned meetinghouse or in a member's home.

In areas where there is a high concentration of LDS youth (such as in Utah, Idaho, Arizona, and other intermountain states), released-time seminary classes are held *during* school hours each day that the local public school is in session. To preserve the separation of Church and state, students are released from the public school campus during one of their regular class periods and allowed to attend their LDS seminary class in a Church-owned building often located adjacent to the public school. Released-time classes are taught primarily by professionally trained LDS religious educators employed by the Church. The entire four-year seminary system does not cost LDS youth a penny; it is paid for through the voluntary tithing offerings made by Latter-day Saints across the world. (See chapter 24 for more on tithing.)

The researchers for the National Study of Youth and Religion credited much of LDS youth's high marks to the LDS seminary program, saying, "'It probably has to do with daily religious training through high school [i.e. seminary]. . . . Daily engagement with people of their own faith, that's an amazing corrective to tip the balance.'"[23]

In released-time seminary, students attend their LDS seminary class in a Church-owned building, often located adjacent to the public school.

Scan this QR code to meet LDS youth **Sean Kimball** and hear his story of how and why he chose to put attending early-morning LDS seminary before being on the school surf team and the blessings that came to him for putting the Lord as the first priority in his life.

21 The Organization of LDS Church Congregations

In the early 1900s, a non-Mormon clergyman commented, "No other organization is so perfect as the Mormon church."[1] Indeed one of the most distinguishing features of the LDS Church its highly efficient, structured, worldwide organization that is almost entirely based upon volunteer labor and a lay ministry, yet is able to function like precision clockwork. The Mormon faith is not just a loose-knit belief system, but a tightly organized body of believers, capable of managing almost limitless growth yet able to account and care for every single member.

Latter-day Saints believe the foundational organization of the Church—with prophets, apostles, seventies, patriarchs, bishops, and so on—was revealed to Joseph Smith as part of the reestablishment of Christ's true Church (see Ephesians 4:11). Although subsequent presidents of the LDS Church have refined aspects of the organization of the Church in order to meet the changing and growing demands of an expanding worldwide faith, the fundamental structure of the Church has remained the same ever since it was first organized.

This chapter outlines the basics of the LDS Church's organization, congregations, and lay ministry.

It's All about the Family

The organizational structure of the LDS Church begins with the fundamental unit of the Church: the family, which is presided over by a father and a mother.

"There have been great movements started in the past but they have died or been modified before they reached maturity. If Mormonism is able to endure, unmodified, until it reaches the third and fourth generation, it is destined to become the greatest power the world has ever known."—Leo Tolstoy, author of *War and Peace*[2]

FIRST PRESIDENCY
Oversee the Twelve Apostles

QUORUM OF THE TWELVE APOSTLES
Oversee the Seventy

AREA
Presided over by the Seventies quorums, which oversee stakes

STAKE	STAKE	STAKE
WARD WARD WARD WARD WARD WARD	WARD WARD WARD WARD WARD WARD	WARD WARD WARD WARD WARD WARD

Multiple families make up the most basic congregation of the LDS Church, which is called a "ward."

Multiple wards (usually about five to twelve) make up a "stake."

Multiple stakes make up a large geographic "area" (such as the Europe East Area or the Africa West Area).

An area is presided over by an Area Presidency composed of members of the Quorums of the Seventy. (There are currently eight quorums of seventy.)

The Quorums of the Seventy are presided over by the Quorum of the Twelve Apostles, who are presided over by the First Presidency of the LDS Church (the prophet and his counselors).

The family is the fundamental unit of the Church, presided over by a father and a mother.

The LDS Congregation— A "Ward"

An LDS "ward" (derived from the old usage of how neighborhoods were divided up for local politics) is the name of the basic local congregation for Latter-day Saints and is composed of a few hundred members. (Smaller congregations are called "branches" before they are recognized as a ward.) An LDS ward varies in geographic size, depending on its location. In

Each ward has its own assigned meetinghouse, such as this one in Manchester, England.

some areas of the world, a ward can cover hundreds of square miles, while in highly concentrated LDS areas, such as suburban Utah, an LDS ward can cover only a quarter of a square mile. (Look! There are LDS meetinghouses on every corner!)

Each ward has its own assigned meetinghouse, where ward members are assigned to attend and worship. There are often a few LDS wards that meet in the same meetinghouse, though their worship services begin and end at different times. A ward is presided over by a bishop (akin to a pastor in other religions) and his two counselors, together called a bishopric.

The major organizations within an LDS ward include:

- The *high priests group* (for men who hold the office of high priest in the Melchizedek Priesthood)
- The *elders quorum* (for men who hold the office of elder in the Melchizedek Priesthood)
- The *Relief Society* (for all women ages eighteen and older)
- The *Sunday School* (for all members ages twelve and up)
- The *Young Men* organization (for male youth ages twelve through eighteen)
- The *Young Women* organization (for female youth ages twelve through eighteen)
- The *Primary* (for children ages one to eleven)

Thus, **a ward is the basic LDS religious community where members meet together** to teach one another the doctrines of the gospel, perform and receive ordinances such as the sacrament, watch over and care for each other, and fellowship and strengthen each other in the faith.

The LDS Stake

Yes, it is called an LDS "stake," not an LDS "steak" (although some Mormons can cook up a very nice tenderloin). The name "stake" comes from the Old Testament prophet Isaiah, who spoke of the spread of the kingdom of God on the earth and said, "Enlarge the place of thy tent, . . . lengthen thy cords, and strengthen thy stakes" (Isaiah 54:2).

LDS Stakes

It's not about this . . .   It's more about this . . .

An LDS stake is comprised of a geographic group of five to twelve wards and usually has a few thousand members in it. A stake is overseen by a stake presidency (a stake president and his two counselors). A high council of twelve high priests help the stake presidency administer the affairs of the stake.

The primary purpose of a stake is to regulate the affairs of the local LDS wards within its jurisdiction. Therefore, an LDS stake will have a stake-level calling to oversee and assist most ward-level callings. For example, there is a stake Primary presidency called to assist all ward Primary presidencies, a stake Relief Society presidency to support all ward Relief Society presidencies, and so on for the Sunday School and the Young Men and Young Women auxiliaries.

All stake and ward leaders serve without remuneration for their services. Twice a year a "stake conference" is held to conduct stake business and to provide teaching and counsel to stake members. These conferences are usually held in a "stake center" (once again, not a place to take your family to dinner), which is usually the largest LDS meetinghouse in the area.

At the close of 2010, there were 28,660 LDS wards and 2,896 stakes across the world.

28,660
wards
2,896
stakes

MORMYTH: LDS ministers are lay ministers and don't get paid by the tithes of the Church.

Answer: True.

One of the miracles of the LDS Church is that its local leaders, teachers, and others who serve in the local congregations do so without any financial remuneration for their service. We have what is called a lay ministry, which means that each LDS ward or stake is run completely by called volunteers who don't receive a dime from the Church or its members for their service, nor do they expect to. Even local congregational positions like the bishop or the stake president—callings which can require around twenty hours per week of service, and often more—do not receive payment for their services. Latter-day Saint congregational donations via tithing or other offerings go primarily to build chapels and temples, print copies of the Book of Mormon, and pay for LDS seminaries and institutes, but are

not used to compensate priesthood or ministerial positions for the Church. (See chapter 24 for more about Mormons and money.)

However, there are a few full-time Latter-day Saint callings—such as being an Apostle, or a member of the First Quorum of the Seventy—that require a member to leave his full-time employment and dedicate all his time to Church service. Members in these situations "receive a modest living allowance provided from income on Church investments."[3] Revelations to Joseph Smith indicate that there are times when LDS Church leaders may receive "a just remuneration for all their services" in the Church (Doctrine and Covenants 42:72). However, the vast majority of Church callings and positions are unpaid, as the Book of Mormon exhorts (see Mosiah 18:24; 27:5).

What Is a "Calling"?

Most Latter-day Saints are given a "calling" within their local ward or stake. A calling is an invitation to serve, extended by the local congregational leaders (usually by members of the bishopric or stake presidency). In any given ward or stake there are hundreds of callings. There are clerks and secretaries, choir directors and pianists, family history consultants and sacrament meeting greeters, as well as presidents and counselors for organizations and auxiliaries, young men and young women leaders, and many, many class teachers. Almost everything that needs to be done to make an LDS congregation function is delegated to someone via a service calling.

A calling is an invitation to serve, usually extended by members of the local bishopric or stake presidency.

It is estimated that **in the average LDS congregation there are between 150 and 250 positions filled, equaling about 400 to 600 hours of voluntary service each week.**[4] That is akin to having ten to fifteen full-time employees to run the congregation.

Callings are not for life, and members rotate from calling to calling as they are released from current assignments and accept new ones given by their local leaders. Depending on the situation, some members serve in a calling for only a few months, while others serve in a position for many years. We believe that our callings come through the authorized inspiration of our local and general Church leaders. Mormons are encouraged to accept all callings that are extended to them,[5] although they are free to decline the position without penalty if they so desire.

Members raise their right hands to indicate their support of the call, or to indicate their opposition to the call.

Each person who is given a calling in the Church is presented before the congregation for a sustaining vote. If the calling is on a ward level, the person's name and calling are presented before the ward. (Likewise, a stake calling is presented before the stake, and a general Church calling is presented before the entire Church at a general conference.) Members raise their right hands to indicate their support of the call, or to indicate their opposition to the call. (Opposition is rare, although it happens.)

After a person is sustained by the congregation, priesthood leaders who are in authority lay their hands upon the person's head and authorize him or her to act in the newly called position. The person will continue to serve in that position until he or she is "released" by authorized priesthood leaders.

Latter-day Saints are discouraged from seeking for leadership callings or prominent congregational positions, and callings are not applied for by congregational members, nor are they to be sought for. As Church leader J. Reuben Clark Jr. (1871–1961) famously said, "In the service of the Lord, it is not where you serve but how."[6]

Why Do Mormons Accept Callings to Serve?

Our desire to serve in assigned callings—giving countless of hours of service throughout our lives—comes from our sincere love for Jesus Christ and our fellow man (see Matthew 22:37–39) and from our belief that this is Jesus' Church. The Lord has said, "If thou lovest me thou shalt serve me and keep all my commandments" (Doctrine and Covenants 42:29). **Mormons view callings as a form of discipleship, dedication, and devotion to Jesus and as a way to fulfill the covenants we have made to serve God and man.**

Our desire to serve in assigned callings—including that of Scoutmaster—comes from our sincere love for Jesus Christ and our fellow man.

When we have an interview and the bishop says, "We would like to call you to teach the fourteen-year-olds in Sunday School," we accept the calling primarily because we view it as though Jesus were saying, "I would like you to teach these good fourteen-year-old youth on Sunday. Will you do that for me?"

Former Scoutmaster, choir director, stake Young Men leader, Primary chorister, missionary

Former mission president, stake president's counselor, bishop, elders quorum secretary, Primary teacher

Former bishopric member, high priests secretary, financial clerk, missionary, Young Men leader, family history coordinator

Former membership clerk, sacrament meeting chorister, employment specialist, Young Men president, Cubmaster

Former girls camp specialist, Relief Society president, Primary pianist, ward music chairman

Former Relief Society teacher, Primary president, Sunday School teacher, welfare coordinator

Former Primary teacher, nursery leader, Young Women leader, Cub Scout leader, ward organist

Former ward clerk, executive secretary, ward mission leader, elders quorum president, Varsity Scout coach

Experience Is the Best Teacher

Imagine the average LDS congregation sitting there each Sunday. In the audience are former bishops and counselors, stake presidents and mission presidents, gospel doctrine teachers and Primary teachers. There are former full-time missionaries. And there is the lifelong member who has had every calling under the sun—twice.

The amount of experience and knowledge, dedication and commitment, that is gained and available to Mormons through countless hours of teaching and leading in various positions of service in the Church is one of Mormonism's greatest strengths.

The Congregational Magic Square: Each Place Holds an Equal Part

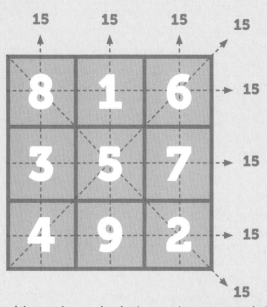

15   15   15   15

8   1   6   → 15

3   5   7   → 15

4   9   2   → 15

15

A "magic square" is a numerical configuration where the numbers in all the rows, columns, and diagonals add up to the same total (in the case on the left, fifteen). Move one number into another location, however, and the square stops functioning.

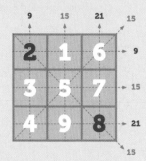

9   15   21   15

2   1   6   → 9

3   5   7   → 15

4   9   8   → 21

15

Similarly, although some callings may be more visible than others in the LDS congregation, no one position is more important than any other. Each calling has its place, purpose, and part in "the perfecting of the saints, for the work of the ministry" (Ephesians 4:12).

Using the New Testament Apostle Paul's analogy, "the eye cannot say unto the hand, I have no need of thee: nor again the head to the feet, I have no need of you" (1 Corinthians 12:21), and neither can the bishop say he has no need of the teacher, or that he is more important, and vice versa. Thus, Latter-day Saints serve in one spot for a while and then are released and are called to a different spot, with each calling fulfilling its needed purpose and place in the Church. **We don't believe it is our *position* in Jesus' Church that will get us to heaven, but rather our *submission* to His teachings.**

Home Teaching and Visiting Teaching: A Watch-care Web of Connection

Al Gore didn't invent the World Wide Web, but through the home and visiting teaching program, you could make the case that the Mormons did. ☺

Each family in an LDS congregation is assigned two priesthood holders—or "home teachers"—to "watch over . . . and be with and strengthen them" (Doctrine and Covenants 20:53) in their homes. Additionally, each woman in the congregation is assigned two women from the Relief Society as "visiting teachers." Young men as young as fourteen can be assigned as home teachers and young women as young as eighteen can be called as visiting teachers.

Once a month, the home and visiting teachers schedule a short visit with the family or individual to whom they are assigned. The purpose of these visits is to extend their love and service, verify that the person or family is well temporally, spiritually, and physically, and offer a brief gospel message. Each month, the visits are reported to priesthood and Relief Society leaders. Thus, if a family or an individual is experiencing problems or difficulties, the home or visiting teachers act as a first line of help and relief and, if necessary can communicate the person's needs to the bishop, other ward leaders, or the congregation, who can provide additional relief.

Home and visiting teachers act as the first line of help and relief when needed.

It Takes a Village to Raise a Child . . . and a Church to Help Save One

Ultimately, the organization of the Church exists to "assist parents."[7] The Church provides the priesthood authority, ordinances, teachings, and doctrines that we believe are necessary for eternal life. All of the Church's programs strive to be "home centered"[8] and provide support and strength to parents as they try to establish successful, faith-

ful, eternal families. For example, if a young woman begins making poor life choices, the Church is set up to help and assist her and her family. There are faithful Young Women leaders, bishops, home teachers, and others who—out of assignment and love—will call and visit her to offer other voices of reason, truth, perspective, help, and friendship. **It indeed takes a village to raise a child, and Latter-day Saints are grateful that they have an LDS congregation in the middle of their villages.**

22 | A Peek inside a Mormon Worship Service

Faithful Mormons gather together once a week on Sunday to worship God the Father and His Son Jesus Christ. We normally meet in a neighborhood LDS chapel with our congregation (called a ward) for a three-hour meeting block where we attend classes and partake of the Lord's Supper to remember Jesus' death and resurrection. Incredibly, the entire Sunday meeting is run and overseen by volunteers who are called as part of a lay, unpaid ministry. (See chapter 21 for more information.) But what exactly do Mormons do during these Sunday meetings?

Here's a quick peek inside our regular three-hour worship service.

Sacrament Meeting— The Pinnacle of the Sabbath Day

This hour-long meeting is the most important part of an LDS Sunday worship service. It can be held either for the first hour of the Sunday block of meetings or the last hour. Here, the entire congregation gathers together (kids included) in a combined service. The meeting begins with the congregation singing a hymn, and then a member of the congregation offers an opening prayer.

The sacrament—or the Lord's Supper—of bread and water is prepared, blessed by a prayer, and then passed to the congregation by authorized priesthood holders (usually the young men). After the bread and water have been offered to those in attendance, the remainder of the meeting is reserved for two or three preselected speakers, usually from the congregation, to deliver gospel-centered messages. Sometimes there is a musical number from the ward choir. The congregation sings a closing hymn, and then the benediction is offered to close the meeting.

On the first Sunday of every month there are no preselected speakers, and, after the sacrament, the remainder of the hour is opened up for members of the congregation to testify of Jesus Christ and His gospel.

Sunday School Classes

During this hour, almost all the adults congregate together in a Sunday School class called Gospel Doctrine, and the youth are divided up by age (twelve to eighteen) in multiple Sunday School classes. Led by a called, volunteer teacher, the Sunday School class studies chapters of scripture to better learn and apply the doctrines and principles of the gospel. The curriculum rotates yearly between a study of the Old Testament, the New Testament, the Book of Mormon, and the Doctrine and Covenants.

Primary Classes

We feel strongly that little children are not only of "the kingdom of heaven" (Matthew 19:14) but that they are also capable of learning about the kingdom of heaven. While adults and youth attend their meetings, children (ages three through eleven) meet in Primary for two hours. The children are divided into age-appropriate classes to learn stories from Jesus' life and basic gospel teachings (such as faith, love, kindness, and prayer) for one hour. During the second hour, they gather together for Sharing Time, where Primary children give brief talks, have a short lesson from an adult, and sing Primary songs together. Some of the best gospel answers you'll ever hear—both profound and funny—are spoken in Primary.

Nursery

A nursery is provided so parents can leave their children (ages eighteen months to three years) for two hours while they attend their adult classes. (Hallelujah!) There are at least two adult volunteers who are called and trained to oversee the nursery. These teachers sing with the kids, teach them a short gospel lesson, give them a snack, and play games with them. As you can imagine, the people who serve in the nursery truly are saints, and they have one of the most important service jobs in the congregation. (The chance to sing "Jesus Wants Me for a Sunbeam" and eat a cookie? Sign me up!)

Young Men and Young Women Meetings

For one hour of the three-hour block of meetings, the youth (ages twelve to eighteen) separate by gender into their own classes.

The young men meet in their respective priesthood quorums (deacon, teacher, and priest) to conduct quorum business, learn their priesthood duties of service toward others, and study the gospel of Jesus Christ.

The young women meet together in their respective Young Women classes (Beehive, Mia Maid, and Laurel) to study Christ's teachings and to strengthen each other in the Young Women Values of the LDS Church, which are faith, divine nature, individual worth, knowledge, choice and accountability, good works, integrity, and virtue. (See chapter 20 for more about LDS teenagers.)

Adult Priesthood Meetings

The adult men (eighteen and older) gather together for a one-hour priesthood meeting. These meetings are usually divided up by priesthood office, with those who hold the authority of elder getting together in one class and those who hold the authority of high priest getting together in another. (See chapter 5 for more about the priesthood offices.) However, adult men who do not hold any priesthood office are welcome to attend these meetings as well.

The purposes of the priesthood meetings are to conduct quorum business, learn priesthood duties of service, strengthen families, and study the gospel of Jesus Christ. The priesthood classes are a great blessing to men in helping them to become better husbands and fathers and to receive support from a brotherhood of men striving to follow Jesus Christ.

The Women's Relief Society Meeting

Relief Society is an hour-long meeting for all women eighteen and older. Together, they learn the gospel of Jesus Christ, increase their faith and personal righteousness, strengthen their families, receive encouragement, and discuss how to help those in need. (See chapter 19 for more about Mormon women.) The Relief Society was established in 1842 by Joseph Smith and today is the largest women's organization in the world. It is a spiritual force of pure religion (see James 1:27) in Mormon congregations worldwide.

All Visitors Welcome

Printed below the Church's logo on our chapels you'll find "Visitors Welcome." That's because you do not have to be a Mormon to come learn and worship together with us, and anyone who wants to come to a Latter-day Saint chapel on a Sunday is appreciated and wanted.

And don't worry, you don't have to participate in the service or classes unless you desire; you can simply come and relax and enjoy the meetings. We don't pass a collection plate or ask you for money. You can come dressed in any modest clothing that you feel comfortable in, but most men come in suits with a shirt and a tie and the women wear dresses or skirts.

Check www.mormon.org to locate a Mormon meetinghouse and its worship service times near you.

23 | Mormons and Missionary Work

Perhaps you have seen LDS missionaries walking or riding their bikes through your neighborhood. Maybe they have even knocked on your door or you've visited with them. All over the world there are pairs of LDS missionaries—mostly young men and young women between nineteen and twenty-five years old, but often senior individuals and couples as well—who have dedicated eighteen to twenty-four months of their life to voluntarily serve others and teach others what Latter-day Saints believe is the restored gospel of Jesus Christ.

Perhaps nothing represents Mormonism to the world more than LDS missionaries.

Although it may seem like a daunting task, the LDS Church and its members take Jesus' mandate to His apostles literally: "Go ye therefore, and teach all nations, baptizing them in the name of the Father, and of the Son, and of the Holy Ghost" (Matthew 28:19). It is estimated that over the past 180 years since Samuel Smith (Joseph Smith's younger brother) was called as the first LDS missionary shortly after the Church was established in 1830, there have been more than one million LDS missionaries who have volunteered to serve.[1] Currently, **there are about 53,000 full-time LDS missionaries assigned to 340 missions** (geographic areas to where a missionary may be called) **in 145 countries.**[2] Through the efforts of these missionaries, each year hundreds and thousands of people join The Church of Jesus Christ of Latter-day Saints; in 2010, there were 272,814 converts baptized.[3]

Here is a little bit about one of the distinctive marvels of the LDS Church: its worldwide missionary program.

Of the 53,000 full-time LDS missionaries, about 80 percent are young, single men, 13 percent are young, single women, and 7 percent are retired couples.[4]

80%

13%

7%

What Do LDS Missionaries Do?

The guidebook for LDS missionaries, *Preach My Gospel*, says that the main job of an LDS missionary is to help people **"come unto Jesus Christ and become converted to His restored gospel."**[5] To accomplish this objective, LDS missionaries leave behind their regular lives and dedicate eighteen to twenty-four months of full-time service to teach others the gospel of Jesus Christ. Missionaries maintain a strict daily routine that looks something like this:

6:30 am Arise and exercise

7:30 am Breakfast

8:00 am–9:30 am Personal and companionship study/prayer

9:30 am–12:00 pm Teach/minister

12:00 pm–1:00 pm Lunch

1:00 pm–5:00 pm Teach/minister

5:00 pm–6:00 pm Dinner

6:00 pm–9:30 pm Teach/minister

9:30 pm–10:30 pm Plan for following day, pray, and retire for bed

LDS missionaries work twelve hours a day, six days a week. They have one day off (a "preparation day" or "P-day" in LDS missionary lingo) to wash clothes, write letters, play sports, or go grocery shopping. Their entire days are dedicated to trying to act and do as Christ would do: serving others, blessing them, praying with and for them, and teaching them. The work of an LDS missionary is entirely selfless in its nature and is truly a labor of love. Contrary to the societal notion that self-indulgence and ease make people happy, most LDS missionaries refer to their years of dedicated, disciplined, and difficult missionary service as the "best two years" of their lives.

Preach My Gospel

Preach My Gospel is the guide LDS missionaries use for their study, preparation, and teaching. The book contains the five main lessons that LDS missionaries teach to those who are interested in learning the basic doctrine of The Church of Jesus Christ of Latter-day Saints.

In the past, LDS missionaries gave specific "discussions" in a specific order—sometimes the lessons were memorized and delivered word for word—but *Preach My Gospel* tells LDS missionaries: "Which lesson you teach, when you teach it, and how much time you give to it" are up to the inspiration of the missionaries based on the situation. Missionaries are told "not to memorize the entire lesson"[6] but to speak in their own words and from the heart.

The missionary lessons and other chapters in *Preach My Gospel* are not confidential or available only to LDS missionaries; anyone—Latter-day Saint or not—can receive a copy of *Preach My Gospel* and study its content. It is available for download for free at http://lds.org.

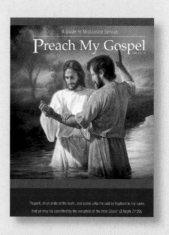

A Guide to Missionary Service

Preach My Gospel

"Repent, all ye ends of the earth, and come unto me and be baptized in my name, that ye may be sanctified by the reception of the Holy Ghost" (3 Nephi 27:20)

What Would Missionaries Do If I Invited Them In?

The main thing that a pair of LDS missionaries would do if invited into your home is simply **teach you a brief message about God the Father and His plan for His children** (see chapter 4), about the reestablishment of Jesus Christ's authorized Church on earth (see chapter 2), and try to answer any questions you may have about Mormonism. They won't ask you to buy anything or make a donation, and rarely will their visit last longer than forty-five minutes[7] (it can even be shorter if you would like it to be). The missionaries would probably leave you a free copy of the Book of Mormon and invite you to read a chapter or two in it and pray about the truthfulness of what you read.

If you are interested in learning more from the missionaries, you can schedule another appointment to talk with them. If you want to get in touch with the LDS missionaries in your area and they don't happen to be strolling down your street at that very moment (but who knows, providentially they just might be), you can request that LDS missionaries be sent to your home at www.mormon.org/missionaries or you can chat with official LDS missionaries online at the same site.

So Who's in Charge of All These Missionaries?

Each of the 340 LDS missions is presided over by a mission president—a mature man who is called and assigned by the Church to voluntarily administer the various affairs of an LDS mission for up to three years. The mission president (with his wife) helps train, teach, and watch over the missionaries who are serving in the mission field. He acts as the missionaries' ecclesiastical leader, and also helps to ensure that the missionaries are living the rules and standards that apply to LDS missionary service.

How Are LDS Missionaries Chosen and Called?

When the LDS Church was first established, people were sometimes called on the spot in the middle of meetings to serve missions. One time the Prophet Joseph Smith simply walked up to Heber C. Kimball (one of the original Mormon apostles) and said to him: "Brother Heber, the Spirit of the Lord has whispered to me: 'Let my servant Heber go to England and proclaim my Gospel, and open the door of salvation to that nation.'"[8] Shortly after that, Heber was on his way to England as a missionary.

However, today the process is a little different, and **those who serve LDS missions proactively volunteer for the call.** An unmarried LDS young man between the ages of nineteen and twenty-five is eligible for missionary service, and an unmarried LDS young woman aged twenty-one or older is also eligible.[9] The missionary is interviewed by his or her local bishop or stake president to ensure that the prospective missionary has faith in Jesus Christ and His restored Church, that he or she is living a life that is in harmony with the standards of the LDS Church, and that he or she is worthy to represent Jesus Christ and teach others of Him. The prospective missionary then fills out and sends in his or her "papers" (all the necessary forms and recommendations) to LDS Church headquarters in Salt Lake City, Utah.

There, a member of the Quorum of the Twelve Apostles reviews the papers and personally assigns each LDS missionary to his or her field of service, which could be anywhere in the world—from somewhere as exotic as the Caribbean to well, not-as-exotic Salt Lake City, Utah. (Believe it or not, there are many full-time missionaries sent to work in Salt Lake City.) Fifty percent of LDS missionaries end up serving somewhere in their home country, although usually not in their home city.[10] We believe that these assignments are made by heavenly inspiration, by prophecy, and by revelation, ensuring that the missionary is sent to where he or she is needed most.[11]

An official letter from LDS Church headquarters informs the future LDS missionary where he or she has been called to serve.

A short time after the mission assignment is made, an official letter from LDS Church headquarters is sent, informing the future LDS missionary where he or she has been called to serve and when to report to the missionary training center. Receiving this letter containing a mission call is one of the most anticipated and anxious days in the lives of prospective Latter-day Saint missionaries and their families.

Missionary Training Centers

A missionary training center (or an "MTC" as it is often referred to) is where full-time missionaries are sent at the beginning of their missions. Depending on where they are called to serve, missionaries will usually spend between three and twelve weeks in a missionary training center. There are fifteen MTCs around the world, the largest being in Provo, Utah. **At the MTC, missionaries better learn the doctrines of the LDS Church and how to teach others more effectively.**

The largest missionary training center is in Provo, Utah, adjacent to the Brigham Young University campus.

When a missionary has been called to serve in a foreign country, their training in the MTC also consists of state-of-the-art language training. It is not uncommon for an LDS missionary to enter the MTC without any previous training in their new foreign language, only to leave two months later able to communicate on a sufficient level to teach the gospel in a foreign tongue. (Many Latter-day Saints see this as the true reason for and a manifestation of the gift of tongues spoken of in the scriptures [see Acts 2:1–17; 1 Corinthians 12:10; Doctrine and Covenants 46:24]). Missionaries spend up to nine hours per day in MTC classes, which are taught primarily by former LDS missionaries.

Missionary Training Center by the Numbers

Here is a quick glimpse inside the Provo, Utah, Missionary Training Center:

1,800–2,500
Number of missionaries at the Provo MTC at any given time (the center has the capacity to handle up to 4,000 missionaries)

300–400
New missionaries that arrive every Wednesday

20,000
Missionaries that are trained at the Provo MTC each year

50
Number of languages taught at the MTC (including the more common, such as Spanish, but also the more rare, such as Icelandic)

19
Number of buildings on the Provo MTC campus, which covers more than thirty acres of property

4,000
Letters delivered and sorted each day (500 packages)

8,000–10,000
Meals served at the Provo MTC cafeteria each day

47,000
Gallons of milk (chocolate included) consumed in 2010 by Provo MTC missionaries[12]

Meet Your New Shadow: LDS Missionary Companions

Just as Jesus called His disciples "and began to send them forth by two and two" (Mark 6:7), LDS missionaries serve with a "companion" of the same gender during their entire mission; senior couples, though, serve with their spouses. Missionaries do not pick their companions, but are assigned who they will work with and for how long. (Talk about developing social skills!)

Throughout the entire mission, an LDS missionary is practically never alone and is always within earshot or eyesight of a companion. They live with their companions, eat with their companions, pray with, teach with, and serve with them all day, every day. There is obvious protection, support, and sustaining that comes from a missionary serving with a companion, but the reason for having missionaries

An LDS missionary is practically never alone.

paired up in twos has more to do with preaching than practicality. Jesus said **"that in the mouth of two or three witnesses every word may be established"** and "where two or three are gathered together in my name, there am I in the midst of them" (Matthew 18:16, 20). There is added protection that comes in twos, but, more importantly, there is added power.

In 2010, the number of LDS Church-service missionaries was 20,813.

Senior Couples and Church-Service Missionaries

Not only do single LDS young men and women serve missions, but so do many senior couples and individuals. Most of them fulfill what are known as "Church-service" missions: nonproselytizing missions where the missionaries simply volunteer and help serve in various ways in different communities. There are medical service missions, welfare service missions, and educational missions where people are taught to read and write. There are public affairs missions and accounting missions and landscaping missions and hosting missions. And that only scratches the surface. If you visit some of the major LDS sites in Salt Lake City, you will find Church-service missionaries everywhere. That nice old lady who took you on a tour of the LDS Church's Conference Center? She's a Church-service missionary. The nice man who helped you research your ancestry at the Family History Library? He's a Church-service missionary too. In 2010, the number of LDS Church-service missionaries was 20,813.[13]

MORMYTH: LDS missionaries can't date others during their mission, be romantically involved with someone, watch TV, listen to the radio, or call home during their missions.

Answer: True, true, true, true, and . . . mostly true.

Latter-day Saint missionaries follow strict rules that govern their behavior and help them remain focused on their missions. During their years of ordained missionary service, missionaries are forbidden to date or engage in intimate physical contact (a handshake is about as much physical affection as an LDS missionary is allowed). Missionaries don't watch TV shows, go to the movies, or listen to popular music. They don't surf the Internet. And speaking of surfing, they don't go swimming or hang out at the beach, even when they are called to serve in places like Hawaii (our dual respect and condolences go out to all tropical-sent missionaries).

Although they are allowed and encouraged to write or e-mail their parents and family members on a weekly basis, missionaries are usually limited to only a few phone calls home a year, traditionally on special occasions like Mother's Day and Christmas. All of these rules are designed to help LDS missionaries concentrate on their dedicated work to God and to minimize things that might distract them from their purpose and calling.

> The Prophet Joseph Smith reminded Latter-day Saints: "After all that has been said, [our] greatest and most important duty is to preach the Gospel."[14]

Why Do LDS Missionaries Wear Such Conservative Clothes?

The way an LDS missionary dresses reflects the seriousness of what Mormons feel is a sacred calling to represent the Lord Jesus Christ and teach His gospel. Everything about the appearance of an LDS missionary is therefore conservative in order to maintain the dignity of their call. LDS missionaries are counseled not to wear anything that is vain, faddish, immodest, sloppy, overly casual, or which might call attention to the messenger and detract from the message.[15] Maintaining high standards of dress and grooming helps our missionaries earn the trust and respect of those they teach and serve. Additionally, the

Everything about the appearance of an LDS missionary is therefore conservative in order to maintain the dignity of their call.

white shirts, dark suits, professional ties, and clean-cut hairstyles of the male missionaries and the modest and professional dresses of the female missionaries—along with the iconic black name tag, of course—help to clearly identify young men and women as missionaries for The Church of Jesus Christ of Latter-day Saints.

What's Your Name?

Ah, the Mormon missionary name tag. Each full-time missionary wears a black name badge with his or her last name along with the title of "Elder" (for young men) or "Sister" (for young women). (And yes, there are LDS young men with the last name of Elder, so for two years they have the pleasure of being called "Elder Elder." Let us know if you ever meet a Sister Sister.) "Elder" is a young man's priesthood title as a missionary. A missionary's name tag also bears the official name of the LDS Church on it.

How Much Do LDS Missionaries Get Paid?

Aside from the plane ticket to and from the mission, the missionary bears the entire cost of funding his or her mission.

Zip, zilch, nada, nothing. Yep, you read that right: **All LDS missionary service is free, gratis.** No bonuses for baptisms; no remuneration for reactivation. Oh, and get this: Not only do LDS missionaries serve for free, but they actually pay their own way for the opportunity to serve. Aside from the plane ticket to and from the mission, the missionary bears the entire cost of funding his or her mission. Currently the cost of a mission is $400 per month, which means that the average eighteen-month mission for a sister costs $7,200 and a twenty-four-month mission for an elder costs $9,600.

Why, you may ask, would a nineteen-year-old man or a twenty-one-year-old woman voluntarily give up two years of their life and pay their own way to serve an LDS mission? Well, just ask them; they'd be happy to tell you.

Do Mormons Have to Serve a Mission?

The requirement to serve a mission depends on whether you are a young man or a young woman. Latter-day Saint males who are ordained to priesthood offices make an oath and a covenant that they will use their priesthood to serve and bless others' lives by "bear[ing] this ministry and Priesthood unto all nations" (Abraham 2:9) and providing people with the ordinances of the gospel (i.e., baptism and conferral of the gift of the Holy Ghost). Therefore **an LDS young man who has been ordained to the priesthood is under a divine obligation and mandate to serve as a full-time LDS missionary.**

However, women in the LDS Church are not ordained to priesthood offices and therefore are not expected or required to serve as full-time missionaries, although they may do so if they choose to and if it does not interfere with an imminent marriage prospect.[16] It is estimated that currently about one-third of eligible LDS young men serve as full-time missionaries for the LDS Church.[17] Some young men are worthy to serve, but simply choose not to go; others are disqualified for a lack of worthiness or for immoral conduct. And some young men are honorably excused from serving for physical, mental, or emotional reasons.[18]

Some young men are honorably excused from serving for physical, mental, or emotional reasons.

Scan this QR code to meet **Tyler Haws**, a young Latter-day Saint who put his promising college basketball career on hold in order to serve an LDS mission.

24 Mormons and Money

Socrates said that a rich man's wealth "should not be praised until it is known how he employs it."[1] The same could be said about the wealth of an organization, including the LDS Church. Many people have commented over the years about the Church's abundant financial resources. In August 1997, *TIME* magazine's cover article, "Mormons, Inc.," called us "America's most prosperous religion," and reported that, based on financial figures provided by the Church, the LDS Church's assets were worth "a minimum of $30 billion" and that it had an "estimated $5.9 billion in annual gross income."[2]

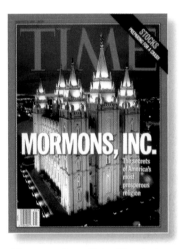

Time magazine called us "America's most prosperous religion."

Although it is difficult to estimate what the figure actually is—President Gordon B. Hinckley said the *Time* article "grossly exaggerated the figures"[3]—it is accurate to say that the LDS Church has money and knows how to manage it and use it.

Which leads us back to Socrates: Before we praise the Church's financial prowess—the "General Electric of American religion,"[4] as *Newsweek* said in 2011—just what does the Church do with all that wealth?

This chapter provides some important answers about Mormons and money.

Tithing

Most of the LDS Church's financial assets come from the voluntary payment of tithes by its members.[5] **Latter-day Saints pay "one-tenth of all their interest [income] annually" to the Church,** and the law of tithing is "a standing law . . . forever" to all members, rich or poor (Doctrine and Covenants 119:4). The marvelous thing about tithing is that faithful Latter-day Saints actually do this *voluntarily*. There is no collection plate passed around LDS congregations, and there are no Mormon tithing tax collectors in dark suits and sunglasses who are sent door-to-door to enforce payment. There are simply some small slips and envelopes outside the bishop's office so members can privately put money into an envelope, seal it, and turn it in to the bishop or to one of his two counselors. All tithes are then carefully accounted for by at least two persons.

At the end of each calendar year, Latter-day Saints have an interview, called "tithing settlement," with their bishop. Here, the bishop provides an individual with a report of all the moneys he or she has turned in for the year and asks if that amount represents a full tithe. If the member says "yes," he or she is considered a full-

There are some small slips and envelopes outside the bishop's office so members can privately put money into a sealed envelope and turn it in.

tithe payer. Once again, there is no verification and no pay-stub comparisons. Just a person's voluntary and faithful word.

One of the primary uses of tithing money is building and maintaining LDS temples.

Money that is collected from tithing is sent directly to Church head-quarters, where the First Presidency, the Quorum of the Twelve, and the Presiding Bishopric decide by inspiration where and how that sacred money should be spent.[6] **Tithing money is used primarily to build and maintain LDS meetinghouses and temples, fund family history work, provide religious education through the Church Educational System, conduct worldwide missionary work, and translate and publish the scriptures and other Church manuals.**[7] Tithing money is not used to pay for LDS clergy, as local congregations are run by a lay ministry, and full-time General Authorities' modest living allowances are paid by Church investments.[8] (See chapter 21 for more about the LDS lay ministry.)

A Chapel a Day Keeps the Devil Away

With the money collected from tithing, it is estimated that the LDS Church builds, on average, **one chapel every day** somewhere in the world.[9] In 1998, President Gordon B. Hinckley (1910–2008) reported that "'we will finish or dedicate 600 new buildings this year. This is a tremendous undertaking.'"[10]

Church Education

Much of tithing money is also used to finance the LDS Church Educational System. The Church owns and operates hundreds of LDS seminaries and institutes of religion across the world, and hires professional religious educators and staff to teach the youth and young adults gospel doctrine and principles.

Additionally, the Church owns and operates elementary and secondary schools in Fiji, Mexico, and the Polynesian islands. The Church also owns the largest private university in America[11]—Brigham Young University in Provo, Utah—and subsidizes its tuition and costs with tithing money. Thanks to this subsidy, Brigham Young University has been rated as one of the best-value, bang-for-your-buck private universities in the country.[12] Other Church universities and colleges include BYU–Hawaii, BYU–Idaho, and LDS Business College.

Fast Offerings

The first Sunday of each month, Latter-day Saints across the world choose to go without food or drink for two consecutive meals, or twenty-four hours.

The Doctrine and Covenants tells Latter-day Saints: "Thou wilt remember the poor, and consecrate of thy properties for their support that which thou hast to impart unto them" (Doctrine and Covenants 42:30). One of the ways we fulfill this Christlike directive is by fasting once a month and paying a fast offering (see Isaiah 58:7). The first Sunday of each month, members of Latter-day Saint congregations across the world choose to go without food or drink for two consecutive meals, or twenty-four hours. They then contribute the money they would have spent on food during their fast and donate it to the Church as a fast offering, which money is then used directly to help the poor and the needy within their own congregations and communities.

President Gordon B. Hinckley (1910–2008) said, "Think, my brethren, of what would happen if the principles of fast day and the fast offering were observed throughout the world. The hungry would be fed, the naked clothed, the homeless sheltered. Our burden of taxes would be lightened. The giver would not suffer but would be blessed by his small abstinence. A new measure of concern and unselfishness would grow in the hearts of people everywhere. Can anyone doubt the divine wisdom that created this program which has blessed the people of this Church as well as many who are not members of the Church?"[13]

"Think . . . of what would happen if the principles of fast day and the fast offering were observed throughout the world."—President Gordon B. Hinckley

Want to Earn a Nobel Prize and Quickly End World Hunger?

The United Nations estimates that it would cost about $195 billion to completely end world hunger, along with other diseases related to poverty and hunger.[14] If just the wealthiest 20 percent of the world fasted once each month, this problem could be solved.

- $195,000,000,000: Cost to end world hunger per year.
- $16,250,000,000: Cost to end world hunger per month.
- $13.54: Cost per month to end world hunger, per person for 1,200,000,000 people (20 percent of the world's population), if they fasted and gave that amount as a fast offering each month.

This map shows the percentage of those living on less than $1 per day, as of 2007.[15]

The LDS Welfare System

The Book of Mormon admonishes Latter-day Saints: "I would that ye should impart of your substance to the poor, every man according to that which he hath, such as feeding the hungry, clothing the naked, visiting the sick and administering to their relief, both spiritually and temporally, according to their wants" (Mosiah 4:26). Thus, one of the areas where the LDS Church spends its money—primarily fast offering money—is in the operation of a world-class welfare system, which was established during the Great Depression to help the poor and the needy. Since then, government leaders have taken note of this remarkable system. President Franklin D. Roosevelt had members of his staff meet for an hour with LDS Church leaders to discuss the Church's welfare program.[16] And when President Ronald Reagan came to Utah, he personally visited LDS Church welfare facilities, commenting, "'What I think is that if more people had this idea back when the Great Depression hit, there wouldn't be any government welfare today, or need for it. . . . **[It's] far superior to anything the government has been able to manage. . . . Oh, that our federal welfare worked so perfectly.'**"[17]

When President Ronald Reagan came to Utah, he personally visited LDS Church welfare facilities.

One thing that makes the LDS Church's welfare system so unique is that it not only grows, produces, and provides much of its own food to those in need—done almost entirely through volunteer efforts and service—but also that this system is set up to do away with the dole, not foster it. As the LDS Church First Presidency said in 1936: "Our primary purpose [is] to set up, in so far as it might be possible, a system under which the curse of idleness would be done away with, the evils of a dole abolished, and independence, industry, thrift and self respect be once more established amongst our people. **The aim of the Church is to help the people to help themselves.** Work is to be re-enthroned as the ruling principle."[18]

The LDS welfare system isn't intended just to help people, it is intended to help people help themselves. In LDS welfare, a person who needs assistance is authorized by the bishop to get food or financial assistance free of charge, but through the Church the bishop also helps provide opportunities for the person to work for what they receive to the extent possible. Additionally, the person is usually put in contact with LDS employment specialists and attends networking and employment training at LDS employment centers to help them obtain work and provide for themselves. **It is estimated that the average person spends only ten to twelve weeks receiving LDS assistance before they no longer need welfare.**[19]

Where's the Beef?

The LDS Church also owns and operates income-producing[20] investments and businesses in fields such as agribusiness, media, insurance, travel, and real estate. The Church has one of the top beef ranches in the world—the Deseret Cattle and Citrus Ranch—covering 312,000 acres in Orlando, Florida.

Mmm, I Love Mormon Pasta

Through its dairy, pasta, bakery, and canning facilities and plants, the LDS Church produces much of the food items it distributes, such as cheese, milk, jam, chili, peaches, soup, and spaghetti just to name a few (and they are good too!). These items are sent to hundreds of bishops' storehouses around the world, where the food items are given to the poor and needy free of charge.

28,000 LDS Bishops Seeking Out the Poor and the Needy

LDS bishops—all 28,000 of them[21]—have a divine mandate to seek out the poor and the needy in their congregations (see Doctrine and Covenants 84:112). To accomplish this task, LDS bishops enlist priesthood and Relief Society leaders, the ward council, and home and visiting teachers to identify those within the congregation who need welfare assistance (see chapter 21 for more on these organizations). The bishop then arranges to meet with those in need to determine what the Church can provide or assist with to sustain life (but not lifestyle). Before he offers Church help, the bishop ascertains first if extended family may help. If not, then the bishop provides commodities of food and other needed items through the bishops' storehouse and various Church services, directing those who are receiving assistance to work to the extent possible for the help they receive.

The LDS Church welfare system also provides additional services that can be of help to families.

LDS Family Services: LDS Family Services helps people resolve social and emotional challenges in life through professional counseling services, including counseling for marital and family issues, and addiction recovery. It also provides counseling services to unwed mothers and helps place children with adoptive parents.

Deseret Industries: At Deseret Industries, people donate their used clothing and household items, which are then sold in secondhand thrift stores operated by the LDS Church. The stores and donation program help provide work and vocational training for people who are currently unemployable in the market, allowing them to gain job skills and experience and become more self-reliant.

Employment Centers: There are about 300 LDS employment centers around the world that help those in need with employment and education. The centers have local job postings, provide one-on-one coaching, help people prepare resumes and for job interviews, and provide phone lines, copiers, Internet access, and fax machines for those who are searching for jobs. The centers also provide career workshops and training programs to help people network and expand their employable capacities.[22]

2010 LDS Welfare System Facts

777,381	Days of labor donated to LDS Church welfare facilities
168,713	Employment placements
8,583	LDS missionaries serving in welfare service missions (such as teaching English, parenting skills, etc.)
326	Employment resource centers
143	Bishops' storehouses
79	LDS Family Services offices
43	Deseret Industries thrift stores
23	Processing facilities for producing food and other items[23]

This silo at Salt Lake City's Welfare Square contains enough grain to feed a small city for about six months.

The Lord's Storehouse

Although it is not a formal operation in the LDS Church's welfare program, the Lord's storehouse is the system that is probably called upon most often to help others. The Lord's storehouse is different from the bishops' storehouse. In LDS lingo, **the Lord's storehouse is the combined and consecrated talents, time, means, and materials of all the members of the LDS Church.**

Latter-day Saint scripture teaches us that our talents are "to be cast into the Lord's storehouse, . . . every man seeking the interest of his neighbor, and doing all things with an eye single to the glory of God" (Doctrine and Covenants 82:18–19). This means that when a poor and needy Latter-day Saint family has a hole in their roof and lacks the money to fix it, the problem may be brought before the congregation through the various LDS Church quorums and auxiliaries. In this case, not only could money be gathered and given, but members of the congregation would use their talents and experience, their tools and materials, and their time, and get up on the roof and get it fixed. The Relief Society might organize the effort, the young men and the elders quorum might actually fix the roof, and the young women might provide refreshments and water. That is one small example of how the Lord's storehouse could and does work in the LDS Church. The Lord's storehouse exists in each LDS congregation and is called upon often.[24]

Provident Living

A vital part of the LDS Church's welfare system is teaching its members how to live providently so they are self-reliant and self-sufficient to the greatest extent possible. There are six primary areas the Church emphasizes with its members to facilitate self-reliance.[25]

Here's a brief summary of two of these six areas of self-reliance.

Latter-day Saints try to live providently in six primary areas.

Home Food Storage

Latter-day Saints are counseled to store food in their homes. The LDS First Presidency in 2007 said: "We encourage members worldwide to prepare for adversity in life by having a basic supply of food and water and some money in savings."[26] **Latter-day Saints are encouraged to build up a three-month supply of food that is consumed in a regular, daily diet and then to rotate through that food regularly.** (Think of it like a home grocery store, where you can take what is needed from storage and then replace what was taken.) Additionally, when circumstances make it possible, Church members are also counseled to store a one-year's supply of the basic food necessary to sustain life, such as wheat, rice, and beans (items that can last thirty years or more without spoilage).[27]

Personal Finances

LDS Church members are taught the basics of family finances to help ensure self-sufficiency and to provide for themselves and their families. **Mormons are taught to avoid consumer debt, pay their tithing, set a budget, build up a savings reserve, and teach family members about finances.**[28] The LDS First Presidency said: "We encourage you wherever you may live in the world to prepare for adversity by looking to the condition of your finances. We urge you to be modest in your expenditures; discipline yourselves in your purchases to avoid debt. . . . If you have paid your debts and have a financial reserve, even though it be small, you and your family will feel more secure and enjoy greater peace in your hearts."[29]

LDS Humanitarian Aid

The Prophet Joseph Smith said, "A man filled with the love of God, is not content with blessing his family alone, but ranges through the whole world, anxious to bless the whole human race."[30] Aside from its welfare services, **the LDS Church strives to bless the whole human race through its humanitarian efforts** for people of all faiths who are suffering in various parts of the world. Recently, the humanitarian efforts of The Church of Jesus Christ of Latter-day Saints provided disaster relief after the earthquakes in Haiti, Indonesia, and Chile and after the 2009 tsunami in Samoa.

Latter-day Saint congregations are mobilized all over the world during disasters to provide service. They often wear bright yellow T-shirts with "Mormon Helping Hands" printed on them.

The LDS Church reports that its humanitarian efforts have donated $1.3 billion in assistance in 178 different countries between 1985 and 2010.[31] It has also given

- 14,345 tons of medical supplies
- 63,377 tons of food
- 93,196 tons of clothing
- 11.1 million hygiene, newborn, and school kits.[32]

To date, the Church's humanitarian efforts have also drilled and dug wells that have helped seven million people in 5,000 communities gain access to clean water,[33] aided 54,080 people in eleven countries in receiving vision care (such as cataract surgery to heal preventable blindness), and provided medical training, such as in neonatal resuscitation, for more than 30,000 medical personnel in developing countries, saving countless lives.[34] The Church does all of this (and much more) free of charge and for people of all faiths.

The Prophet Joseph Smith taught that a true Latter-day Saint "is to feed the hungry, to clothe the naked, to provide for the widow, to dry up the tear of the orphan, to comfort the afflicted, whether in this church, or in any other, or in no church at all, wherever he finds them."[35]

Meet some people who have been helped by the Mormons!

Scan this QR code to watch a video of the effect that an LDS Church-provided well has on a group of people in Sierra Leone.

MORMYTH: The LDS Church cares more about building its temples and churches than caring for the poor and the needy.

Answer: False.

The LDS Church has a broad mission that includes not only caring for the poor and the needy but three other areas that also bless people's lives: "helping members live the gospel of Jesus Christ, gathering Israel through missionary work, . . . and enabling the salvation of the dead by building temples and performing vicarious ordinances."[36]

While much of the Church's money and assets are consumed in areas not directly involved with caring for the needy, when the LDS Church welfare system was established just after the Great Depression, President **Heber J. Grant** said the Church was to "reach out and take care of the people" no matter what the cost even if it had to

go so far as to "close the seminaries, shut down missionary work for a period of time, or even close the temples. . . . They would not let the people go hungry."[37]

In 2011, LDS Presiding Bishop H. David Burton (who oversees temporal welfare matters for the entire LDS Church) said: "No matter how many temples we build, no matter how large our membership grows, no matter how positively we are perceived in the eyes of the world—should we fail in this great core commandment to 'succor the weak, lift up the hands which hang down, and strengthen the feeble knees' (Doctrine and Covenants 81:5), or turn our hearts from those who suffer and mourn, we are under condemnation and cannot please the Lord."[38]

25 Mormons, Politics, and America

It's said that people should avoid discussing religion and politics in polite company. Well, how about we talk about both, and then add a little American nationalism to the mix? Ready?

Mormons have a notable and colorful past when it comes to politics, religion, and America. (For example, consider the establishment of Zion, the Missouri extermination order, the Utah War, the practice of polygamy and the Edmunds–Tucker Act, just to name a few.) Although today many view Latter-day Saints as good citizens,[1] some people still wonder about the Church's position on politics and religion, especially as Latter-day Saints such as Mitt Romney, Harry Reid, and others participate in the political spotlight.

Mormons have a notable and colorful past when it comes to politics, religion, and America.

Can a Mormon politician sign a bill that is against what the LDS Church teaches? Can a faithful Mormon be a Democrat? Do Latter-day Saints want to mix church and state?

Before you cast your next ballot in the election booth, here are some facts about the Church's official position on matters relating to politics, government, and America.

Did you know that between 1857 and 1858 there was a war called the Utah War? After receiving exaggerated and sensationalized reports of a Mormon rebellion against the United States, President James Buchanan sent armed forces to Utah to quell it. With the LDS Church still reeling from the Missouri extermination order and their forced exodus from Illinois, and unsure of the federal government's motives and reasons for sending a federal army to Utah—Buchanan had failed, after all, to notify Brigham Young that he was replacing him with Alfred Cumming as the territorial governor of Utah—the Saints feared another governmental extermination and prepared to defend themselves. Although a few skirmishes took place, no actual battles occurred, and the "war" ended peacefully through negotiations as Brigham Young stepped down as governor and turned the office over to Cumming.

America in LDS Church Doctrine

Latter-day Saint theology teaches that the United States of America is a promised land.

Latter-day Saint theology teaches that the United States of America is a promised land and "a land which is choice above all other lands" (Ether 2:10). Joseph Smith taught that **"the whole of America is Zion itself from north to south"**[2] and that the latter-day city of Zion spoken of in the scriptures will be built in the United States of America (see Revelation 3:12; 21:2; Ether 13:3–10; Doctrine and Covenants 42:9; Articles of Faith 1:10).

A recurring theme in the Book of Mormon is that **America is a choice land, with God leading chosen groups of people to it,** including the Jaredites (a group of people led here during the biblical Tower of Babel dispersion) and Lehi and his family (the principal group in the Book of Mormon). America is a land "consecrated unto him whom [God] shall bring" (2 Nephi 1:7). We believe that many people and groups, including Columbus, the Pilgrims, and others, came to America (see 1 Nephi 13:12–13) and were "wrought upon" by the Spirit of God in their journeys (1 Nephi 13:12). **We believe that God had a hand in establishing the United States of America as a land of liberty to act as a "prologue for the restoration of the gospel."**[3]

We believe that many people and groups, including Columbus, came to America and were "wrought upon" by the Spirit of God in their journeys.

The Book of Mormon declares: "For it is wisdom in the Father that [the founders] should be established in this land, and be set up as a free people by the power of the Father, that these things [the Book of Mormon and the reestablishment of Christ's Church] might come forth" (3 Nephi 21:4). However, this land of liberty comes with a condition: "And now," warned the Book of Mormon prophet Moroni, "we can behold the decrees of God concerning this land, that it is a land of promise; and whatsoever nation shall possess it shall serve God, or they shall be swept off when the fulness of his wrath shall come upon them. And the fulness of his wrath cometh upon them when they are ripened in iniquity" (Ether 2:9).

Scriptural Teachings Regarding Government

The types, systems, and roles of governments are a recurring theme in LDS scriptures. The Book of Mormon speaks at length about kings and monarchs, beginning with Nephi's declaration that his people "should have no king" (2 Nephi 5:18) although they considered him such. Later, the Book of Mormon teaches that "because all men are not just it is not expedient that ye should have a king or kings to rule over you" and warns about "how much iniquity doth one wicked king cause to be committed" (Mosiah 29:16–17).

The Book of Mormon says to "do your business by the voice of the people" (Mosiah 29:26).

The Book of Mormon people implemented a system of judges who were selected "by the voice of the people"—a phrase mentioned in the Book of Mormon twenty-two times. The Book of Mormon says this about democracy: "Now it is not common that the voice of the people desireth anything contrary to that which is right; but it is common for the lesser part of the people to desire that which is not right; therefore this shall ye observe and make it your law—to do your business by the voice of the people" (Mosiah 29:26). However, the Book of Mormon teaches that if "they who chose evil [are] more numerous than they who chose good" then the people are "ripening for destruction" (Helaman 5:2; see also Mosiah 29:27).

There is an entire section of the Doctrine and Covenants (section 134) dedicated to politics, providing twelve statements of LDS belief regarding governments, some of which are that:

■ "Governments were instituted of God for the benefit of man; and that he holds men accountable for their acts in relation to them" (verse 1).

■ Governments should "secure to each individual the free exercise of conscience, the right and control of property, and the protection of life" (verse 2).

■ "We do not believe it just to mingle religious influence with civil government, whereby one religious society is fostered and another proscribed in its spiritual privileges" (verse 9), and that governments should stay out of religion unless religious worship causes a person "to infringe upon the rights and liberties of others" (verse 4).

■ "We believe that all men are bound to sustain and uphold the respective governments in which they reside" (verse 5).

Or, in the words of one of the Articles of Faith, "We believe in being subject to kings, presidents, rulers, and magistrates, in obeying, honoring, and sustaining the law" (Articles of Faith 1:12).

Our scriptures teach us that in selecting government officials, "honest men and wise men should be sought for diligently, and good men and wise men ye should observe to uphold" (Doctrine and Covenants 98:10). Ultimately, regarding government, we believe that one day Jesus will return to earth and "that Christ will reign personally upon the earth" (Articles of Faith 1:10) and assume His rightful role as King of kings and Lord of lords over the whole earth.

The US Constitution and Freedom

A 2011 *Newsweek* article accurately stated that "the theme of freedom—and the threat of losing it—runs through much of Mormonism."[4] One of our core doctrines is that of "agency"—the power of a person to exercise independent action and choice. Latter-day Saints believe that, in the premortal existence before we came to earth, Satan "sought to destroy the agency of man" (Moses 4:3) and that all mankind fought a war against Satan and his followers in order to protect our freedom to choose. Thus, we believe one reason **God inspired the Constitution of the United States**—and its subsequent effect in liberating other nations—was **so people could be "free to choose"** (2 Nephi 2:27) **and exercise their moral agency.**

We believe that God inspired the Constitution of the United States of America.

Latter-day Saint scriptures teach that God suffered the "constitution . . . to be established" and that it "should be maintained for the rights and protection *of all flesh*, according to just and holy principles; that every man may act . . . according to the moral agency which I have given unto him" (Doctrine and Covenants 101:77–78; emphasis added).

Latter-day Saints believe that God had His hand in the founding of America and the framing of its Constitution, complete with its inherent rights and freedoms. Mormon doctrine states that the great pantheon of Founding Fathers who established America and its Constitution—Washington, Jefferson, Adams, Franklin, Madison, and Hamilton, among others—were "wise men whom [God] raised up unto this very purpose" (Doctrine and Covenants 101:80). LDS Church President Wilford Woodruff (1807–1898) declared that "those men who laid the foundation of this American government . . . were the best spirits the God of heaven could find on the face of the earth. They were choice spirits [and] were inspired of the Lord."[5]

In his 1789 inaugural address, George Washington said: "No people can be bound to acknowledge and adore the invisible hand, which conducts the Affairs of men more than the People of the United States. Every step, by which they have advanced to the character of an independent nation, seems to have been distinguished by some token of providential agency."[6]

James Madison, often referred to as the Father of the Constitution, wrote, "It is impossible for the man of pious reflection not to perceive in it a finger of that Almighty hand which has been so frequently and signally extended to our relief in the critical stages of the revolution."[7]

Charles Pinckney, a very active participant during the Constitutional Convention and the author of the Pinckney Plan, said: "When the great work [of the Constitution] was done and published, . . . I was struck with amazement. Nothing less than the superintending Hand of Providence, that so miraculously carried us through the war . . . could have brought it about so complete, upon the whole."[8]

In short, Mormons believe the Constitution of the United States to be, in the words of Joseph Smith, "a glorious standard; . . . a heavenly banner."[9] Our hope and prayer is the same as what Joseph Smith prayed at the dedication of the first LDS temple, in Kirtland, Ohio, in 1836: "May those principles, which were so honorably and nobly defended, namely, the Constitution of our land, by our fathers, be established forever" (Doctrine and Covenants 109:54).

Will the Constitution "Hang by a Thread"?

There is a persistent rumor that "the Constitution will hang by a thread" and that the Latter-day Saints will rescue it from ruin. This prophecy is attributed to Joseph Smith and is sometimes called the White Horse Prophecy. However, it has been refuted by Church authorities on multiple occasions as unofficial. The idea was apparently written down by a man named Edwin Rushton nearly fifty years after Joseph Smith's death.[10]

Political Neutrality

The LDS First Presidency repeatedly emphasizes the Church's official position of political neutrality, which is that The Church of Jesus Christ of Latter-day Saints does not officially support any political party or any candidate. In their own words, the LDS Church "does not:

- "Endorse, promote or oppose political parties, candidates or platforms.

- "Allow its church buildings, membership lists or other resources to be used for partisan political purposes.

- "Attempt to direct its members as to which candidate or party they should give their votes. This policy applies whether or not a candidate for office is a member of The Church of Jesus Christ of Latter-day Saints.

- "Attempt to direct or dictate to a government leader. . . .

"In the United States, where nearly half of the world's Latter-day Saints live, it is customary for the Church at each national election to issue a letter to be read to all congregations encouraging its members to vote, but emphasizing the Church's neutrality in partisan political matters."[11]

That being said, Mormons—and Utah in particular—are one of the "most conservative major religious groups in [America]," with 59 percent of LDS respondents identifying themselves as "conservative" and 31 percent identifying themselves as "moderate," according to a 2010 Gallup poll.[12] A 2007 Pew study found that about two-thirds (65 percent) of Mormons identify with the Republican party, which is 15 percent higher than evangelicals (50 percent) and 30 percent higher than the general population (35 percent). Only one-fifth of Mormons (22 percent) say they are Democrats, and the remainder say they do not favor either party.[13]

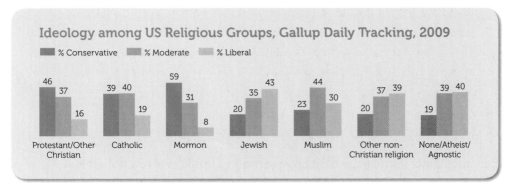

Ideology among US Religious Groups, Gallup Daily Tracking, 2009

■ % Conservative   ■ % Moderate   ■ % Liberal

	Conservative	Moderate	Liberal
Protestant/Other Christian	46	37	16
Catholic	39	40	19
Mormon	59	31	8
Jewish	20	35	43
Muslim	23	44	30
Other non-Christian religion	20	37	39
None/Atheist/Agnostic	19	39	40

Conservative

☐ **Moderate**

☐ **Liberal**

If the LDS Church Has a Position of Political Neutrality, Then Why Do They Speak Out on Political Issues?

Polls show that Mormons are one of the most conservative major religious groups in America.

The Prophet Joseph Smith said: "It is our duty to concentrate all our influence to make popular that which is sound and good, and unpopular that which is unsound. 'Tis right, politically, for a man who has influence to use it. . . . From henceforth I will maintain all the influence I can get."[14] **Although the LDS Church has a position of political neutrality when it comes to parties and candidates, that doesn't mean they are politically neutral or must keep silent when it comes to public policy on moral or ethical issues.**

The LDS Church leadership can and often does speak out on moral or ethical issues and makes their stance known.

Like any other individual or group involved in a democratic republic, the LDS Church leadership can, should, and often does speak out on moral or ethical issues and make their stance known. The Church has spoken out on a variety of moral issues, ranging from alcohol and gambling laws to abortion and, most recently, on same-gender marriage. The Church's formal statement declares that the LDS Church will "reserve the right as an institution to address, in a nonpartisan way, issues that it believes have significant community or moral consequences or that directly affect the interests of the Church."[15]

Mormons in Government Office

Latter-day Saints have been involved in local and national government since the earliest days of the Church. Joseph Smith was the mayor of Nauvoo, Illinois, and Brigham Young was the first governor of the territory of Utah. There have been Mormons in the US House of Representatives, the Senate, and the Cabinet. Mormons have even campaigned for the office of United States president. As of 2011, there are fifteen Latter-day Saints in the 112th Congress, with five in the Senate (two Democrats and three Republicans, including current Democratic Senate Majority Leader Harry Reid) and ten in the House (eight Republicans and two Democrats).[16]

Ezra Taft Benson served as Secretary of Agriculture in President Dwight D. Eisenhower's cabinet while he was also serving as a member of the LDS Church's Quorum of the Twelve Apostles.

Latter-day Saint Mike Leavitt, former governor of Utah, served as the Secretary of Health and Human Services in President George W. Bush's Cabinet.

There are some people who fear Latter-day Saint participation in government, falsely believing that a Mormon candidate's first loyalties are to the LDS Church and its directives, rather than to their constituents or the Constitution. The LDS Church's official statement declares: **"Elected officials who are Latter-day Saints make their own decisions and may not necessarily be in agreement with one another or even with a publicly stated Church position.** While the Church may communicate its views to them, as it may to any other elected official, it recognizes that these officials still must make their own choices based on their best judgment and with consideration of the constituencies whom they were elected to represent."[17]

Orrin Hatch, the ranking member of the Senate Committee on Finance and former chairman of the Senate Judiciary Committee, is a Latter-day Saint.

A Mormon US President?

Former Massachusetts governor Mitt Romney is a Mormon.

In the 1960s and 1970s, many minority and religious groups faced an unfair political bias, with 20 percent to 30 percent of the country saying they would not vote for a United States president who was, for example, a woman or an African-American or Jewish. Yet today, long after the political bias against those groups has dwindled, there seems to still be some resistance to voting for a Mormon president.

A 2011 Gallup poll found that 22 percent of Americans still would discriminate against a Mormon candidate in the 2012 presidential election. (Only two subgroups fared worse than Mormons—32 percent of Americans said they would not vote for a gay or lesbian candidate, and 49 percent said they would not vote for an atheist candidate.)[18] There is hope that the American bias will subside for Mormonism the way it has for other subgroups. In 1959, the year before John F. Kennedy won the presidency, 25 percent of Americans said they would not vote for a Catholic. By 1961, that number had dropped to 13 percent. And as of 2011, it is only 7 percent.

In 1959, the year before John F. Kennedy won the presidency, 25 percent of Americans said they would not vote for a Catholic.

Interestingly, it appears that those who are less likely to vote for a Mormon president do so more out of a misunderstanding about the LDS Church's doctrinal belief in salvation through Christ than anything else (see chapter 3). A 2007 Pew Forum poll found that 42 percent of those who believe the Mormon religion is not Christian say they would not vote for a Mormon president, whereas only 16 percent of those who believe Mormonism *is* a Christian faith would not vote for a Mormon.[19]

A 2011 Gallup poll found that 22 percent of Americans would not vote for a Mormon candidate in the 2012 presidential election.

Willingness to Vote for Person of Various Characteristics for President

	Yes, would vote for	No, would not	No opinion
	%	%	%
Black	94	5	1
A woman	93	6	1
Catholic	92	7	1
Baptist	92	7	1
Jewish	89	9	2
Hispanic	89	10	1
Mormon	76	22	2
Gay or lesbian	67	32	2
An atheist	49	49	3

July 9–12, 2011

26 The Weird and Wonderful World of Mormon Culture

Over the years, Mormons have developed some distinct and peculiar cultural quirks. Some of these aspects of Mormon culture can be found around the world, but others are more prevalent in the American West—Utah, in particular—where Mormons have been rubbing off on each other for more than a century and a half. **These cultural idiosyncrasies are not officially taught by LDS Church leaders as part of Church doctrine, but they still find their way into the LDS lifestyle.** For example, nowhere in the scriptures will you find a verse that says, "Thou shalt eat 'funeral potatoes,'" and yet most Mormons cheerfully continue to cook and eat the unique dish that combines potatoes, crushed corn flakes, and cheese at congregational picnics, at baby blessings, and, yes, at funerals too.

Some aspects of Mormon culture are more prevalent in the American West—Utah, in particular.

We're not afraid to laugh at ourselves or poke a little fun at some of these social traditions that are common to Mormonism, so sit back and enjoy a smattering of some of the unofficial, peculiar, eccentric, and sometimes downright weird cultural aspects of the LDS Church.

The 24th of July

Betcha didn't know that Utahns and many Mormons have their own holiday that rivals the Fourth of July, did ya? Yep. Parades, floats, barbeques, fireworks—the works. It's July 24th, the day when the Mormon pioneers entered the Salt Lake Valley after their epic journey across the American wilderness. Don't get us wrong, we celebrate the Fourth of July to its fullest along with the rest of the country (well, minus the alcoholic beverages, of course). But twenty days later, the state of Utah—and many non-Utah Mormons as well—celebrate all over again, but this time there are bonnets and covered wagons mixed in with the stars and stripes in the parades.

Pioneer Trek

To commemorate and remember the Mormon pioneer exodus west in the 1800s, many LDS congregations take their youth on a pioneer trek. For a few days, LDS youth leave behind their iPods, cell phones, cozy beds, and other comforts of modern living and voluntarily trudge for miles through the wilderness in pioneer clothing, pulling handcarts, eating hardtack, and sleeping on the ground.

To commemorate and remember the Mormon pioneer exodus west in the 1800s, many LDS congregations take their youth on a pioneer trek.

Although it may seem bizarre to have our youth voluntarily slap on bonnets and pull handcarts, they learn a lot of lessons along the way, most notably about the fire of faith that caused thousands of Mormons in the 1800s to choose to make the same trek, but for real.

Culturally weird? Perhaps. Culturally significant? Without a doubt.

The "Holy War"

This war has nothing to do with the Crusades. For many Mormons, the "Holy War" repeats each year when LDS-Church-owned Brigham Young University (BYU) and the University of Utah (U of U) square off in college football. The two universities—known simply as the "Y" and the "U"—are both located in Utah, about forty-five miles apart, but there is no love lost between their fans. The added religious aspect of the rivalry can make Ohio State versus Michigan seem like a grade-school game of kickball. Some BYU fans think that

For many Mormons, the "Holy War" repeats each year when BYU and the U of U square off in college football.

the "Y" has a divine destiny to win because of the school's religious affiliation (especially against those heathens at the U of U—a university, ironically, that was started by Brigham Young and that boasts a large number of Mormon students, fans, and players). And most U of U fans want nothing more than to put BYU fans in their supposedly stuffy, strict, self-righteous place. For a week, fans and players talk friendly trash, cite past triumphs, and then watch the teams battle it out on the field. Then many U of U fans and BYU fans get up the next morning and go to church together and call each other brother and sister. It's fun, and a little bizarre. We admit it.

"Obviously, when you're doing what's right on and off the field, I think the Lord steps in and plays a part in it. Magic happens."
—Former BYU wide receiver Austin Collie, after a BYU win over the U of U

"When Brigham Young came into the valley, he pointed to where the University of Utah would be and said, 'This is the place.' Provo was just an afterthought."—Former Utah head coach Ron McBride

Ice Cream, Cookies, and Jell-O—Oh, My!

Did you know that Utah leads the nation in sales of ice cream? And that in 2011, Utah also led the nation in Girl Scout cookie sales?[1] And don't even get us started on green Jell-O, which Utahns consume at a higher rate per capita than any other place, not only in the United States but in the *world*. In 2001, Jell-O was actually designated as the official Utah state snack.[2] You know you're a Mormon when Jell-O mixed with shaved carrots makes you go, "Mmm, pass that bad boy over here."

In 2001, Jell-O was actually designated as the official Utah state snack.

What's under Your Bed?

Because LDS prophets have counseled us to store food both as a principle of provident living and in case of emergency, many Mormons have a storage of food set aside in their homes. Some Mormons gather as much as a two-year supply of food, which means white buckets of oats get crammed into all sorts of nooks and crannies. (How resourceful, a five-gallon lamp stand! You fit all those boxes of powdered milk under your bed? You are a Tetris master.) All that two-year-old Top Ramen should be used and rotated regularly, which means there are actual cookbooks specifically designed for LDS food storage items. Yummy, do I smell cracked wheat delight?

Where to fit all those five-gallon buckets of wheat? A lampstand! How resourceful!

CTR Ring Bling

Mormons have a familiar saying that even Primary kids know: Choose the Right. We even sing a little song, "Choose the right when a choice is placed before you."[3] To help them remember to try to choose the right, we give our Primary kids little rings with the acronym CTR on it. The kids love those rings. But so do some Mormon youth, and adults too. Lately all sorts of cool-looking CTR rings have popped up, many on par with rings sold at a jewelry store instead of the kind worn by a preschooler. So, if you bump into a Mormon sporting a pure sterling silver ring with the letters CTR, those are not the initials of a spouse (although that would be convenient!). The person is simply wearing a reminder to try to make good choices.

Helpful? Sometimes. Culturally weird? Just slightly.

"The Best Two Years"

If you are with a Mormon man and you ask him what the best two years of his life were, get ready to hear about slammed doors, barking dogs, unusual cuisine, and days spent preaching the gospel. The phrase "the best two years" is a common summary applied to the years spent serving an LDS mission. (See chapter 23 for more about LDS missionary work.) It's such a well-known phrase that there is even a popular Mormon movie called *The Best Two Years*. Obviously the best two years of a Latter-day Saint's life are not restricted to their early twenties, but those years of service often provide some of the best opportunities for spiritual growth and personal development in a young person's life. So, unless you want to hear about their LDS missionary service (and maybe you do), we'd recommend you avoid combining "best" and "two" and "years" in any sentence during a discussion with a former Mormon missionary.

Play Ball!

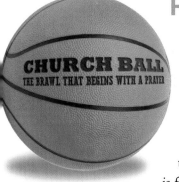

Each year many LDS congregations form a team and play other local congregations in (ideally) friendly games of basketball and other sports. These games are meant to foster congregational unity and love—and they often do—but they can also bring about temper tantrums and trips to the hospital. Although there is no money paid or press coverage, for some Mormons the idea of taking first place in the "stake" is more important than taking state is for school athletes. Many church ballers are determined to prove to their spouses and fellow Mormons that if Coach would have just put them in the big game back in high school they coulda gone pro. Mormons often joke that Church ball is the only brawl that begins with a prayer.

Mormons often joke that Church ball is the only brawl that begins with a prayer.

Wedding Receptions in a Gym?

Many of our American LDS churches have a basketball court (or a "cultural hall" as they are officially called) smack in the middle of the building. The LDS Church allows their buildings to be used for wedding receptions for free, so it is not uncommon for Mormons to hold their reception in the cultural hall of their local LDS meetinghouse. In other words, you might see beautiful white streamers running through a basketball hoop while attending a Mormon wedding reception.

Economical? Definitely. A little weird when you think about it? Ditto.

These Are My Kids—Moroni, Mosiah, and Mahonri Moriancumr

Lots of people give their kids biblical names (Adam, Dan, or Sarah, for example). Mormons do that too, but we also give our kids scriptural names from the Book of Mormon. If you are at a soccer game and you hear a mom yell, "Go get him, Nephi!" or "Nice shot, Helaman!" you know there's a Mormon on the field. Also—like many families with a lot of children—some Mormons have this alliteration thing with naming their kids. If you meet your new neighbors and they have five kids with names that all begin with the same letter ("This is Ammon, Alyssa, Adrian, Alvin, and Adam"), then odds are some good ol' Mormon culture is being put to use.

If you are at a soccer game and you hear a mom yell, "Go get him, Nephi!" or "Nice shot, Helaman!" you know there's a Mormon on the field.

Fold Your Arms and Bless That Donut

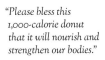

"Please bless this 1,000-calorie donut that it will nourish and strengthen our bodies."

Mormons pray in much the same way as everyone else who believes in God does, but some things are uniquely part of the LDS culture of prayer. For example, mainstream Christians will often join hands in a circle or put their arm on the person they are praying with. Mormons? We fold our arms tight and squint our eyes closed. We don't have to do this, but for some reason it's a culturally common way of trying to be reverent. Also, you'll probably hear this unofficial phrase almost word for word in many Mormon prayers over food (even if it's a 1,000-calorie donut): "Please bless this food that it will nourish and strengthen our bodies." Mmm, fold my arms and let me eat.

Arts and Crafts—Not Just for School Projects Anymore

Some Mormon women love their arts and crafts, and even have designated "Super Saturdays" where they get together and make handmade items for their homes. We make things like family home evening charts (see chapter 7), Mod Podge pictures of Jesus on ceramic tiles, and use vinyl letters to write familiar sayings like "Families Are Forever" on our walls. These craft events are wonderful, fun, social, and creative, but they also make for some downright bizarre decorations in the homes of some Mormons. (Are those Joseph Smith and Brigham Young bookends? Nice!)

Brigham Young and Joseph Smith bookends? Nice!

Mormon Blogs

For years Mormons have been counseled to keep a journal and record their life experiences and thoughts. Then, lo and behold, blogs were invented! Hallelujah! Now, countless Mormons document their daily musings, detail their do-it-yourself projects, share family happenings, and post cute photos of their kids online. There are Mormon mommy blogs, Mormon cooking blogs, Mormon design blogs, and even a large group of blogs known collectively as "The Bloggernacle" (a pun off of the Mormon Tabernacle). So, thanks to the Internet, Mormons can now

There are so many Mormon blogs out there that they have earned their own collective name.

keep in contact with their extended families, spread the joy of living the gospel, and keep a journal of their lives, all with a click of a mouse. Now that's *efficient* cultural weirdness!

Countless Mormons document their daily musings, detail their do-it-yourself projects, share family happenings, and post cute photos of their kids online.

Notes

Preface

1. As quoted in Scott D. Pierce, "Conan O'Brien mocks Orrin Hatch—and the Mormons," *Deseret News,* December 17, 2009, http://www.deseret news.com/article/705352005/Conan-OBrien -mocks-Orrin-Hatch-2-and-the-Mormons.html.

2. "Public Expresses Mixed Views of Islam, Mormon-ism," September 26, 2007, http://pewforum.org /Public-Expresses-Mixed-Views-of-Islam -Mormonism.aspx.

3. Ibid.

4. Gary C. Lawrence, *How Americans View Mormon-ism* (Orange, CA: The Parameter Foundation, 2008), 54.

5. *Cheers,* episode no. 166, "Call Me Irresponsible," first broadcast April 13, 1989, by NBC. Directed by James Burrows and written by Dan O'Shannon and Tom Anderson, http://www.imdb.com/title /tt0539707/quotes?qt0152771.

6. See Walter Kirn, "Mormons Rock!" *Newsweek,* June 5, 2011, http://www.thedailybeast.com /newsweek/2011/06/05/mormons-rock.html.

Introduction

1. See Allison Pond, "A Portrait of Mormons in the U.S.," July 24, 2009, http://pewresearch.org /pubs/1292/mormon-religion-demographics -beliefs-practices-politics.

2. "Church Now Fourth Largest in the U.S.; Growth Continues Worldwide," in "News of the Church," *Liahona,* August 2005, N2, http://lds.org/liahona /2005/08/news-of-the-church.

3. See Rodney Stark, "The Rise of a New World Faith," in *The Rise of Mormonism,* ed. Reid L. Neilson (New York: Columbia University Press, 2005), 140.

4. See Pond, "Portrait of Mormons in the U.S."

5. See "First Presidency Celebrates 10-Year Anniver-sary," in "News of the Church," *Liahona,* August 2005, N2.

6. See "Statistics of the Church," http://lds.org/church /statistics.

7. Stark, *Rise of Mormonism,* ix.

8. *Merriam-Webster Dictionary,* s.v. "cult."

9. See "Who Are the Mormons?" http:// newsroom .lds.org/article/who-are-the-mormons.

10. See *Deseret News 2010 Church Almanac* (Salt Lake City: Deseret News, 2009), 4–5.

11. See Henry B. Eyring, "Hearts Bound Together," *Ensign,* May 2005, 77.

12. See "LDS population of Utah declining," *Deseret News,* November 29, 2008, http://www.deseret news.com/article/705266634/LDS-population-of -Utah-declining.html.

Chapter 2: The Message of Mormonism

1. See Gary C. Lawrence, *How Americans View Mormonism* (Orange, CA: The Parameter Founda-tion, 2008), 42.

2. Some oppose the idea of an "organized" or official church. However, if one believes in divine author-ity being given from God, and also that ordinances (such as baptism) are required, then an organiza-tion is necessary to oversee the use of authority and the ordinances those in authority perform. Thus, because Latter-day Saints believe that ordi-nances (such as baptism) are necessary, and that authority is necessary to perform such ordinances, we believe an organized church is also necessary.

3. Lawrence, *How Americans View Mormonism,* 89.

4. There are too many scriptures to provide a com-prehensive list, but the following biblical scriptures indicate a growing apostasy threatening Jesus' original Church: Acts 20:28–30; Galatians 1:6–7;

1 Timothy 4:1–3; 2 Timothy 1:15; 4:3–4; 2 Peter 2:1–3; Jude 1:4.

5. Philip Smith's classic work *The History of the Christian Church during the First Ten Centuries* says: "The sad truth is that, as soon as Christianity was generally diffused, it began to absorb corruptions from all the lands in which it was planted, and to reflect the complexion of all their systems of religion and philosophy." New York: Harper & Brothers, 1879, 49.

6. Thomas Jefferson, *The Writings of Thomas Jefferson* (New York: Derby & Jackson, 1859), 7:210, 257.

7. Quoted in William Cullen Bryant, ed., *Picturesque America: or, the Land We Live In,* 2 vols. (New York: D. Appleton and Co., 1872–74), 1:502.

8. Quoted in Ezra Taft Benson, *Come unto Christ* (Salt Lake City: Deseret Book, 1983), 71.

9. *The Works of the Revered John Wesley,* 7 vols. (New York: Carlton & Porter, 1856), 2:266.

10. See David Barrett, et al., *World Christian Encyclopedia: A Comparative Survey of Churches and Religions—A.D. 30 to 2200* (Oxford University Press, 2001), http://www.religioustolerance.org/worldrel.htm.

11. In David Daniell, *Introduction to Tyndale's New Testament* (London: Yale University Press, 1989), viii.

12. The Mormon prophet Brigham Young said of John Wesley that he was "as good [a man] as ever walked the earth." In *Journal of Discourses,* 26 vols. (Liverpool: Latter-day Saints' Book Depot, 1854–86), 7:5.

13. US Constitution, amend. I, http://www.usconstitution.net/xconst_Am1.html.

14. Doctrine and Covenants 110:11–16 details Joseph Smith's visitations from Moses, Elias, and Elijah, who restored certain powers (authority, or "keys" in LDS terminology) they once held, such as the power to gather scattered Israel.

15. The book of LDS scripture entitled the Doctrine and Covenants is a compilation of many of these revelations received by Joseph Smith.

16. Orson F. Whitney, in Conference Report, April 1927, 96.

17. *Handbook 2: Administering the Church* (Salt Lake City: The Church of Jesus Christ of Latter-day Saints, 2010), 188.

18. Gordon B. Hinckley, "The Marvelous Foundation of Our Faith," *Ensign,* November 2002, 81.

Chapter 3: Are Mormons Christian? Latter-day Saints and the Gospel of Jesus Christ

1. Joseph Smith, *Teachings of the Prophet Joseph Smith,* comp. Joseph Fielding Smith (Salt Lake City: Deseret Book, 1976), 121.

2. *Preach My Gospel* (Salt Lake City: The Church of Jesus Christ of Latter-day Saints, 2004), 61.

3. LDS theology teaches that the Lord taught Adam and Eve faith in Jesus Christ from the very beginning (see Moses 5:6–8), and that Adam was baptized (see Moses 6:62–65).

4. Mormon theology teaches that in the premortal life (where we were born as God's spirit children) we worshipped Jesus and through "the blood of the Lamb" defeated a rebellion led by Satan (Revelation 12:11).

5. The Book of Mormon teaches that after Jesus visited His people in the Americas, He went and ministered to the lost ten tribes of Israel scattered throughout the world (see 3 Nephi 17:4). The Doctrine and Covenants gives a parable suggesting Christ's visitations to different peoples and concludes: "And thus they all received the light of the countenance of their lord, every man in his hour, and in his time, and in his season." Doctrine and Covenants 88:58; see also vv. 46–61.

6. The Doctrine and Covenants teaches "that by [Christ], and through him, and of him, the worlds are and were created, and the inhabitants thereof are begotten sons and daughters unto God." 76:24.

7. "Unbounded space, time, or quantity" is the dictionary definition of "infinity," http://www.thefreedictionary.com/infinity.

8. It is interesting to note how often Jesus uses the marriage covenant as a metaphor for our covenant relationship with Him. For example, see Jeremiah 3:1–11, the metaphor of Hosea (Christ) and Gomer (Israel), and the parable of the ten virgins (Matthew 25:1–13). For an excellent reading on the saving power of covenants, see Mosiah 5:1–8 in the Book of Mormon.

9. *Teachings of Gordon B. Hinckley* (Salt Lake City: Deseret Book, 1997), 182.

10. See Howard W. Hunter, "'Exceeding Great and Precious Promises,'" *Ensign,* November 1994, 8.

11. See Jeffrey R. Holland, "'Abide in Me,'" *Ensign,* May 2004, 30.

12. See Gordon B. Hinckley, "The Symbol of Christ," *Ensign,* May 1975, 92.

Chapter 4: What Is the Purpose of Life?

1. Gary C. Lawrence, *How Americans View Mormonism* (Orange, CA: The Parameter Foundation, 2008), 48.

2. Ibid.

3. Joseph Smith, *Teachings of the Prophet Joseph Smith,* comp. Joseph Fielding Smith (Salt Lake City: Deseret Book, 1976), 354.

4. See Frank Newport, "Americans More Likely to Believe in God Than the Devil, Heaven More Than Hell," June 13, 2007, http://www.gallup.com/poll/27877/americans-more-likely-believe-god-than-devil-heaven-more-than-hell.aspx. It is interesting to note that this figure has increased nearly 20 percent since 1991.

5. Naomi W. Randall, "I Am a Child of God," in *Hymns of The Church of Jesus Christ of Latter-day Saints* (Salt Lake City: The Church of Jesus Christ of Latter-day Saints, 1985), no. 301.

6. C. S. Lewis, *The Weight of Glory* (New York: HarperCollins, 2001), 45–46; emphasis in original.

7. "Plan of Salvation," in *True to the Faith* (Salt Lake City: The Church of Jesus Christ of Latter-day Saints, 2004), 115; emphasis added.

8. "The Family: A Proclamation to the World," *Ensign,* November 1995, 102.

9. Smith, *Teachings of the Prophet Joseph Smith,* 345.

10. Russell M. Nelson, "Where Is Wisdom?" *Ensign,* November 1992, 6.

11. *Preach My Gospel* (Salt Lake City: The Church of Jesus Christ of Latter-day Saints, 2004), 50.

12. "The Family: A Proclamation to the World."

13. "Agency," in *True to the Faith,* 12.

14. See ibid.

15. Smith, *Teachings of the Prophet Joseph Smith,* 181.

16. Orson F. Whitney, quoted in *Improvement Era,* March 1966, 211.

17. Smith, *Teachings of the Prophet Joseph Smith,* 255.

18. Joseph Smith, *History of The Church of Jesus Christ of Latter-day Saints,* 7 vols., ed. B. H. Roberts (Salt Lake City: The Church of Jesus Christ of Latter-day Saints, 1932–51), 5:135.

Chapter 5: LDS Priesthood Authority and Ordinances

1. Boyd K. Packer, *That All May Be Edified: Plans for Building Spirituality* (Salt Lake City: Bookcraft, 1982), 28.

2. As cited by Jeffrey R. Holland in "Our Most Distinguishing Feature," *Ensign,* May, 2005, 44.

3. *Handbook 2: Administering the Church* (Salt Lake City: The Church of Jesus Christ of Latter-day Saints, 2010), 8.

4. *Handbook 2: Administering the Church,* 40.

5. See *Preach My Gospel* (Salt Lake City: The Church of Jesus Christ of Latter-day Saints, 2004), 9.

6. LDS Apostle Dallin H. Oaks said: "When we renew our baptismal covenants in this way [through the sacrament], the Lord renews the cleansing effect of our baptism. In this way we are made clean and can always have His Spirit to be with us." "The Aaronic Priesthood and the Sacrament," *Ensign,* November 1998, 38.

7. See *Handbook 2: Administering the Church,* 8.

8. LDS Apostle Boyd K. Packer taught: "Your authority comes through your ordination; your power comes through obedience and worthiness." "The Aaronic Priesthood," *Ensign,* November 1981, 32.

9. The Book of Mormon teaches that the Lord "denieth none that come unto him, black and white, bond and free, male and female; and he remembereth the heathen; and all are alike unto God, both Jew and Gentile." 2 Nephi 26:33.

10. LDS Apostle Jeffrey R. Holland said, speaking of the black priesthood restriction: "I have to concede to my earlier colleagues. . . . They, I'm sure, in their own way, were doing the best they knew to give shape to [the policy], to give context for it, to give even history to it. All I can say is however well intended the explanations were, I think almost all of them were inadequate and/or wrong." Transcript from PBS Interview, "The Mormons," http://www.pbs.org/mormons/interviews/holland.html#1.

    An official statement by the LDS Church on why black Africans were denied the priesthood says: "It is not known precisely why, how or when this restriction began in the Church. . . . Some explanations with respect to this matter were made in the absense of direct revelation." "Race and the Church: All Are Alike Unto God," http://www.mormonnewsroom.org/article/race-church.

11. For a full, open, and well-researched reading on the history of the LDS policy restricting blacks from the priesthood and the events leading up to its change, please see Edward L. Kimball, "Spencer W. Kimball and the Revelation on the Priesthood," *BYU Studies* 47, no. 2 (2008): 4–78. Much of the information summarized in this book on the LDS

black priesthood policy is taken from that article. See also Armand L. Mauss, "The Fading of the Pharaoh's Curse: The Decline and Fall of the Priesthood Ban against Blacks in the Mormon Church," *Dialogue: A Journal of Mormon Thought* 14, no. 3 (Fall 1981): 10–45; see also Armand L. Mauss, summarized in *All Abraham's Children: Changing Mormon Conceptions of Race and Lineage* (Urbana, Ill.: University of Illinois Press, 2003), 231–41.

12. Much of the law of Moses may be seen as such a revelation given because of the conditions and situation of God's people, which policies and practices Jesus later changed (see Matthew 5–7). The Book of Mormon teaches that "by faith was the law of Moses given. But in the gift of his Son hath God prepared a more excellent way; and it is by faith that it hath been fulfilled" (Ether 12:11). Similarly, Jesus originally commanded his disciples to "go not into the way of the Gentiles, and into any city of the Samaritans enter ye not: but go rather to the lost sheep of the house of Israel" (Matthew 10:5–6). Yet after His Resurrection and Ascension, the Lord commanded Peter to reverse this policy and to openly teach and baptize Gentiles into the Church (see Acts 10–11).

13. While the LDS Church does not offer membership numbers by race, on October 14, 2009, the *Church News* stated: "A rough estimate would place the number of Church members with African roots at year-end 1997 at half a million [10 million total membership at the time], with about 100,000 each in Africa and the Caribbean, and another 300,000 in Brazil." "Top 10 Stories of the 20th Century," www.ldschurchnews.com/articles/58064/Top -10-Stories-of-the-20th-Century.html.

Chapter 6: Mormons and Marriage

1. Latter-day Saints believe that God married Adam and Eve in the Garden of Eden prior to their fall (see "Marriage: Eternal Marriage," in *Encyclopedia of Mormonism*, 4 vols., ed. Daniel H. Ludlow [New York: Macmillan, 1992], 2:857–59).

2. "The nature of male and female spirits is such that they complete each other. Men and women are intended to progress together toward exaltation." *Handbook 2: Administering the Church* (Salt Lake City: The Church of Jesus Christ of Latter-day Saints, 2010), 3.

3. See Bruce A. Chadwick, Brent L. Top, and Richard J. McClendon, *Shield of Faith: The Power of Religion in the Lives of LDS Youth and Young Adults* (Provo,

Utah: Religious Studies Center; Salt Lake City: Deseret Book, 2010), 263.

4. The LDS handbook of instructions for leaders of its local congregations says that those "whose circumstances do not allow them to receive the blessings of eternal marriage and parenthood in this life will receive all promised blessings in the eternities, provided they keep the covenants they have made with God." *Handbook 2: Administering in the Church* (Salt Lake City: The Church of Jesus Christ of Latter-day Saints, 2010), 4.

5. See "Summary of Key Findings," 2007 Pew Study Religious Landscape Survey; http://religions.pew forum.org/reports.

6. See Chadwick, Top, and McClendon, *Shield of Faith*, 222.

7. See "Dating," in *For the Strength of Youth* (Salt Lake City: The Church of Jesus Christ of Latter-day Saints, 2011), 4.

8. See Deborah Bulkeley, "Utah's birthrate is tops," *Deseret News*, October 13, 2005, www.deseret news.com/article/635/152902/Utahs-birthrate-is -tops.html.

9. "The Family: A Proclamation to the World" specifically warns "that the disintegration of the family will bring upon individuals, communities, and nations the calamities foretold by ancient and modern prophets." *Ensign*, November 1995, 102.

10. Researchers predict the overall divorce rate of Latter-day Saints to be about two-thirds the national average (see Chadwick, Top, and McClendon, *Shield of Faith*, 260; see also "Divorce," in *Encyclopedia of Mormonism*, 1:392).

11. It is estimated that the LDS temple divorce rate "is somewhere in the teens and probably no higher than 20%." Chadwick, Top, and McClendon, *Shield of Faith*, 261.

12. Gordon B. Hinckley, "Loyalty," *Ensign*, May 2003, 59.

13. The LDS handbook of instructions to its local leaders says, "All members, even if they have never married or are without family in the Church, should strive for the ideal of living in an eternal family." *Handbook 2: Administering the Church*, 4. LDS Apostle Richard G. Scott (1928–) defined the ideal eternal family thus: "Through the restored gospel we learn there is an *ideal family*. It is a family composed of a righteous Melchizedek Priesthood bearer with a righteous wife sealed to him and children born in the covenant or sealed

to them." "First Things First," *Ensign,* May 2001, 6; emphasis in original.

14. "The Divine Institution of Marriage," http://news room.lds.org/article/the-divine-institution-of -marriage.

15. "The Family: A Proclamation to the World."

16. LDS President and prophet Gordon B. Hinckley (1910–2008) said: "Logic and reason would certainly suggest that if we have a Father in Heaven, we have a Mother in Heaven. That doctrine rests well with me." "Daughters of God," *Ensign,* November 1991, 100. However, we do not pray to our Heavenly Mother, as Jesus (both in the Bible and Book of Mormon) instructed His followers: "After this manner therefore pray ye: Our Father which art in heaven." Matthew 6:9; 3 Nephi 13:9.

    Although there is not much official LDS doctrine regarding a Heavenly Mother, she is sometimes referred to in LDS general conferences and in the popular LDS hymn, "O My Father" by Eliza R. Snow in *Hymns of The Church of Jesus Christ of Latter-day Saints* (Salt Lake City: The Church of Jesus Christ of Latter-day Saints, 1985), no. 292.

17. *Handbook 2: Administering the Church,* 196.

18. Ibid.

19. See "The Divine Institution of Marriage."

20. Ibid.

21. See Aaron Falk and Scott Taylor, "Mormon church supports Salt Lake City's protections for gay rights," *Deseret News,* November 11, 2009, http://www .deseretnews.com/article/705343621/Mormon -church-supports-Salt-Lake-Citys-protections-for -gay-rights.html.

22. "The Divine Institution of Marriage."

23. A 2007 Gallup Poll found that 18 percent of respondents mentioned "polygamy" when asked what word comes to mind when thinking about Mormonism. The next highest was "Salt Lake City" at 10 percent. Frank Newport, "Americans' Views of the Mormon Religion," March 2, 2007, http://www .gallup.com/poll/26758/americans-views-mormon -religion.aspx.

24. See *Encyclopedia of Mormonism,* 3:1095.

25. One source estimates that "66.3 percent of Utah polygamists had two wives, and another 21.2 percent had three wives." Richard Lloyd Anderson and Scott H. Faulring, *The Prophet Joseph Smith and His Plural Wives,* in *FARMS Review of Books* 10, no. 2 (1998): 67–104.

26. Joseph Smith recorded a revelation given to him about the practice of plural marriage in 1843 (see Doctrine and Covenants 132). It appears that Joseph Smith understood the principles of plural marriage as early as 1831. Although some LDS Church leaders (beginning with Joseph Smith) entered into plural marriages in the 1830s and 1840s, the LDS Church did not openly teach and practice plural marriage until 1852. For a more complete reading on LDS plural marriage, see "Plural Marriage," in *Encyclopedia of Mormonism,* 3:1095.

27. "Official Declaration 1," found at the end of the Doctrine and Covenants, describes the revelation received by LDS President Wilford Woodruff (1807–1898) to end the LDS Church's practice of plural marriage in response to the consequences of the 1887 Edmunds–Tucker act.

28. Gordon B. Hinckley, "What Are People Asking About Us?" *Ensign,* November 1998, 71.

Chapter 7: Mormons and Family

1. See Christopher Smith, "LDS Ads the Message: Family First," *Salt Lake Tribune,* June 15, 2002, http://www.freerepublic.com/focus/f-religion /700831/posts.

2. Gary C. Lawrence, *How Americans View Mormonism* (Orange, CA: The Parameter Foundation, 2008), 26. Twenty-one percent of respondents (N=250) mentioned something related to family-oriented values, while the next highest category was "helpful," which was mentioned by 11 percent of the sample.

3. "The Family: A Proclamation to the World," *Ensign,* November 1995, 102.

4. John Wilmot, http://thinkexist.com/quotation /before_i_got_married_i_had_six_theories _about/12508.html.

5. "The Family: A Proclamation to the World."

6. See ibid.

7. "Monday evening [is] a sacred time." "Family Home Evening," *True to the Faith* (Salt Lake City: The Church of Jesus Christ of Latter-day Saints, 2004), 65.

8. "The Family: A Proclamation to the World."

9. *Handbook 2: Administering the Church* (Salt Lake City: The Church of Jesus Christ of Latter-day Saints, 2010), 9.

10. "The Family: A Proclamation to the World."

11. Brigham Young, *Teachings of the Presidents of the Church: Brigham Young* (Salt Lake City: The Church of Jesus Christ of Latter-day Saints, 1997), 337.

12. See Bible Dictionary, s.v. "temple," 781.

13. Although fertility rates for Latter-day Saints are higher in the US and Canada, "Mormon fertility in the United States has moved in tandem with non-Mormon fertility." Rodney Stark, *The Rise of Mormonism*, ed. Reid L. Neilson (New York: Columbia University Press, 2005), 89.

14. See Stark, *Rise of Mormonism*, 89.

15. "The Family: A Proclamation to the World."

16. "Unlike their non-Mormon counterparts, higher-income Mormon families average more children . . . and they are demanded in greater numbers by those households that can better afford them, so that Mormon professionals average significantly larger families than do Mormon laborers." Stark, *Rise of Mormonism*, 89.

17. *Handbook 2: Administering the Church*, 195.

18. The percentage of births to unmarried women in the US for 2007 was 39.7 percent of all births. In Utah, it was 19.6 percent. See Lee Davidson, "Almanac bursting with Utah trivia," *Deseret News*, December 16, 2009, http://www.deseretnews.com /article/705351848/Almanac-bursting-with-Utah -trivia.html.

19. "The Family: A Proclamation to the World."

20. See *Handbook 2: Administering the Church*, 195.

21. See ibid., 196.

22. Quoted from J. E. McCulloch, *Home: The Savior of Civilization* (Washington, DC: Southern Co-operative League, 1924), 42; in Conference Report, April 1964, 5.

23. *Handbook 2: Administering the Church*, 3.

24. "Letter from the First Presidency," *Liahona*, December 1999, 1.

25. The LDS Church has information regarding more than 3 billion deceased people. See http://news room.lds.org/topic/genealogy.

Chapter 8: What Happens inside LDS Temples?

1. See Thomas S. Monson, "The Holy Temple—a Beacon to the World," *Ensign*, May 2011, 92.

2. See "Temples of The Church of Jesus Christ of Latter-day Saints," http://www.ldschurchtemples .com/maps/.

3. Boyd K. Packer, "The Holy Temple," *Ensign*, February 1995, 32.

4. "Temples," in *True to the Faith* (Salt Lake City: The Church of Jesus Christ of Latter-day Saints, 2004), 171.

5. *Teachings of Gordon B. Hinckley* (Salt Lake City: Deseret Book, 1997), 148.

6. *Preparing to Enter the Holy Temple* (Salt Lake City: The Church of Jesus Christ of Latter-day Saints, 2002), 35.

7. See Carl Haub, "How Many People Have Ever Lived on Earth?" http://www.prb.org/Articles/2002/How ManyPeopleHaveEverLivedonEarth.aspx.

8. See Scott Taylor, "Oquirrh Mountain Temple open house begins today," June 1, 2009, http://www .deseretnews.com/article/705307771/Oquirrh -Mountain-Temple-open-house-begins-today.html.

9. See "Entering the Temple," http://lds.org/church /temples/why-we-build-temples/entering-the -temple?lang=eng.

10. Packer, "The Holy Temple," 30–31.

Chapter 9: LDS Scriptures and Sources of Truth

1. Joseph Smith, *History of The Church of Jesus Christ of Latter-day Saints*, 7 vols., ed. B. H. Roberts (Salt Lake City: The Church of Jesus Christ of Latter-day Saints, 1932–51), 4:461.

2. The Doctrine and Covenants also contains a few other revelations from subsequent LDS prophets, including Brigham Young, Joseph F. Smith, Wilford Woodruff, and Spencer W. Kimball.

3. LDS President and prophet Ezra Taft Benson (1899–1994) said, "The living prophet is more important to us than a dead prophet. . . . The most important prophet, so far as you and I are concerned, is the one living in our day and age to whom the Lord is currently revealing His will for us." "Fourteen Fundamentals in Following the Prophet," in *1980 Devotional Speeches of the Year* (Provo: BYU Press, 1981), 27.

4. *Teachings of Presidents of the Church: John Taylor* (Salt Lake City: The Church of Jesus Christ of Latter-day Saints, 2001), 153.

5. "Approaching Mormon Doctrine," May 4, 2007, http://newsroom.lds.org/ldsnewsroom/eng /commentary/approaching-mormon-doctrine.

6. "General Conference Interpretation Fact Sheet," September 12, 2011, http://newsroom.lds.org/article/general-conference-interpretation-fact-sheet.

7. "The prophets of the present dispensation, from Joseph Smith onward, have championed the idea that the Latter-day Saints have no exclusive access to truth. God enlightens people everywhere." "Truth," in *Encyclopedia of Mormonism*, 4 vols., ed. Daniel H. Ludlow (New York: Macmillan, 1992), 1490.

8. President Brigham Young said that "God has revealed all the truth that is now in the possession of the world, whether it be scientific or religious. The whole world [is] under obligation to him for what they know and enjoy; they are indebted to him for it all." In *Journal of Discourses*, 26 vols. (Liverpool: Latter-day Saints' Book Depot, 1854–86), 8:162.

9. George Albert Smith, in *Journal of Discourses*, 14:368.

10. "Approaching Mormon Doctrine," http://newsroom.lds.org/ldsnewsroom/eng/commentary/approaching-mormon-doctrine.

11. Bruce A. Chadwick, Brent L. Top, and Richard J. McClendon, *Shield of Faith: The Power of Religion in the Lives of LDS Youth and Young Adults* (Provo, Utah: Religious Studies Center; and Salt Lake City: Deseret Book, 2010), 157.

12. See ibid.

13. See "Science and Scientists," in *Encyclopedia of Mormonism*, 1272–74.

Chapter 10: The Mormon View of the Afterlife

1. See Frank Newport, "Americans More Likely to Believe in God Than the Devil, Heaven More Than Hell," June 13, 2007, http://www.gallup.com/poll/27877/americans-more-likely-believe-god-than-devil-heaven-more-than-hell.aspx.

2. See Gary C. Lawrence, *How Americans View Mormonism* (Orange, CA: The Parameter Foundation, 2008), 48.

3. "Death, Physical," in *True to the Faith* (Salt Lake City: The Church of Jesus Christ of Latter-day Saints, 2004), 46–47.

4. See *Preach My Gospel* (Salt Lake City: The Church of Jesus Christ of Latter-day Saints, 2004), 59. See also 3 Nephi 26:5.

5. James E. Talmage, "The Eternity of Sex," in *Young Woman's Journal*, October 1914, 603.

6. Quentin L. Cook, "Our Father's Plan—Big Enough for All His Children," *Ensign*, May 2009, 37.

7. It is true that Joseph Smith answered the question, "'Will everybody be damned, but Mormons?'" with, "Yes, and a great portion of them, unless they repent, and work righteousness." *Teachings of the Prophet Joseph Smith*, comp. Joseph Fielding Smith (Salt Lake City: Deseret Book, 1976), 119. But his statement makes it clear that he meant that all must obey the true gospel of Jesus Christ to be saved, which he believed was found in The Church of Jesus Christ of Latter-day Saints. He did not mean that the 99.98 percent of the world who are not members of the LDS Church will not or cannot be saved in the celestial kingdom.

8. Bible Dictionary (Salt Lake City: The Church of Jesus Christ of Latter-day Saints, 1985), s.v. "Hell," 700.

9. Dallin H. Oaks, "The Challenge to Become," *Ensign*, November 2000, 32; emphasis in original.

Chapter 11: The History of the LDS Church in Thirty Seconds

1. Information on LDS Church history facts, dates, and places were obtained primarily from *Church History in the Fulness of Times* (Salt Lake City: The Church of Jesus Christ of Latter-day Saints, 2003), as well as from Christopher Bigelow, *The Timechart History of Mormonism from Premortality to the Present*, ed. Jana Riess (Hertfordshire, United Kingdom: Worth Press Ltd., 2007).

2. The order stated that "'the Mormons must be treated as enemies, and *must be exterminated* or driven from the state, if necessary for the public good.'" *Church History in the Fulness of Times*, 201; emphasis in original. In 1976, Missouri governor Christopher S. Bond issued an executive order repealing the unconstitutional Extermination Order, formally apologizing on behalf of the state of Missouri to the Latter-day Saints for the injustices and suffering the original Extermination Order caused.

3. Quoted in *Teachings of Presidents of the Church: Wilford Woodruff* (Salt Lake City: The Church of Jesus Christ of Latter-day Saints, 2004), 146.

4. See "Who Are the Mormons?" http://newsroom.lds.org/article/who-are-the-mormons.

Chapter 12: The Joseph Smith Story

1. As quoted in B. H. Roberts, *A Comprehensive History of The Church of Jesus Christ of Latter-day*

Saints, 6 vols. (Salt Lake City: Deseret Book, 1930), 2:349.

2. For a sociological analysis of Mormonism's growth as the first new world faith since Islam, see Rodney Stark, "The Rise of a New World Faith," in *The Rise of Mormonism,* ed. Reid L. Neilson (New York: Columbia University Press, 2005).

3. Joseph Smith, in *Personal Writings of Joseph Smith,* ed. Dean C. Jessee (Salt Lake City: Deseret Book, 2002), 10.

4. *Personal Writings of Joseph Smith,* 11.

5. Joseph Smith, *History of The Church of Jesus Christ of Latter-day Saints,* 7 vols., ed. B. H. Roberts (Salt Lake City: The Church of Jesus Christ of Latter-day Saints, 1932–51), 4:537.

6. Joseph Smith, *Teachings of the Prophet Joseph Smith,* comp. Joseph Fielding Smith (Salt Lake City: Deseret Book, 1976), 361.

7. Smith, *History of the Church,* 4:492–93.

8. See Stephen L Richards, in Conference Report, October 1936, 32. LDS scholar Robert J. Matthews said, "I suppose the number of pages of scripture produced through Joseph Smith exceeds that of any other prophet." *Selected Writings of Robert J. Matthews* (Salt Lake City: Deseret Book, 1999), 534.

9. See section heading to Doctrine and Covenants 132.

10. Richard Lyman Bushman, *Joseph Smith: Rough Stone Rolling* (New York: Knopf, 2005), 326.

11. Todd Compton puts the number of Joseph Smith's plural wives at thirty-three (see *In Sacred Loneliness: The Plural Wives of Joseph Smith* [Salt Lake City: Signature Books, 1997], 1), while Richard L. Anderson and Scott H. Faulring put it at twenty-nine (see "The Prophet Joseph Smith and His Plural Wives," *FARMS Review of Books* 10, no. 2 (1998): 67–104).

12. See "U.S. Religious Knowledge Survey," September 28, 2010, http://pewforum.org/Other-Beliefs-and-Practices/U-S-Religious-Knowledge-Survey.aspx.

13. Noam Chomsky, http://www.brainyquote.com/quotes/keywords/prophets.html.

14. See "Joseph Smith Historic Sites: Missouri, Liberty Jail," http://josephsmith.net.

15. Smith, *History of the Church,* 1:88.

16. Ibid., 5:336.

17. Truman G. Madsen, *Joseph Smith the Prophet* (Salt Lake City: Bookcraft, 1989), 64.

18. Ibid., 37.

19. Joseph Smith, in *Millennial Star,* July 11, 1863, 439.

20. Smith, *History of the Church,* 5:394.

21. Ezra Taft Benson, "Joseph Smith: Prophet to Our Generation," *Ensign,* November 1981, 63.

22. Smith, *History of the Church,* 6:555.

23. Ibid., 5:85.

24. Joseph Smith, as quoted by Wilford Woodruff, in Conference Report, April 1898, 57.

25. See "Who Are the Mormons?" http://www.newsroom.lds.org/article/who-are-the-mormons.

26. John Needham to Thomas Ward, July 7, 1843, *Latter-Day Saints' Millennial Star* 4 (October 1843): 89.

27. Edwin F. Parry, comp. *Stories about Joseph Smith the Prophet* (Salt Lake City: Deseret News Press, 1934), 17–18.

28. Madsen, *Joseph Smith the Prophet,* 26.

29. Parley P. Pratt, in *Discourses of the Prophet Joseph Smith,* comp. Alma P. Burton (Salt Lake City: Deseret Book, 1977), 4.

30. In ibid., 5.

31. As quoted in ibid., 10.

32. Smith, *Teachings of the Prophet Joseph Smith,* 275.

33. Madsen, *Joseph Smith the Prophet,* 59.

34. Ibid., 33.

35. Smith, *History of the Church,* 4:80.

36. "Praise to the Man," in *Hymns of The Church of Jesus Christ of Latter-day Saints* (Salt Lake City: The Church of Jesus Christ of Latter-day Saints, 1985), no. 27.

37. *Teachings of the Prophet Joseph Smith,* 175.

38. Ibid., 255–56.

39. Ibid., 216–17.

40. Ibid., 181.

41. Ibid., 326.

42. Ibid., 354.

43. Smith, *History of the Church,* 2:170.

44. As quoted by Joseph F. Merrill, in Conference Report, April 1947, 136.

45. George Wharton James, quoted by Alvin R. Dyer, in Conference Report, October 1959, 21.

46. Harold Bloom, *The American Religion: The Emergence of the Post-Christian Nation* (New York: Simon & Schuster, 1992), 82, 95, 97.

Chapter 13: The Book of Mormon

1. Noted sociologist Rodney Stark, a non-Mormon who studies Mormonism's growth extensively, put forth the idea that Joseph Smith produced the Book of Mormon in a surge of literary genius, similar to Mozart's or Gershwin's musical compositions (see *The Rise of Mormonism*, ed. Reid L. Neilson [New York: Columbia University Press, 2005], 40–41). Although for Mormons this theory is preferable than theories that paint Joseph Smith as a cunning and duplicitous fraud, the "literary inspiration" theory does not account for the sworn testimonies of numerous witnesses who saw and handled the physical evidence related to an actual Book of Mormon (i.e., the golden plates and the Urim and Thummim used to translate them).

2. "The Book of Mormon is a Satanic wonder, intended to deceive." http://www.lds-mormon.com/satan.shtml.

3. See John L. Sorenson, *Mormon's Map* (Provo, Utah: FARMS, 2000), 78.

4. See "U.S. Religious Knowledge Survey," September 28, 2010, http://pewforum.org/Other-Beliefs-and-Practices/U-S-Religious-Knowledge-Survey.aspx.

5. While we do feel that some verses of the Bible have been mistranslated over the years or that there are missing portions that the original inspired writer intended, this doesn't diminish our belief in the divinity of the Bible.

6. Joseph Smith, *History of The Church of Jesus Christ of Latter-day Saints,* 7 vols., ed. B. H. Roberts (Salt Lake City: The Church of Jesus Christ of Latter-day Saints, 1932–51), 4:461.

7. Smith, *History of the Church,* 2:52.

8. See Frank Newport, "Americans More Likely to Believe in God Than the Devil, Heaven More Than Hell, June 13, 2007, http://www.gallup.com/poll/27877/americans-more-likely-believe-god-than-devil-heaven-more-than-hell.aspx.

9. See Hugh Nibley, *Since Cumorah* (Salt Lake City: Deseret Book, 1967), 56–57, 220.

10. Francis W. Kirkham, "The Manner of Translating the Book of Mormon," *Improvement Era* 42, no. 10 (October 1939): 630. In that same interview, Emma Smith said that the Book of Mormon "is marvelous to me, 'a marvel and a wonder,' as much so as to

anyone else. . . . It would have been improbable that a learned man could do this; and, for one so . . . unlearned as [Joseph] was, it was simply impossible." Ibid., 631.

11. As quoted in Terryl L. Givens, *By the Hand of Mormon: The American Scripture That Launched a New World Religion* (New York: Oxford University Press, 2002), 22.

12. *Improvement Era* 32, no. 10 (1939). In that same article, it is recorded that an interviewer asked Emma Smith, "Had he [Joseph] not a book or manuscript from which he read or dictated to you?" Emma answered, "He had neither manuscript nor book to read from. . . . If he had had anything of the kind he could not have concealed it from me."

13. Oliver Cowdery endnote in Joseph Smith—History, 58.

14. See Neal A. Maxwell, "'By the Gift and Power of God,'" *Ensign,* January 1997, 39.

15. See "I Have a Question: 'How long did it take Joseph Smith to translate the Book of Mormon?'" *Ensign,* January 1988, 47.

16. Smith, *History of the Church,* 4:461.

17. See "Book of Mormon Editions," in *Encyclopedia of Mormonism,* 4 vols., ed. Daniel H. Ludlow (New York: Macmillan, 1992), 175–76.

18. Jeffrey R. Holland, "A Standard unto My People," CES Symposium on the Book of Mormon, Brigham Young University, August 9, 1994, 6; emphasis in original.

19. David Whitmer, as cited by Joseph Fielding Smith, in Conference Report, October 1956, 20.

20. Quoted in C. M. Nielsen, "Oliver Cowdery for the Defense," *Improvement Era* 8 (August 1943): 464.

21. Givens, *By the Hand of Mormon,* 25.

22. Quoted in Richard Lyman Bushman, *Joseph Smith: Rough Stone Rolling* (New York: Alfred A. Knopf, 2005), 57.

23. Givens, *By the Hand of Mormon,* 40.

24. John L. Hilton, "On Verifying Wordprint Studies: Book of Mormon Authorship," *BYU Studies* 30, no. 3 (1990): 101.

25. Wayne A. Larsen, Alvin C. Rencher, and Tim Layton, "Who Wrote the Book of Mormon? An Analysis of Wordprints," *BYU Studies* 20, no. 3 (Spring 1980): 225–45.

26. See Ryan Kunz, "180 Years Later, Book of Mormon Nears 150 Million Copies," *Ensign,* March 2010,

74–76; Gordon B. Hinckley, "A Testimony Vibrant and True," *Ensign,* August 2004, 4.

27. See Susan Easton Black, *Finding Christ through the Book of Mormon* (Salt Lake City: Deseret Book, 1987), 15.

28. See "Research and Perspectives: Book of Mormon Update," *Ensign,* April 1992, 63.

29. Mark Twain, *Roughing It,* 2 vols. (Hartford, Conn.: American Publishing, 1873), 1:127.

30. University of North Carolina professor and respected author Grant Hardy argues this position, and he has produced an entire book examining the literary qualities of the Book of Mormon: *Understanding the Book of Mormon: A Reader's Guide* (New York: Oxford University Press, 2010).

31. "20 Books That Changed America," *Barnes & Noble Presents Book* (July/August 2003): 58–61; reprinted January 7, 2006, http://abcnews.go.com/WNN/story?id=132737&page=1.

Chapter 14: Latter-day Prophets

1. Ralph Waldo Emerson's Harvard Divinity School Address, Sunday Evening, July 15, 1838, http://www.emersoncentral.com/divaddr.htm.

2. "Prophets," in *True to the Faith* (Salt Lake City: The Church of Jesus Christ of Latter-day Saints, 2004), 129.

3. David A. Bednar, "Special Witnesses of the Name of Christ," *The Religious Educator* 12, no. 2 (2011): 2.

4. LDS First Presidency member James E. Faust said that divine revelation comes to modern prophets "by the guidance of the Holy Ghost (which is perhaps most common)." "Continuous Revelation," *Ensign,* November 1989, 9.

5. Gordon B. Hinckley, "'This Thing Was Not Done in a Corner,'" *Ensign,* November 1996, 50–51.

6. Dates and summaries for this section were taken primarily from the institute student manual prepared by the Church Educational System entitled *Presidents of the Church* (Salt Lake City: The Church of Jesus Christ of Latter-day Saints, 2003).

7. "The friendship between Lyndon B. Johnson and David O. McKay was the strongest bond between a Church president and U.S. President in history." Michael K. Winder, *Presidents and Prophets: The Story of America's Presidents and the LDS Church* (American Fork, Utah: Covenant Communications, Inc, 2007), 301.

8. See Winder, *Presidents and Prophets,* 301.

9. See "Memories of a Prophet," *Improvement Era,* February 1970, 72.

10. J. E. McCulloch, quoted in *Teachings of Presidents of the Church: David O. McKay* (Salt Lake City: The Church of Jesus Christ of Latter-day Saints, 2003), 153.

11. Ezra Taft Benson, "Flooding the Earth with the Book of Mormon," *Ensign,* November 1988, 5.

12. Howard W. Hunter, "'Exceeding Great and Precious Promises,'" *Ensign,* November 1994, 8.

13. See "Today in Church History," in *Church News,* June 23, 2010, www.ldschurchnews.com/articles/59532/Today-in-Church-history-Pres-Hinckley-born-100-years-ago.html.

14. *Handbook 2: Administering the Church* (Salt Lake City: The Church of Jesus Christ of Latter-day Saints, 2010), 9.

15. See "80 over 80: 2010, *Slate's* list of the most influential octogenarians in America," November 30, 2010, http://www.slate.com/id/2276194/.

16. See Cathy Lynn Grossman, "Obama, Clinton top most-admired lists for 2011," *USA Today,* December 27, 2011, http://www.usatoday.com/news/nation/story/2011-12-27/most-admired-people-2011/52243574/1.

17. For detailed information on the succession of an LDS Church president, see "Succession in the Presidency of The Church of Jesus Christ of Latter-day Saints," http://newsroom.lds.org/additional-resource/succession-in-the-presidency-of-the-church-of-jesus-christ-of-latter-day-saints.

18. Joseph Smith said: "I told them I was but a man, and they must not expect me to be perfect; if they expected perfection from me, I should expect it from them; but if they would bear with my infirmities and the infirmities of the brethren, I would likewise bear with their infirmities." *History of The Church of Jesus Christ of Latter-day Saints,* 7 vols., ed. B. H. Roberts (Salt Lake City: The Church of Jesus Christ of Latter-day Saints, 1932–51), 5:181. Elder James E. Faust said, "We make no claim of infallibility or perfection in the prophets, seers, and revelators." "Continuous Revelation," *Ensign,* November 1989, 11.

19. Faust, "Continuous Revelation," 10.

20. Brigham Young, *Discourses of Brigham Young,* ed. John A. Widtsoe (Salt Lake City: Deseret Book, 1941), 135.

Chapter 15: Temple Square

1. Aaron Falk, "Temple Square Ranks 16th in visitors," *Deseret News,* March 12, 2009, http://www.deseret news.com/article/705290247/Temple-Square -ranks-16th-in-visitors.html.

2. Most statistics and facts on Temple Square buildings were summarized from http://newsroom.lds .org/article/temple-square and http://www.visit templesquare.com/.

3. Statistics on the Tabernacle and organ summarized from http://mormontabernaclechoir.org and http://newsroom.lds.org/topic/mormon-tabernacle -choir.

4. Statistics on the Mormon Tabernacle Choir summarized from http://mormontabernaclechoir.org and http://newsroom.lds.org/topic/mormon -tabernacle-choir.

Chapter 16: Mo-cabulary: Understanding Mormon Vernacular

1. Many of the doctrinal definitions are summarized from entries in the LDS scriptures and Bible Dictionary, or from *Handbook 2: Administering the Church* (Salt Lake City: The Church of Jesus Christ of Latter-day Saints, 2010), *True to the Faith* (Salt Lake City: The Church of Jesus Christ of Latter-day Saints, 2004), or *Preach My Gospel* (Salt Lake City: The Church of Jesus Christ of Latter-day Saints, 2004).

Chapter 17: What Does It Take to Be a Mormon? LDS Standards

1. See Gary C. Lawrence, *How Americans View Mormonism* (Orange, CA: The Parameter Foundation, 2008), 32.

2. The Prophet Joseph Smith taught "that a religion that does not require the sacrifice of all things never has power sufficient to produce the faith necessary unto life and salvation." *Lectures on Faith* (Salt Lake City: Deseret Book, 1985), 69.

3. Gordon B. Hinckley, interview by Larry King on *Larry King Live,* September 8, 1998, http://www.lds -mormon.com/lkl_00.shtml.

4. See Rodney Stark, *Rise of Mormonism* (New York: Columbia University Press, 2005), 94.

5. See Stark, *Rise of Mormonism,* 92.

6. See "Faith," in *True to the Faith* (Salt Lake City: The Church of Jesus Christ of Latter-day Saints, 2004), 54.

7. "Baptism," in *True to the Faith,* 22.

8. See David A. Bednar, "Receive the Holy Ghost," *Ensign,* November 2010, 95.

9. Neal A. Maxwell, "'A Brother Offended,'" *Ensign,* May 1982, 38.

10. "Sabbath Day Observance," in *For the Strength of Youth* (Salt Lake City: The Church of Jesus Christ of Latter-day Saints, 2011), 31.

11. Ibid.

12. See *Preach My Gospel* (Salt Lake City: The Church of Jesus Christ of Latter-day Saints, 2004), 204.

13. See The Urban Institute, National Center for Charitable Statistics, http://nccsdataweb.urban.org /kbfiles/421/stgive_02.pdf.

14. *Preach My Gospel,* 206.

15. "Chastity," in *True to the Faith,* 29.

16. The Pew Forum on Religion & Public Life, "A Portrait of Mormons in the U.S.," July 24, 2009, http:// pewforum.org/Christian/Mormon/A-Portrait-of -Mormons-in-the-US--Religious-Beliefs-and -Practices.aspx.

17. Lawrence, *How Americans View Mormonism,* 34.

18. "Entertainment and Media," in *For the Strength of Youth,* 11.

19. The 2011 *For the Strength of Youth* booklet does not say anything specific about rated-R movies. However, the subject has been specifically mentioned repeatedly in LDS general conferences by various speakers including Mary Ellen W. Smoot, Elder David E. Sorensen, and Elder John H. Groberg in 2001. Most notable was President Ezra Taft Benson's conference address to the youth of the Church when he said, "Don't see R-rated movies or vulgar videos or participate in any entertainment that is immoral, suggestive, or pornographic." "To the Young Women of the Church," *Ensign,* November 1986, 84.

20. "Scriptures," in *True to the Faith,* 156.

21. The Pew Forum on Religion & Public Life, "A Portrait of Mormons in the U.S."

22. Joseph Smith, *History of The Church of Jesus Christ of Latter-day Saints,* 7 vols., ed. B. H. Roberts (Salt Lake City: The Church of Jesus Christ of Latter-day Saints, 1932–51), 5:401.

23. Gordon B. Hinckley, "'I Am Clean,'" *Ensign,* May 2007, 62.

24. See "Physical and Emotional Health," in *For the Strength of Youth,* 25–27.

25. James E. Enstrom, "Health practices and cancer mortality among active California Mormons," *J. Natl. Cancer Inst.* 81, no. 23 (6 December 1989): 1807–14. See also Foundation for Christian Studies, "Doctrinal Study: Church Practices: Health of the Body," http://www.studychristianity.com/health_body.html.

26. Nicholas O. Rule, James V. Garrett, and Nalini Ambady, "On the Perception of Religious Group Membership from Faces," 2010, http://www.plosone.org/article/info%3Adoi%2F10.1371%2Fjournal.pone.0014241#pone-0014241-t001.

27. "Service," in *For the Strength of Youth,* 32.

28. Robert D. Putnam and David E. Campbell, *American Grace: How Religion Divides and Unites Us* (New York: Simon and Schuster, 2010), 452.

29. Sean Gregory, "Brandon Davies: Is BYU's Premarital Sex Controversy Good for College Sports?" *Time,* March 14, 2011, http://www.time.com/time/arts/article/0,8599,2057184,00.html.

Chapter 18: Mormons and Sex

1. According to 2009 US Census Bureau data, Utah had a birthrate of 19.4 births per 1,000 residents. See http://www.census.gov/compendia/statab/2012/tables/12s0082.pdf.

2. "The Family: A Proclamation to the World," *Ensign,* November 1995, 102.

3. "Sexual Purity," in *For the Strength of Youth* (Salt Lake City: The Church of Jesus Christ of Latter-day Saints, 2011), 35; see also "Chastity," in *True to the Faith* (Salt Lake City: The Church of Jesus Christ of Latter-day Saints, 2004), 29.

4. See *Handbook 2: Administering the Church* (Salt Lake City: The Church of Jesus Christ of Latter-day Saints, 2010), 195.

5. See Nicholas Bakalar, "U.S. Births Rise in All Age Groups," in the *New York Times,* March 1, 2010.

6. See Guttmacher Institute, "Facts on Induced Abortion in the United States," August 2011; http://www.guttmacher.org/pubs/fb_induced_abortion.html#1.

7. See Lawrence K. Altman, "Sex Infections Found in Quarter of Teenage Girls," in the *New York Times,* March 12, 2008; http://www.nytimes.com/2008/03/12/science/12std.html.

8. See http://www.census.gov/compendia/statab/2012/tables/12s0085.pdf.

9. See Dean M. Busby, Jason S. Carroll, Brian J. Willoughby, "Compatibility or restraint? The effects of sexual timing on marriage relationships," *Journal of Family Psychology* 24, no. 6 (2010), doi: 10.1037/a002/690.

10. Marianne Holman, "BYU Study: Sexual abstinence until marriage leads to stability and trust," January 8, 2011, http://www.ldschurchnews.com/articles/60338/BYU-Study-Sexual-abstinence-until-marriage-leads-to-stability-and-trust.html.

11. Ezra Taft Benson, *The Teachings of Ezra Taft Benson* (Salt Lake City: Bookcraft, 1988), 285.

12. "Abortion," in *True to the Faith,* 4.

13. Ibid.

14. Ibid., 4–5.

15. "The worth of souls is great in the sight of God." Doctrine and Covenants 18:10.

16. "Birth Control," in *True to the Faith,* 26.

17. See "Birth Control," in *Encyclopedia of Mormonism,* ed. Daniel H. Ludlow, 4 vols. (New York: Macmillan, 1992), 1:116.

18. The standard for single Mormons before marriage is this: "Do not participate in passionate kissing, lie on top of another person, or touch the private, sacred parts of another person's body, with or without clothing." "Sexual Purity," in *For the Strength of Youth,* 36.

19. For a few examples, see Mosiah 13:22 and Doctrine and Covenants 42:24.

20. See John Hilton III and Anthony Sweat, *Why? Powerful Answers and Practical Reasons for Living LDS Standards* (Salt Lake City: Deseret Book, 2009), 89.

21. Dallin H. Oaks, "Pornography," *Ensign,* May 2005, 89.

22. The US Census reports that Utah had the lowest average age of first marriage (21.9 for women and 23.9 for men). Utah also had the highest percentage of married households, and the lowest unwed birthrate (only 15 percent of Utah moms were unwed) and the lowest teen birthrate (see Deborah Bulkeley, "Utah's birthrate is tops," *Deseret News,* October 13, 2005, http://www.deseretnews.com/article/635152902/Utahs-birthrate-is-tops.html.

23. "Same-Gender Attraction," http://www.mormonnewsroom.org/official-statement/same-gender-attraction.

24. *God Loveth His Children* (Salt Lake City: The Church of Jesus Christ of Latter-day Saints, 2007), 6.

25. *Handbook 2: Administering the Church* (Salt Lake City: The Church of Jesus Christ of Latter-day Saints, 2010), 196.

Chapter 19: Mormon Women

1. Wallace Stegner, *The Gathering of Zion: The Story of the Mormon Trail* (Lincoln, Nebraska: University of Nebraska Press, 1964), 13.

2. Emily Matchar, "Why I can't stop reading Mormon housewife blogs," January 15, 2011, http://www.salon.com/life/feature/2011/01/15/feminist_obsessed_with_mormon_blogs.

3. See "The Family: A Proclamation to the World," *Ensign,* November 1995, 102.

4. "Message of the First Presidency," *Deseret News Weekly Church Edition,* October 1942, 5.

5. See Sheri L. Dew, "Are We Not All Mothers?" *Ensign,* November 2001, 96–98.

6. Julie B. Beck, "Mothers Who Know," *Ensign,* November 2007, 76.

7. See 2007 Pew Forum U.S. Religious Landscape Survey, http://religions.pewforum.org/reports.

8. Neal A. Maxwell, "The Women of God," *Ensign,* May 1978, 10–11.

9. *Handbook 2: Administering the Church* (Salt Lake City: The Church of Jesus Christ of Latter-day Saints, 2010), 4.

10. See "Frequently Asked Questions," http://mormon.org/faq/#Women. See also Gordon B. Hinckley, "'This Thing Was Not Done in a Corner,'" *Ensign,* November 1996, 48; Julie B. Beck, "Using Relief Society Meetings to Teach and Inspire," *Liahona,* September 2010, 35.

11. See "Relief Society History," http://lds.org/pa/display/0,17884,8211–1,00.html.

12. See *Handbook 2: Administering the Church,* 64.

13. See "Frequently Asked Questions," http://mormon.org/faq/#Women.

14. Joseph Smith, *Teachings of Presidents of the Church: Joseph Smith* (Salt Lake City: The Church of Jesus Christ of Latter-day Saints, 2007), 452–53.

15. See *Handbook 2: Administering the Church,* 68–69.

16. See ibid., 65.

17. See Robert D. Putnam and David E. Campbell, *American Grace: How Religion Divides and Unites Us* (New York: Simon and Schuster, 2010), 245.

18. The LDS Church's official handbook says that in ward council, "Women should feel that their comments are valued as full participants. The bishop seeks input from Relief Society, Young Women, and Primary leaders in all matters considered by the ward council." *Handbook 2: Administering the Church,* 17.

19. Putnam and Campbell, *American Grace,* 245.

20. See "Relief Society History," http://lds.org/pa/display/0,17884,8211–1,00.html.

21. See "Young Women," in *Encyclopedia of Mormonism,* 4 vols., ed. Daniel H. Ludlow (New York: Macmillan, 1992), 4:1616.

22. See "One in a Million Shares Children's Stories," February 11, 2011, http://lds.org/church/news/one-in-a-million-shares-childrens-stories?lang=eng.

23. LDS Apostle Neal A. Maxwell (1926–2004) said, "'We know so little about the reasons for the division of duties between womanhood and manhood as well as between motherhood and priesthood. These were divinely determined in another time and another place.'" In "Gospel Principles and the Roles of Women," *Encyclopedia of Mormonism,* 4 vols., ed. Daniel H. Ludlow (New York: Macmillan, 1992), 4:1576.

24. Gordon B. Hinckley, quoted in "Frequently Asked Questions," http://mormon.org/faq/#Women|question=/faq/women-in-the-church/.

25. See "Woman Suffrage," in *Encyclopedia of Mormonism,* 4 vols., ed. Daniel H. Ludlow (New York: Macmillan, 1992), 1572–73.

26. See "Women, Role of," in Arnold K. Garr, Donald Q. Cannon, and Richard O. Cowan, *Encyclopedia of Latter-day Saint History* (Salt Lake City: Deseret Book, 2000), 1358.

27. "Feminism," http://www.thefreedictionary.com/feminism.

28. "The Family: A Proclamation to the World."

29. Ibid.

30. Quentin L. Cook, "LDS Women Are Incredible!" *Ensign,* May 2011, 21.

31. "O My Father," in *Hymns of The Church of Jesus Christ of Latter-day Saints* (Salt Lake City: The Church of Jesus Christ of Latter-day Saints, 1985), no. 292.

32. "The Family: A Proclamation to the World."

33. Spencer W. Kimball, *The Teachings of Spencer W. Kimball,* ed. Edward L. Kimball (Salt Lake City: Bookcraft, 1982), 25.

34. "The Origin of Man," *Improvement Era,* November 1909, 78.

35. "Eve," in *Encyclopedia of Mormonism,* 4 vols., ed. Daniel H. Ludlow (New York: Macmillan, 1992), 2:476.

36. Gordon B. Hinckley, quoted in Sheri L. Dew, *Go Forward with Faith: The Biography of Gordon B. Hinckley* (Salt Lake City: Deseret Book, 1996), 526.

37. Putnam and Campbell, *American Grace,* 233.

38. James E. Faust, "What It Means to Be a Daughter of God," *Ensign,* November 1999, 101.

39. Gordon B. Hinckley, *Teachings of Gordon B. Hinckley* (Salt Lake City: Deseret Book, 1997), 387.

40. Brigham Young, *Teachings of Presidents of the Church: Brigham Young* (Salt Lake City: The Church of Jesus Christ of Latter-day Saints, 1997), 135.

41. Kimball, *Teachings of Spencer W. Kimball,* 320.

42. "Education," in *For the Strength of Youth* (Salt Lake City: The Church of Jesus Christ of Latter-day Saints, 2011), 9.

43. The Express Scripts report did not specify why Utah led the nation in depression rates, nor did it provide information divided by religion or gender. Some people have theorized that Utah has higher rates of depression-related prescriptions simply because Utahns are less likely to self-medicate through alcohol or drugs. Another is that because Utahns are more generally educated, perhaps they understand their symptoms, report them, and seek professional medical help more often than in other areas. This explanation is plausible as the Express Scripts report also indicated that Utah leads the nation in prescribed antibiotics and anti-inflammatory drugs. See Bruce A. Chadwick, Brent L. Top, Richard J. McClendon, *Shield of Faith: The Power of Religion in the Lives of LDS Youth and Young Adults* (Provo, Utah: Religious Studies Center; and Salt Lake City: Deseret Book, 2010), 313.

44. See *Religion, Mental Health, and the Latter-day Saints,* ed. Daniel K Judd (Provo, Utah: BYU Religious Studies Center, 1999), 33.

45. Chadwick, Top, and McClendon, *Shield of Faith,* 304, 312.

46. Sarah Osmotherly, "Hi, I'm Sarah," http://mormon.org/me/4SD4/.

Chapter 20: LDS Teenagers

1. Quoted at http://www.quotegarden.com/teenagers.html.

2. Elaine Jarvik, "LDS teens tops in living faith," *Deseret News,* March 15, 2005, A01. See also Christian Smith and Melinda Lundquist Denton, *Soul Searching: The Religious and Spiritual Lives of American Teenagers* (New York: Oxford University Press, 2005).

3. As reported in "Studies Show LDS Youth Are Living Their Religion," *News from the Church,* April 13, 2005, see also http://ldswhy.com/qu/why-mormon-youth-rock.

4. "Physical and Emotional Health," in *For the Strength of Youth* (Salt Lake City: The Church of Jesus Christ of Latter-day Saints, 2011), 25–26.

5. "Health & Science," *Time,* July 11, 2011, 19.

6. Table summarized from Bruce A. Chadwick, Brent L. Top, and Richard J. McClendon, *Shield of Faith: The Power of Religion in the Lives of LDS Youth and Young Adults* (Provo, Utah: Religious Studies Center; and Salt Lake City: Deseret Book, 2010), 102.

7. National Survey of Youth and Religion, 2002–2003, 2007–2008, Christian Smith and Patricia Snell, *Souls in Transition: The Religious and Spiritual Lives of Emerging Adults* (New York: Oxford University Press, 2009), 116.

8. See Chadwick, Top, and McClendon, *Shield of Faith,* 201.

9. "Repentance," in *For the Strength of Youth,* 28.

10. See "Repentance," in *True to the Faith* (Salt Lake City: The Church of Jesus Christ of Latter-day Saints, 2004), 132–35.

11. "Dating," in *For the Strength of Youth,* 4.

12. Ibid.

13. See Kate Fogarty, "Teens and Dating: Tips for Parents and Professionals," University of Florida IAF Extension, http://edis.ifas.ufl.edu/fy851.

14. International Communications Research National Omnibus Survey, "Parents of Teens and Teens Discuss Sex, Love, and Relationships: Polling Data," April 1998, http://www.icrsurvey.com/Study.aspx?f=Teenpreg.html.

15. "Agency and Accountability," in *For the Strength of Youth,* 2.

16. "Boy Scouts of America Membership Report—2007," P.R.A.Y., January 7, 2008, http://

www.praypub.org/pdf_docs/BSA_Membership
_Report_2007.pdf.

17. Thomas S. Monson, in Julie Dockstader Heaps,
"Role models needed for youth; fewer critics," in
Church News, June 7, 2003, www.ldschurchnews
.com/articles/43875/Role-models-needed-for
-youth-fewer-critics.html.

18. See *Fulfilling My Duty to God: For Aaronic Priesthood Holders* (Salt Lake City: The Church of Jesus
Christ of Latter-day Saints, 2010), 7.

19. "Young Women Theme," *Young Women Personal
Progress* (Salt Lake City: The Church of Jesus
Christ of Latter-day Saints, 2009), 3.

20. "The Objective of Seminaries and Institutes of Religion" (Salt Lake City: Church Educational System,
2009), 1; see also http://seminary.lds.org.

21. *A Current Teaching Emphasis for the Church
Educational System* (Salt Lake City: The Church of
Jesus Christ of Latter-day Saints, 2004), 1.

22. "Seminaries and Institutes of Religion Annual
Report for 2010" (Salt Lake City: Seminaries and
Institutes of Religion, 2011), 2.

23. Quoted in Jarvik, "LDS teens tops in living faith,"
Deseret News, March 15, 2005, A01; emphasis
added.

Chapter 21: The Organization of LDS Church Congregations

1. Nels L. Nelson, *Scientific Aspects of Mormonism*
(New York: G. P. Putnam's Sons, 1904), 1.

2. Quoted in Thomas J. Yates, "Count Tolstoi and the
'American Religion,'" *Improvement Era* 42
(February 1939): 94.

3. "Financial Contributions," in *Encyclopedia of Mormonism,* 4 vols., ed. Daniel H. Ludlow (New York:
Macmillan, 1992), 2:510.

4. See Rodney Stark, *The Rise of Mormonism* (New
York: Columbia University Press, 2005), 90.

5. See Boyd K. Packer, "Called to Serve," *Ensign,*
November 1997, 6–8.

6. J. Reuben Clark Jr., in Conference Report, April
1951, 154.

7. *Handbook 2: Administering the Church* (Salt Lake
City: The Church of Jesus Christ of Latter-day
Saints, 2010), 4.

8. *Handbook 2: Administering the Church,* 4.

Chapter 23: Mormons and Missionary Work

1. See "One Million Missionaries, Thirteen Million
Members," The Church of Jesus Christ of Latter-
day Saints Newsroom, June 25, 2007, http://news
room.lds.org/article/one-million-missionaries
-thirteen-million-members.

2. See "Basic Facts about the Church," http://lds.org
/church/facts?lang=eng.

3. See "Statistical Report, 2010," *Ensign,* May 2011, 28.

4. See Peggy Fletcher Stack, "Mission Metamorphosis," *Salt Lake Tribune,* June 30, 2007, http://www
.religionnewsblog.com/18597/mormon
-missionaries-3.

5. *Preach My Gospel* (The Church of Jesus Christ of
Latter-day Saints: Salt Lake City, 2004), 2.

6. Ibid., vii.

7. See ibid.

8. As quoted in Orson F. Whitney, *Life of Heber C.
Kimball* (Salt Lake City: Deseret Book, 1945), 104.

9. An oft-asked question is why the age for missionary service is twenty-one for an LDS young
woman, which is two years later than the age
for a young man's missionary service. President
Gordon B. Hinckley explained: "Missionary work is
essentially a priesthood responsibility. As such, our
young men must carry the major burden. This is
their responsibility and their obligation. . . . Over a
period of many years, we have held the age level
higher for [young women] in an effort to keep the
number going relatively small." "Some Thoughts
on Temples, Retention of Converts, and Missionary
Service," *Ensign,* November 1997, 52.

10. See Neil L. Andersen, "Preparing the World for the
Second Coming," *Ensign,* May 2011, 51.

11. See Ronald A. Rasband, "The Divine Call of a Missionary," *Ensign,* May 2010, 51–53.

12. See Provo Missionary Training Center statistics,
http://www.mtc.byu.edu/themtc-virtualtour.htm,
http://www.mtc.byu.edu/miss-president.htm, and
http://www.ksl.com/?nid=148&sid=14504817.

13. See "Statistical Report, 2010," *Ensign,* May 2011, 28.

14. Joseph Smith, *The History of The Church of Jesus
Christ of Latter-day Saints,* 7 vols., ed. B. H. Roberts
(Salt Lake City: The Church of Jesus Christ of
Latter-day Saints, 1932–51), 2:478.

15. For dress and grooming standards for LDS sister
missionaries, see http://missionary.lds.org/dress

-grooming/faq/ and for elders, see http://www
.mtc.byu.edu/doc/elders.pdf.

16. See Richard G. Scott, "Now Is the Time to Serve a Mission!" *Ensign,* May 2006, 88.

17. See Stack, "Mission Metamorphosis." See also Rodney Stark, *The Rise of Mormonism* (New York: Columbia University Press), 2005, 126.

18. "Your physical or emotional circumstance may be such that you have been excused by the President of the Church from full-time missionary service (see 'Statement on Missionary Work' attached to First Presidency letter, 11 Dec. 2002)." Richard G. Scott, "Realize Your Full Potential," *Ensign,* November 2003, 43.

Chapter 24: Mormons and Money

1. Socrates, http://thinkexist.com/quotationswealth /4.html.

2. David Vav Biema, S. C. Gwynne, and Richard N. Ostling, "Kingdom Come," *Time,* Monday, August 4, 1997, 4, http://www.time.com/time/magazine /article/0,9171,986794,00.html; see also lds -mormon.com/time.shtml.

3. Gordon B. Hinckley, "Latter-day Saints in Very Deed," *Ensign,* November 1997, 85.

4. Walter Kirn, "Mormons Rock!" *Newsweek,* June 5, 2011, 3, http://www.thedailybeast.com/news week/2011/06/05/mormons-rock.html.

5. "Our major source of revenue is the ancient law of the tithe." Gordon B. Hinckley, http://mormon.org /faq/church-operations/.

6. See "Tithing," in *True to the Faith* (Salt Lake City: The Church of Jesus Christ of Latter-day Saints, 2004), 180–82.

7. See ibid; see also Dallin H. Oaks, "Tithing," *Ensign,* May 1994, 35.

8. See "Financial Contributions," in *Encyclopedia of Mormonism,* 4 vols., ed. Daniel H. Ludlow (New York: Macmillan, 1992), 2:510.

9. The number of buildings the Church completes each year fluctuates based on worldwide economic conditions and membership needs, but as early as 1979 the Church was reporting building a chapel a day. See LeGrand Richards, "The Gift of the Holy Ghost," *Ensign,* November 1979, 78.

10. Gordon B. Hinckley, "News of the Church," *Ensign,* November 1998, 108.

11. See "Intellectual History," in *Encyclopedia of Mormonism,* 2:688; see also Gordon B. Hinckley, "This Work Is Concerned with People," *Ensign,* May 1995, 52.

12. See Wendy Leonard, "BYU Ranks Among Best-Value Private Schools in the Nation," *Deseret News,* January 9, 2009, http://www.deseretnews.com /article/705276182/BYU-ranks-among-best-value -private-schools-in-the-nation.html.

13. Gordon B. Hinckley, "The State of the Church," *Ensign,* May 1991, 52–53.

14. See "Help End World Hunger," http://www.squidoo .com/world-hunger.

15. See World Resource Institute, http://www.wri.org.

16. See Michael K. Winder, *President and Prophets* (American Fork, Utah: Covenant Communications, 2007), 248.

17. Ronald Reagan, quoted in Winder, *Presidents and Prophets,* 352, 354.

18. First Presidency, in Conference Report, October 1936, 3.

19. See Biema, Gwynne, and Ostling, "Kingdom Come."

20. In 1997, *Time* magazine estimated the Church's business income (nontithing or other donations) at about $600 million per year. See Biema, Gwynne, and Ostling, "Kingdom Come."

21. See H. David Burton, "The Sanctifying Work of Welfare," *Ensign,* May 2011, 82.

22. See LDS Employment Resource Services, https:// www.ldsjobs.org/.

23. See "Welfare Services Fact Sheet—2010," http:// www.providentliving.org/pdf/2010_WELFactSheet _English.pdf.

24. See *Providing in the Lord's Way* (Salt Lake City: The Church of Jesus Christ of Latter-day Saints, 2009), 3.

25. See ibid., 1.

26. "Home Storage," http://lds.org/family/family-well -being/home-storage?lang=eng.

27. See "Longer-Term Supply," http://www.provident living.org/content/list/0,11664,7448–1,00.html.

28. See *All Is Safely Gathered In: Family Finances* (Salt Lake City: The Church of Jesus Christ of Latter-day Saints, 2007), 2. Although Mormons are taught this doctrine, there is some evidence that personal finances may be an area where some Latter-day Saints need to better apply the counsel of Church

leaders. From 2002 to 2004, Utah (60 percent LDS) repeatedly had the dubious honor of leading the nation in bankruptcy rates. See "Utah Bankruptcies Lead Nation," *Deseret News,* December 9, 2002, http://www.deseretnews.com/article/952991/Utah -bankruptcies-lead-nation.html. Although Utah's ranking slipped to fifteenth nationwide in 2007, it was back in third in 2011. Although some hypoth-esize why this is the case—often linking the cause to tithing, large families, and couples who marry young—to date, no known data significantly correlates high bankruptcy rates with higher religiosity in the LDS Church. In fact, one study finds no such link exists. See "LDS faith, bank-ruptcy: No link," http://www.freerepublic.com /focus/f-religion/1858323/posts.

29. *All Is Safely Gathered In,* 1.

30. Joseph Smith, *The History of The Church of Jesus Christ of Latter-day Saints,* 7 vols., ed. B. H. Roberts (Salt Lake City: The Church of Jesus Christ of Latter-day Saints, 1932–51), 4:227.

31. See "Welfare Services Fact Sheet—2010."

32. Ibid.

33. See "Hope in the World" video, http://www.lds philanthropies.org/humanitarian-services/news -features/video-hope-in-the-world.html.

34. See Latter-day Saint Charities, "Neonatal Resusci-tation Training," http://www.ldsphilanthropies.org /humanitarian-services/funds/neonatal -resuscitation.html.

35. Joseph Smith, *Teachings of Presidents of the Church: Joseph Smith* (Salt Lake City: The Church of Jesus Christ of Latter-day Saints, 2007), 426.

36. *Handbook 2: Administering the Church* (Salt Lake City: The Church of Jesus Christ of Latter-day Saints, 2010), 9.

37. Heber J. Grant, in Glen L. Rudd, *Pure Religion: The Story of Church Welfare since 1930* (Salt Lake City: The Church of Jesus Christ of Latter-day Saints, 1995), 34.

38. David H. Burton, "The Sanctifying Work of Welfare," *Ensign,* May 2011, 82.

Chapter 25: Mormons, Politics, and America

1. Of the top word associations related to Mormon-ism, "family values," "dedicated," "devout," "good," "strict," and "faithful" were in the top nine. See Pew Forum, "Public Expresses Mixed Views of Islam, Mormonism," September 25, 2007, http://pew forum.org/Public-Expresses-Mixed-Views-of -Islam-Mormonism.aspx.

2. Joseph Smith, *Teachings of the Prophet Joseph Smith,* comp. Joseph Fielding Smith (Salt Lake City: Deseret Book, 1976), 362.

3. Ezra Taft Benson, "I Testify," *Ensign,* November 1988, 87.

4. Walter Kirn, "Mormons Rock!" *Newsweek,* June 5, 2011, 3, http://www.thedailybeast.com/news week/2011/06/05/mormons-rock.html.

5. Wilford Woodruff, in Conference Report, April 1898, 89.

6. George Washington, in *The Papers of George Washington,* "Washington's First Inaugural Ad-dress—Final Version," April 30, 1789, http://gw papers.virginia.edu/documents/inaugural/final. html.

7. Alexander Hamilton, James Madison, and John Jay, *The Federalist: A Commentary on the Consti-tution of the United States,* ed. Henry Cabot Lodge (New York: G. P. Putnam's Sons, n.d.), 222.

8. *Essays on the Constitution of the United States,* ed. Paul L. Ford (Brooklyn, NY: Historical Printing Club, 1892), 412.

9. Smith, *Teachings of the Prophet Joseph Smith,* 147.

10. See George Cobabe, "The White Horse Prophecy," The Foundation for Apologetic Information and Research (F.A.I.R.), http://www.fairlds.org/pubs /whitehorse.pdf. See also Kate Ensign-Lewis, "The Truth about Mormon Myths," *LDS Living* (May/June 2011): 56–57.

11. "Political Neutrality," http://newsroom.lds.org /official-statement/political-neutrality.

12. See Frank Newport, "Mormons Most Conservative Major Religious Group in U.S.," January 11, 2010, http://www.gallup.com/poll/125021/Mormons -Conservative-Major-Religious-Group.aspx.

13. See Allison Pond, "A Portrait of Mormons in the U.S.," Pew Forum on Religion and Public Life, July 24, 2009, http://pewresearch.org/pubs/1292 /mormon-religion-demographics-beliefs -practices-politics.

14. Joseph Smith, *The History of The Church of Jesus Christ of Latter-day Saints,* 7 vols., ed. B. H. Roberts (Salt Lake City: The Church of Jesus Christ of Latter-day Saints, 1932–51), 5:286.

15. "Political Neutrality."

16. See Pew Forum, "Faith on the Hill: The Religious Composition of the 112th Congress," updated February 28, 2011, http://pewforum.org /Government/Faith-on-the-Hill--The-Religious -Composition-of-the-112th-Congress.aspx.

17. "Political Neutrality."

18. See Lydia Saad, "In U.S., 22% Are Hesitant to Support a Mormon in 2012," June 20, 2011, http:// www.gallup.com/poll/148100/hesitant-support -mormon-2012.aspx.

19. See Pew Forum, "Public Expresses Mixed Views of Islam, Mormonism," September 26, 2007, http:// pewforum.org/Public-Expresses-Mixed-Views-of -Islam-Mormonism.aspx.

Chapter 26: The Weird and Wonderful World of Mormon Culture

1. See Kathy Stephensen, "Utah devours Girls Scouts cookies," March 11, 2011, http://www.sltrib.com /sltrib/blogsbitebybite/51406446–60/cookies -cookie-girl-scout.html.csp.

2. See Katty Kay, "Utah loves Jell-O—official," February 2, 2001, http://news.bbc.co.uk/2/hi/americas /1156021.stm.

3. "Choose the Right," in *Hymns of The Church of Jesus Christ of Latter-day Saints* (Salt Lake City: The Church of Jesus Christ of Latter-day Saints, 1985), no. 239.

Photo and Image Credits

Images courtesy of Anthony Sweat: 34 (family photo), 47 (sacrament trays), 61 (painting of family), 72–73 (interiors of Salt Lake Temple), 118 (Book of Mormon display), 177 (girls attending the temple), 193 (welcome sign), 194 (missionaries), 225 (Joseph and Brigham bookends)

Images courtesy of Barry Hansen: 62 (family photo), 197 (mission call letter), 199 (DeVar and Patricia Cluff), 204 (tithing slips), 222 (lamp and bucket)

Images courtesy of Shauna Gibby: 15 (Sacred Grove), 69 (Palmyra chapel), 97 (Grandin press; Kirtland Temple), 115 (handwritten Book of Mormon pages)

iStock: 1, 3, 5, 8, 10, 14, 15, 16, 27, 31, 38, 39, 40, 45, 48, 50, 64, 74, 75, 81, 82, 83, 85, 87, 89, 90, 92, 96, 97, 102, 108, 110, 118, 120, 123, 125, 126, 131, 132, 135, 142, 146, 157, 158, 159, 160, 161, 162, 163, 165, 169, 180, 183, 184, 186, 194, 198, 202, 222

Mormon.org: 4, 18, 37, 41, 54, 61, 85, 89, 121, 172, 181, 202. Used by permission.

Shutterstock: ix, 8, 9, 19, 32, 35, 36, 44, 47, 50, 51, 57, 58, 61, 64, 65, 66, 69, 70, 71, 74, 75, 76, 77, 78, 83, 88, 93, 98, 106, 108, 111, 113, 114, 120, 121, 125, 135, 139, 141, 143, 144, 145, 146, 147, 148, 150, 155, 164, 171, 174, 175, 186, 199, 200, 204, 212, 214, 217, 220

Thinkstock: x, 4, 9, 18, 23, 24, 27, 29, 30, 31, 46, 49, 52, 53, 55, 58, 59, 60, 62, 66, 68, 70, 74, 79, 80, 85, 86, 90, 105, 107, 118, 119, 120, 122, 123, 125, 130, 134, 138, 141, 142, 143, 148, 149, 150, 151, 152, 153, 154, 155, 156, 160, 162, 166, 170, 173, 175, 176, 179, 180, 182, 183, 184, 185, 187, 189, 190, 191, 192, 193, 195, 198, 201, 205, 213, 215, 221, 223, 224, 225

Wikimedia: 68, 97, 134, 135, 197, 201, 204, 206, 210, 218, 219

Page x: *Newsweek,* June 13 & 20, 2011.
Page 3, 19: portraits of Christ by Heinrich Hofmann. Public domain.
Page 11: *Christ Ordaining the Apostles* by Harry Anderson © by Intellectual Reserve, Inc. Used by permission.
Page 14: portrait of Joseph Smith; Gutenberg press; and portrait of Christopher Columbus. Public domain.
Page 20: painting of lilies by Monet. Public domain.
Page 20: *The Oath of the Horatii* by David Jacque. Public domain.
Page 21: stained glass of the First Vision. Public domain.
Page 23: *Christ on the Cross* by Carl Bloch. Public domain.
Page 23: *The Apparition of Christ to Mary Magdalen* by Alexander Ivanov. Public domain.
Page 24: image of Christ in Gethsemane. Public domain.
Page 37: *Adam and Eve* by Wenzel Peter. Public domain.
Page 42: Priests blessing the sacrament (photo); Bishop receiving tithing (photo); David A. Bednar. © by Intellectual Reserve, Inc. Used by permission.
Page 43: *Melchizedek Priesthood Restoration* by Kenneth Riley; *John the Baptist Conferring the Aaronic Priesthood* by Del Parson. © by Intellectual Reserve, Inc. Used by permission.
Page 46: Girl being baptized (photo); Girl confirmation (photo). © by Intellectual Reserve, Inc. Used by permission.
Page 47: Statue of Peter by Bertel Thorvaldsen. Public domain.
Page 49: 1978 Nigerian baptism (photo) © by Intellectual Reserve, Inc. Used by permission.

Page 56: "Mormon Family"; photographer: Kean Collection; collection: Archive Photos. Courtesy Getty Images.

Page 67: "Illustration of the Israelite's Tabernacle, high angle view," photographer: Dorling Kindersley; collection: Dorling Kindersley RF. Courtesy Getty Images.

Page 96: *Winter Quarters; Carthage;* and *Crossing the Mississippi* by C.C.A. Christensen. Public domain.

Page 96: image of Brigham Young. Public domain.

Page 96: world map from http://lds.org/maps/.

Page 97: *Hill Cumorah; Liberty Jail;* and *Nauvoo Temple* by C.C.A. Christensen. Public domain.

Page 97: image of sailing ship by Frederick Tudgay. Public domain.

Page 98: portrait of Joseph Smith © by Intellectual Reserve, Inc. Used by permission.

Page 99: image from JosephSmith.net.

Page 99: *The Desire of My Heart* by Walter Rane. Used by permission.

Page 100: *Moroni Appears to Joseph Smith* by Tom Lovell. Used by permission.

Page 101: *Joseph Receives the Gold Plates* by Kenneth Riley. Used by permission.

Page 103: *Joseph in Liberty Jail* by Danquart Weggeland. Public domain.

Page 104: Joseph Smith after the martyrdom from JosephSmith.net.

Page 107: *Going As a Lamb* by Liz Lemon Swindle. Used by permission.

Page 115: image of translation pen. Public domain.

Page 118: fingerprint cartoon by Veer. Used by permission.

Page 122: President Thomas S. Monson (photo). © by Intellectual Reserve, Inc. Used by permission.

Page 124: The First Presidency and the Quorum of the Twelve (photo). © by Intellectual Reserve, Inc. Used by permission.

Page 127: *Joseph Smith* by Del Parson; *Brigham Young* by John Willard Clawson; *John Taylor* by John Willard Clawson. © by Intellectual Reserve, Inc. Used by permission.

Page 128: *Wilford Woodruff* by Kenneth Corbett. Used by permission. *Lorenzo Snow* by Lewis Ramsey; *Joseph F. Smith* by A. Salzbrenner; *Heber J. Grant* by C. J. Fox; *George Albert Smith* by Lee Greene Richards. © by Intellectual Reserve, Inc. Used by permission.

Page 129: *David O. McKay* by Alvin Gittins; Spencer W. Kimball (photo); Ezra Taft Benson (photo) by Busath Photography; Howard W. Hunter (photo). © by Intellectual Reserve, Inc. Used by permission. Joseph Fielding Smith (photo) and Harold B. Lee (photo) by Merrett Smith. Used by permission.

Page 130: Gordon B. Hinckley (photo) and Thomas S. Monson (photo). © by Intellectual Reserve, Inc. Used by permission.

Page 131: Jeffrey R. Holland (photo) © by Intellectual Reserve, Inc. Used by permission.

Page 133: *Wilford Woodruff* by Kenneth Corbett. Used by permission.

Page 134–35: map of Temple Square © 2012 Neil Brown.

Page 140: *Ensign,* October 2009.

Page 167: Linda K. Burton (photo); Elaine S. Dalton (photo); Rosemary M. Wixom (photo). © by Intellectual Reserve, Inc. Used by permission.

Page 168: Martha Hughes Cannon © 2004 Utah State Historical Society. All rights reserved. Used by permission.

Page 181: Stansbury Park seminary building from Zwick Construction.

Page 187: Filipino sacrament meeting (photo) by Craig Dimond. © by Intellectual Reserve, Inc. Used by permission.

Page 198: MTC building from mtc.byu.edu/themtc.html.

Page 203: *Time,* August 4, 1997.

Page 206: Ronald Reagan at Ogden Welfare Cannery. Corbis Images. Used by permission.

Page 208: Welfare Square silos (photo). © by Intellectual Reserve, Inc. Used by permission.

Page 211: Sierra Leone from ldsphilanthropies.com.

Page 221: image of youth on trek (photo) by Joshua Jensen.

Page 222: CTR ring from BuyLDS.com.